History of Football in Europe

History of Football in Europe

Stephane Boswell

Larsen & Keller
www.larsen-keller.com

History of Football in Europe
Stephane Boswell
ISBN: 979-8-88836-037-8 (Hardback)

Larsen & Keller
Published by Larsen and Keller Education,
5 Penn Plaza,
19th Floor,
New York, NY 10001, USA

Cataloging-in-Publication Data

History of football in Europe / Stephane Boswell.
p. cm.
Includes bibliographical references and index.
ISBN 979-8-88836-037-8
1. Soccer--Europe. 2. Soccer--Europe--History. I. Boswell, Stephane.
GV944.E8 H57 2023
796.334 094--dc23

For more information regarding Larsen and Keller Education and its products, please visit the publisher's website www.larsen-keller.com

Table of Contents

Preface

Football is a team sport in which players kick a ball to score a goal in various ways. During a match, there are two teams and each team has 11 players. There are different types of football including American football, Australian Rules football, Gaelic football, soccer, rugby union, Canadian football and rugby league. Each kind of football has its own set of rules and guidelines. Britain is the place where modern football first emerged in the 19th century. In 1904, representatives from the football associations of Belgium, Denmark, France, the Netherlands, Spain, Sweden, and Switzerland established the Fédération Internationale de Football Association (FIFA), which is the governing body for football. The concept of football spread from England to Europe and across the Atlantic. The Union of European Football Associations (UEFA) was established in 1954 and it organizes the European championship tournament every four years. The UEFA European Football Championship is also called the Euros. This book provides comprehensive insights into the history of football in Europe. Its extensive content provides the readers with a thorough understanding of the subject.

The information shared in this book is based on empirical researches made by veterans in this field of study. The elaborative information provided in this book will help the readers further their scope of knowledge leading to advancements in this field.

Finally, I would like to thank my fellow researchers who gave constructive feedback and my family members who supported me at every step of my research.

Stephane Boswell

1

An Overview of Dutch Football

I remember being interested in Dutch football from a young age. The first football match I can remember watching was the Italia 1990 World Cup match between England and the Netherlands – although saying I remember 'watching' it is a little inaccurate. To be honest, until I looked up the score, while writing this, I could not remember who had won (actually it was a draw) or who had played for either team. But the match has stuck in my mind, partly because of the vibrant orange shirts of the Dutch team, which, I suppose, for a six-year-old, were particularly attractive and eye-catching. It certainly was not for the memory of a stunning English performance; as much as I like football, goalless draws do not often remain with me long, and I must admit that I have never really supported England in sporting matters – I always chose to be one of those awkward (and rightly derided!) people who picks teams based on what they are like, rather than where they are from. No, I remember this game because of where I watched it – the emergency room of High Wycombe hospital while awaiting stitches for a rather large gash on my leg. The gash itself had been obtained while running around the boundary of my local cricket club, no doubt trying to emulate some of the more scintillating elements from the World Cup. This mix of excitement and injury may in part explain my relationship with sport – it is something I love, but I am not always sure I like it, or whether it is good for me. These sentiments will permeate these histories.

But my interest in Dutch football is not purely based on orange shirts or memories of a hospital waiting room. Being a sporting child, living in Britain in the early 1990s, I had the good fortune of being able to watch *Football Italia* on Channel 4 every Sunday afternoon after returning from playing rugby. Having never supported a football team – my local team Maidenhead United had never quite grabbed me – I became captivated by one team in particular and, above all, two of their star players: the 1992 AC Milan team with Marco van Basten and Ruud Gullit. I did not really know much about them, or the Netherlands, but I knew that I liked what I saw; how could one not like the mixture of beauty and skill that was Van Basten, or the stunning combination of precision and power embodied by Gullit? This Milan team was special and at its heart were three Dutchmen: Van Basten, Gullit and Rijkaard.[1] In 1995, a year after demolishing Johan Cruijff's Barcelona, Milan lost in the European Cup Final to an impressive Ajax side – something for which I am not sure I have ever forgiven the Amsterdam-based team. Later, another three Dutchmen joined the club, all from Ajax: Kluivert, Davids and Reiziger. In many ways, they were not quite the same.

Nearly twenty years later, I found myself in another hospital, after another sporting injury, this time in Van Basten's hometown of Utrecht. My knowledge of Marco gave me something to talk about with the surgeon and I would often find myself debating with others about who was better, Van Basten or Cruijff. In certain parts of the Netherlands, this is not something that should be done without some preparation. At other times, I walked down the street where he grew up, and cycled past the ground where he played as a youth. A chance sighting of Ruud Gullit filming outside the Utrecht *Speelklok* museum was undoubtedly the highlight of my two years living in the Netherlands. That I have constructed these histories about Dutch football at all is the result of many people and many factors, but these visits to hospitals, the bright orange shirt and the magnificence of Marco van Basten and Ruud Gullit all play a central role in their production. At least, that is how I remember it.

But these histories are not concerned with star names. It may seem unwise to say so early in a book on Dutch football, but there will be little discussion of actual football matches in this work. The results, who scored and when, and how 'important' this was for certain clubs will be mentioned only in passing – for instance, there will only be one further mention of Cruijff. There will be no 'in-depth' biographies of the early greats of the games, no explanation for the development of the 'great' clubs of today and no anecdotes about famous victories or infamous losses.

Rather, my aims in this book can be divided broadly into two areas: those relating, on the one hand, to theoretical aspects and, on the other, to practical aspects. Theoretically, I hope to introduce you to my own postmodern approach to history and what purpose I feel history can have. Sport has been an important part of my life and I believe that it can be a valuable location for considering the world around us, yet sporting histories so often seem to be traditional and conservative in their approach. I want to demonstrate that sport can be a place for new, experimental approaches to history. Secondly, I will provide four histories in which early Dutch football, up to 1920, will be a tool to think about wider concepts. My focus will be on various aspects of football culture: the fans; the media; how football interacted with discourses of power, values and space; and some of the many individuals connected, sometimes tangentially, to the game and, on occasions, aspects of the matches themselves.

I believe that these sporting histories will do something different to others. At the heart of this difference is my own belief that the discipline of history, despite many changes in the past decades, is operating under a misapprehension: namely, that it – and more specifically, those described as 'historians' – can explain the past. I believe the true value of history lies in exploring possibilities for the future from the perspective of the present, rather than focusing on the past. In fact, I believe that history is always rooted in the present. The idea of history being about the present and the future is the underlying theme of this work. I think early Dutch football is an important and interesting topic; however, my primary objective is to demonstrate how postmodern history can be put into practice and can help us think about the world around us today.

In writing this book, I have kept quite a broad audience in mind. I hope that it will be useful to academics and students with interests in Dutch history and culture, or to those with an interest in sports history; to undergraduate students and teachers who are looking for practical examples of how to do history in a different, more sceptical style. But I also hope this book will be useful to a wider audience interested in sport or popular culture and who may be unfamiliar with sceptical approaches to history or the use of sport in examining wider concerns. In the rest of this introduction, I will explain in more detail exactly what I hope to achieve with this book and just why it is entitled *Four Histories about Early Dutch Football 1910–1920: Constructing Discourses*.

The postmodern

By saying that history is more connected to the future and present than the past, I am making an important statement about how history – the academic discipline connected to research into the past – functions. It is an assumption that is influenced by what are often termed 'sceptical' and 'postmodern' ideas.[2] The term 'sceptical', while having a long history itself, can be understood as signifying ideas that doubt the ability of history and historians to research *the* past, to *discover* reality, to represent *the* meaning of the past, and which doubt that the process of writing (or reading) is unimportant to how the past is represented and understood. The postmodern is, perhaps deliberately, a little more difficult to define.

The term 'postmodern' is used, by many people, in a variety of contexts. It is used in many different disciplines, often as a shorthand term for a range of ideas which are much more disparate, more nebulous than the use of a single term might suggest.[3] The first, throwaway, use of the term is suggested to have been as far back as 1875, but its use was popularised from the 1960s and especially in the 1980s.[4] In the 1990s, numerous texts appeared in the English language connected to the theory of history, including those which discussed postmodern ideas.[5] The term became ubiquitous in the media, across different cultures and places and in different academic disciplines.[6] But what exactly does it mean?

The term '*post*-modern' suggests that it is in some way linked to another time or quality – it is after the 'modern' – but what this actually means is not entirely clear. At the beginning of his introduction to postmodernism, 'What Then Is Post-Modernism?', Charles Jencks suggested that it was 'ironic to ask this question after so many years, as if there were a clear answer'.[7] How does it relate to the 'modern' and what is (or was) this anyway? Indeed so unclear is the answer, that there are multiple spellings of 'postmodern'. Is it the 'Post-Modern', 'post-modern', 'postmodern', 'PM' or the sarcastic 'Po-Mo'?[8] As Malpas summarises, the term has been used to think about the world in a variety of ways:

> [T]he postmodern has been defined in a huge variety of different ways: as a new aesthetic formation (Hassan, 1982, 1987), a condition (Lyotard, 1984; Harvey, 1990), a culture (Connor, 1997), a cultural dominant (Jameson, 1991), a set of artistic movements employing a parodic mode of self-conscious representation (Hutcheon, 1988, 2002), an ethical or political imperative (Bauman, 1993, 1995), a period in which we have reached the 'end of history' (Baudrillard, 1994; Fukuyama, 1992; Vattimo, 1988), a 'new horizon of our cultural, philosophical and political experience' (Laclau, 1988), an 'illusion' (Eagleton, 1996), a reactionary

political formation (Callinicos, 1989), or even just a rather unfortunate mistake (Norris, 1990, 1993).[9]

While the term is often linked to 'irony, disruption, difference, discontinuity, playfulness, parody, hyper-reality and simulation'[10] there 'is no unified postmodern theory, or even a coherent set of positions', but only a number of diverse, plural, often contradictory ideas.[11]

Despite its vague, contradictory and contentious nature, which should really confine any term to the intellectual dustbin, it has seemingly only become more widely used. In a range of different fields and popular culture, the use of one of the various spellings and meanings of 'postmodern' has become an important, if not always welcome, part of the discourse. In an attempt to locate how this vague notion of postmodern has been considered in different fields, or how these fields can be considered postmodern, Jencks provides a tentative suggestion as to what the term might include. For Jencks, it is something that is a response to, but also intimately linked to and concurrent with, the 'modern' – the two are interdependent. In architecture and literature, Jencks has suggested that the postmodern is concerned with irony and ambiguity while modern values were straightforwardness, transparency and simplicity.[12] In politics, the postmodern could be regional power (like the EU) while the modern was the nation-state; in science, postmodern approaches could be complex and non-linear while the modern was simple and linear; the media world of the postmodern is instantly changing, whilst the modern was fast-changing; postmodern culture could be said to embrace multiple taste-cultures, where the modern was elitist.[13] Jencks's self-consciously ironic and selective attempt to suggest what the postmodern and modern might include – and their interdependency – highlights the range and scope of areas in which the postmodern has become used.

Within the humanities, postmodernism is understood and applied differently between and within fields such as sociology, philosophy, theology or history.[14] Within history, 'postmodern' has become an umbrella term for a variety of approaches, as Bowen Raddeker notes.[15] It can include poststructuralism, deconstruction and the linguistic turn, indicating that language and how it relates to the world is a central aspect.[16] Lyotard saw the postmodern as something connected to representing the unrepresentable in art and literary forms. It was a necessary response to the nineteenth and twentieth centuries, which provided their 'fill of terror'; a response to the failed project of universal, rational modernity, for which the horrific murder-machine of Auschwitz could be seen as a symbol.[17]

For Lyotard, then, postmodernism was a positive response to the past, linked to a desire to change how it was represented and researched.

One of the most vocal postmodern critics of history, Jenkins has noted that postmodern concepts have questioned the nature and purpose of academic history. To use his terminology, they have dismissed the concept of 'uppercase History', which places events within a larger scheme of development.[18] This 'incredulity toward metanarratives', as Lyotard famously described postmodernism, includes a rejection of orthodox Marxist approaches or those that see a path of progression in the past.[19] But Jenkins notes that postmodern concepts have also dismissed 'lowercase history' – the idea that history can be studied objectively, academically or for its own sake.[20] Postmodern ideas have shown a suspicion of fixed concepts of meaning, reality, knowledge, facts and truth; of the concepts of Reason, rationality and the Enlightenment; in short, a suspicion of what many people associate with the discipline of history.[21] I am sympathetic to these postmodern views. There may be those who see such ideas as unwanted and as a destructive, vapid and troublesome offering, giving criticism without substance or values, without any suggestion of what it wants to bring about.[22]

But the difficulty of definition is, in my view, part of the point. Part of what those who are associated with postmodern ideas set out to challenge is the 'clear and concise process of identification and definition [which] is one of the key elements of rationality'.[23] That I refer to my ideas as postmodern indicates that I believe there is some value in the use of the term; this is because of its contentious, fuzzy and indefinable nature.

I use the term to refer to a spirit of investigation, of scepticism (some may even say cynicism), of doubt in existing explanations and a lack of certainty about my own position. I am not satisfied with how we represent the past, how it is 'understood' and the processes by which we try to do this. To me, postmodernity means the need to represent the individual, the fragmented and the contradictory, and an attempt to provide a personal, self-reflective and consciously flawed response to how the world is constructed. Notions of permanence or transcendental truth have little place here, and concepts such as 'identity', 'values' and especially 'power' are constructed and relative. At the heart of the histories proposed in this book is the need to question how constructs operate, whether they are historical or current, institutional or even my own. I believe history is important. As Southgate suggests, it is at the heart of our contemporary education systems and is fundamental to concepts of identity and culture.[24] I think that the importance of history to contemporary culture, society and identities means that it is something that needs to be challenged, reconsidered and adapted. It is something too important to leave purely to professional historians and those who are given the authority to construct history.

My research has been influenced by many different works, by those who would happily feel part of the postmodern and many who would not. The names of White (the role of narrative and storytelling in determining meaning), Lyotard (an incredulity to the grand narratives of the past), Barthes (language, the 'reader' and 'author'), Ankersmit (the past and history, subjectivity and values), Rail (sport, gender and the postmodern), Jenkins (history as a positioned discipline, morality in history), de Certeau (the place of the author and process of writing), Derrida (binaries and archival technology), Munslow (the story space and history) and Foucault (discourse, language, power) have all been profoundly influential for my histories. Influenced by their work I have outlined six broad themes, which will enable me to highlight important theoretical considerations connected to history and my own approach:

- the past and history
- the archive and history
- the problems of language in history
- narrative, style and history
- places and modes of production
- the historian and history.

The past and history

What is the difference between the 'past' and 'history'? Munslow outlines his view: 'The past is what once was, is no more and has gone for good. History, on the other hand, is a corpus of narrative discourses *about* the once reality of the past produced and fashioned by historians.'[25] In this summation, there is a clear distinction between the 'past' and the account which is constructed about it: 'history'. When we read a history book or see a historical film, we do not believe that we are seeing the past acted out in front of us, as though taken from its own time and transported to ours. What we are seeing, reading or imagining is a constructed representation about the past, an attempt to re-present an aspect which has disappeared and is now absent.[26] Through language, text and sometimes images, history attempts to represent the absent past using a variety of 'traces' gathered from the period in question placed within a wider narrative.

But what is this constructed representation about the past? Does it represent the reality of the past or something different? In short, what is it that we can say about the past? Ankersmit notes that there is a difference between individual statements based on research and the wider historical narratives which link them together.[27] Using Ankersmit's work, Jenkins notes there is a problem when history tries to claim that it represents an objective reality of the past and this problem arises when historians go beyond simple statements of fact to create more complex visions of the past. While it may be possible to make some simple true or false statements about the past – about what happened, who was where, when certain things took place – which can be verified against the traces of the past in the archive, once these statements are sifted, sorted, given priority of importance and combined together to create a 'picture' of the past, they take on a different property. They are no longer statements of fact, but part of a complex text which attempts to tell a story about the past. Within these 'pictures', historians have made selections as to what is relevant or not. Some statements are prioritised, others are ignored and ways of linking the statements are theorised or speculated upon to make up for a lack in evidence. Whereas one can check single statements, at least, to some extent, against traces of the past, there is nothing which permits us to check the wider picture, the history, against the 'real' past.[28]

Jenkins suggests that this picture of the past is as important as the veracity of the individual statements of fact. History is not just a list of established facts but, as Munslow noted above, like Ankersmit and White, it is a constructed narrative, a collection of statements which are given a meaning when they are ordered and linked. These two aspects – the simple statement and the historical text – are two different kinds of information which cannot be reduced to each other; history is not a simple description of the reality of past. Its 'accuracy' cannot be verified against a past reality, as this is gone, or by adding up the number of 'true statements'. Rather, the historical text is a constructed and selective discourse, which uses factual statements as part of a wider 'picture'. Jenkins sums up his reading of Ankersmit on this matter:

> [S]aying *true* things about the past's traces at the level of the statement is easy – 'anybody can do that' – but saying true things about the past's traces at the level of the text is categorically impossible – 'nobody can do that'. For texts are not, sadly, cognitive,

> empirical, epistemological entities, but speculative, imagined 'imaginaries'[.][29]

It is, perhaps, worth noting that Ankersmit does not suggest there is no truth in history, that all histories are equally valid or that there is no connection to reality. In *Historical Representation*, he suggests that we need to consider historical writing as a representation *about* reality, rather than a description *of* it.[30] He notes that individual statements of the past can be considered as 'descriptions', but that the overall historical text is a 'representation'. These are two very different things. While a description may have an object to refer to, history, at the level of the text, is a representation about reality – there is no fixed object to refer to. History is related to reality through historical descriptions and individual statements, but the overall narrative, the product which we call history includes other aspects.[31]

For Ankersmit, historians, like other language users, are not in the position to have both relevance and precision: we can either use representations to get to the 'heart of reality', although this may be vague, or sacrifice relevance for the precision of the true statement.[32] There are three aspects to the relationship between the past and historical representations. The first is the reality of the past (the past), the second are descriptions about the past (traces) and the third are historical representations (texts).[33] These three aspects are fundamentally different, albeit connected. Ankersmit's representational view of history suggests that historical representations are proposals, rather than descriptions – they are proposals on how to link a certain chunk of language to a certain part of the past.[34] Proposals, Ankersmit continues, cannot logically be 'false' or 'true' in the same way simple statements can be, but historical proposals can be discussed rationally and compared to each other. But such a comparison is not a comparison with the past.[35] Ankersmit is not a historical relativist. He is not suggesting that there can be no truth in history, but that the kind of truth we get is not of a traditional, empirical kind which attempts to describe a reified real past.

By viewing historical works as proposals, we obtain a new link between history texts and the past, one which rejects empiricist ideas. It suggests to me that an objective description of the past is not possible in terms of the overall historical text – there is simply no object to check a historical account against to see if it is an accurate description of the past reality; no amount of fact-checking or research in the archive can compensate for this impossibility. The thorny issue of reality in history is still much contested and the extent to which history can link to reality, or what this reality might be, is something which continues to trouble me. In the spirit of openness, it is a link I am still uncertain about. I am still unsure about how we can be certain that individual statements of fact are accurate descriptions of the past. Those who do not share my sceptical view of history may suggest that history can describe a form of past reality, even if only partially; that history can, through detailed research and investigation of the traces, describe what happened and give causes and effects. Ankersmit too would be keen to counter any view in which history had no link to the reality of the past. But given my uncertainty on the link between the past and the real, this style of history is beyond me; it sounds too certain, too final. It seems to ignore the arbitrary cuts, fusions and omissions we make in representations which are simply not made in reality.[36]

If history is not capable of describing the past then there must be another relationship between history and the past, and this means that the historian has a different task. In 'Historiography and Postmodernism', Ankersmit questions what one and a half centuries of 'digging' more attentively into the past, in an effort to scientifically reconstruct the reality of it, has really achieved. It is a provocative statement, but I would suggest that such digging has not brought us any closer to *the* reality of the past – we cannot do this through history. As Ankersmit suggests: 'The time has come that we should *think* about the past, rather than *investigate* it.'[37]

The idea of thinking about the past has been very influential for my own approach. Accepting the idea that history cannot be a direct description of the reality of the past has freed me to think more about my own research and its purpose, to think more about how I relate to the past I am considering, to think about what I have used and ignored, to think how I have combined statements together and to think about the artificial gaps, closures and perspectives I have brought to my histories.[38] After Munslow, I use the term 'representation about the past' in this work to emphasise my lack of certainty with regard to history's ability to objectively describe the past.[39] History is not 'of' the past but 'about' it; histories do not come to the historian from the past but are constructed about it. I believe that, once the historian is freed from the notion that history can describe, reconstruct or understand the past then they may be able to think in new ways, to represent different aspects about the past, to imagine the past and how it is important to us today – at least, this is what I have tried to do. History should not be about narrowing down stories, describing a definitive version or eliminating 'wrong' versions of the past, but should be about an '"explosion" of possible points of view'.[40]

In each of my histories, I have attempted to represent different aspects of the past, using different techniques and imaginaries, accepting that each will be different, contradictory and flawed – not because *my* history is more prone to this than others, but because history can only ever be these things. One of the important questions I want to consider is how can I represent the idea of history as possibilities of the past and give room for different ways of representing the absent and irrecoverable past, informed by my own current concerns?

The archive and history

Ankersmit noted that single statements of fact could be shown to be either true or false by appealing to the traces of the past; therefore, history had, at least to some extent, the possibility of a connection to the past. These traces of the past form part of what is often referred to as the 'archive'. This certainly includes the traces found in official archives, such as the *Nationaal Archief* (Dutch National Archive, NA) in The Hague or the *Stadsarchief Rotterdam* (City Archive of Rotterdam, SAR), where I did much of my own research, but also includes other evidence available to the historian, such as libraries, museums and private collections. I use 'archive' to refer to the traces of the past which historians have access to in order to construct their texts. It is a definition which is contested, especially as the nature of documents and collection practices change.[41] However, there is a more abstract side to the archive, a side which is connected to power, to what can be said and what can be considered 'true'. The archive does not allow the historian unproblematic access to the past but shapes and is shaped by ways of knowing.

Amongst others, Foucault, Derrida and de Certeau were concerned about how archives were formed and what role they played in the formation of knowledge. In 1969, Foucault stated that '[t]he archive is first the law of what can be said, the system that governs the appearance of statements as unique events'.[42] Foucault's archive was not a neutral tool which historians could use to check their stories about the past, but something which formed how the past could be represented and what could be said. The archive's ability to form the stories of the past was not just an accidental sin of omission – it was not just by accident that certain parts of the past did not find their way into the archive. Rather, for Foucault, the archive functions as a way to order the past, to stop it becoming an amorphous mess, a linear stream. The archive gives form to the past. It is connected to power over what can be said, and who can say it.

In a similar vein, Derrida suggests that archival technology shapes the nature of knowledge which can be kept and transmitted. Rather than just recording events, the archive helps to form and construct them. It is not a neutral intermediary between past actions and present traces, but is selective, contingent and forming. If the archive cannot hold, or chooses not to hold, certain records then they cannot form part of the stories of the past.[43] As Manoff indicates, what is omitted or included in the archive is based upon a combination of political, economic, social, technological and academic factors: 'What is considered a legitimate contribution to the archive changes over time and is a function of the transformations of the disciplines and the shifting boundaries among them.'[44]

Similarly, de Certeau noted: 'From collecting documents to writing books, historical practice is entirely relative to the structure of society.'[45] What goes into the archive, or is left out, is connected to shifting perceptions of the importance of different types of material and their perceived social relevance. Filling the archive is an active task – it does not merely fill itself – and this has an impact on what is placed within it. 'In history everything begins with the gesture of *setting aside*, of putting together, of transforming certain classified objects into "documents." […] In reality it consists in *producing* such documents by dint of copying, transcribing, or photographing these objects, simultaneously changing their locus and their status.'[46]

The archive, the basis upon which history is formed and represented, is, even before the historian begins their research, a partial, fragmented and structured representation about the past.[47] While Ankersmit suggested that it was impossible to check the accuracy of the historical text against the past, it may even be impossible to check the accuracy of the single statement. Manoff notes that in women's studies and postcolonial studies there is a 'suspicion of archives', which derives from the selective and positioned nature of the official record – a record which was often collected in order to support a specific view of the world.[48] This places a further barrier between the historian and the ability to describe the past.

It is not just which records are kept or ignored that is a problem for the archive, but in what form these records are kept. A great deal of archival material is in written form and this poses further problems. One is the role of language in the representation of reality. Another is that the written form of recording is already selective in whom it can represent; what of those who did not write their observations, could not write their observations, or whose observations were not deemed worthy of keeping? In Highmore's analysis of de Certeau's work, he emphasises the view that there has been 'little material that hasn't been mediated by the practices and interests of "archivists"'.[49] Quoting de Certeau: 'A massive unawareness consigns the "masses" to oblivion, probably because of the privilege enjoyed by written culture, because of its repression of oral culture and of *different* expressions that then became types of "folklore" along the borderlines of an empire.'[50]

Of course it is possible, as Highmore notes, to use the structured archive to find what it ignores, to read the sources 'against the grain'. In this way, he suggests that the archive while structured and ordered is also messy and available to different readings.[51] But what still concerns me are the gaps in the archives. There will always be gaps in the archive, but I am concerned that these gaps are related to power; they are connected to who was allowed to speak and what was considered worth keeping. Where such gaps exist there is a question about just which histories can be told. If it is only those which can be checked against the archive, we are allowing former, and still effective, power structures to impose a silencing effect over aspects of the past. One of the aims of this work is to consider how we can tell stories about the past when the archive is lacking or asymmetrical in its collection of traces. Do we have to accept that the gaps in the archive make some forms of history – which focus on the ignored, the oppressed or silent – less possible, or is there a way we can represent the gaps? I believe there is.

The problems of language in history

Language, how it links to reality and how it constructs meaning has become particularly important since the linguistic turn – where language became the prime area for consideration in a range of disciplines.[52] Building on structuralist linguistic interpretations of language, poststructuralists and deconstructionists began to question how language, reality and meaning were linked. The answers to these questions, and the fact they were raised at all, had important consequences for how history was thought to operate and how the past could be represented – not only in terms of whether the reality of the world could be represented through language but whether the meaning attributed to language was fixed enough for readers and authors to understand each other.

A fundamental concern of the linguistic turn in history is the confusion between language and reality and the self-referential nature of linguistic descriptions.[53] The work of Ferdinand de Saussure provided a model of how language operates. Integral to this idea was the concept of the word as a 'sign'. In the structuralist representation of language, the sign comprises two further elements: the 'signifier', which is the linguistic representation of the word – the letters and sounds – and the 'signified', which is the concept of the word – the idea we have when we see or hear the word. A third element is the 'referent', the actual real-world object, to which the sign is notionally linked.[54] This model of language views the real-world object as the least important aspect of the structural system. Words did not automatically correspond to their referents but were instead in an arbitrary relationship which was fixed by social and cultural circumstances.[55] Language, then, does not provide us an unproblematic reproduction of reality but rather an incomplete and fluid representation of it. Words do not directly refer to the real world but are part of a differential system which only operates in combination with, and in opposition to, other words.[56]

In the 1960s, Roland Barthes elaborated on this structuralist view of language in relation to the production of history. In three essays, 'The Discourse of History', 'The Death of the Author' and 'The Reality Effect', he outlined how the practice of history needed to reconsider its relationship to the past and to language. Part of his critique was that by turning the past into a subject of study, historians confused the referent and signified, confusing the 'concept of the real' with the 'real' and producing a 'reality effect' from this.[57] In this sense, Barthes saw history as no different to fiction.[58] For Barthes, the very building blocks of history, the 'facts', were also a linguistic construction. Barthes's suspicion of facts came from two places. The first, after Nietzsche, was that the fact was not a simple statement but one imbued with meaning already. A 'fact' existed because it was deemed notable by someone; meaning had to be given to something to make it *into* a fact.[59] His second point, as noted in 'The Discourse of History', was that there was confusion in history between the referent and signifier. He stated that the 'fact never has any but a linguistic existence (as the term of discourse), yet everything happens as if this linguistic existence were merely a pure and simple "copy" of *another* existence, situated in an extra-structural field, the "real"'.[60]

The linguistic description of something should not be mistaken for the item under description; the reality of the past cannot be reached through linguistic descriptions of it. While sceptical of all of Barthes's claims, Ankersmit suggested that history is involved in creating a 'reality effect'.[61] The linguistic formulation of the link between the past and history reiterates the impossibility of having objective, direct access to the past and suggests a change in focus from representing the real to the intelligible.[62]

Barthes's 'Death of the Author' deals with how meaning can be communicated between the author and the reader. Barthes uses the term 'author' to refer to a previous – perhaps mythical – incarnation of writer, someone who believes that they create the single authoritative meaning of the work. As the title suggests, Barthes believed this 'author' was now dead and was replaced by the 'scriptor', someone who was aware of the contingency and intertextuality of their work: 'the text is a fabric of quotations, resulting from a thousand sources of culture'.[63] As such, any attempt to decipher a text becomes meaningless; imposing a single 'author' upon it falsely attempts to remove the influences of other work and to create a falsely coherent corpus of work. In place of the 'author', Barthes places the 'reader' at the centre of the creation of meaning. It is the reader who gives the text a unity, not the author.[64] And this means that each separate reader will bring their own ideas, texts and beliefs to each work; for everyone, there will be a new and different representation of the past.

Poststructuralists have taken on the ideas of structuralists such as Barthes and continued to question the link between language and reality. As Munslow notes, poststructuralism has 'further emphasised the problematical, aporetic connections between reality, reference and representation by emphasising the nature of texts (sources and history books) as being replete with gaps, silences and hesitation over meaning(s) and signification'.[65] Poststructuralist ideas have centred on the way in which knowledge is shaped by our understanding of language and the opaque and fluid nature of language. Meanings that are understood by one reader in one way may be understood by another in a different one. In this way, it is impossible for any author, or reader, to state they understand the true, unambiguous meaning of any text. How language is related to power, to constructions of the world and the possible ways of expressing it has also been a key aspect of poststructuralist works, especially those of Foucault.[66]

How language was used in the past is a central concern to the present histories, but so too is my awareness that any meaning I may give the histories is opaque and fluid. The role of the reader in this creation of meaning is also important; the possibilities for new thoughts provided by the opacity of language, even those with which I disagree or have not intended, is something I welcome rather than fear.

Narrative, style and history

> Content is a derivative of style.[67]
>
> Ankersmit, 'Historiography and Postmodernism'

Barthes suggests that the role of narrative in history is part of a 'reality effect', an integral part of providing history with a sense of the real.[68] Ankersmit reinforces the link between how history is represented through its form and what it says in its content. In both cases, the narrative function of history is integral to how it represents the past and how it constructs meanings for the past. The style with which historians construct their stories is not just a neutral way of imparting information or argument; it is not a way of reflecting reality, but an intrinsic part of the constructed representation about the past.

Narrative can be understood as the relating of a sequence of happenings or events by establishing a meaningful connection between them.[69] The way narrative constructs historical meaning has been explored in great detail by White. He accepts that there is a link between the archive and the past. He does not deny the reality of the past, or that events happened, and he also accepts that events happened outside of a linguistic framework. However, he is concerned with how the events of the past are layered together to form historical narratives. Central to White's work is the idea that the same events can be constructed in multiple, sometimes contradictory, ways in different narratives. It is the process of creating a narrative from the events of the past which, for White, inscribes meaning upon them and can do so in a variety of ways.[70] For White, the historical narrative is not a question of 'true' or 'false', but of how the story has been constructed and which type of story is being told. While different stories can be told, they are limited by the 'modes of emplotment which the myths of Western literary tradition sanctioned as appropriate ways of endowing human processes with meanings'.[71]

Historians, then, do not discover or find meaning in the events of the past; they construct it and it is narrative which, according to White, makes this happen. The events of the past are transformed by narrative into a story of a specific type which is then understandable to the reader.[72] It is worth quoting White at some length here:

> The production of meaning, in this case, can be regarded as a performance, because any given set of real events can be emplotted in a number of ways, can bear the weight of being told as any number of different kinds of stories. Since no given set or sequence of real events is *intrinsically* 'tragic,' 'comic,' or 'farcical,' but can be constructed as such only by the imposition of the structure of a given story-type on the events, it is the choice of the story-type and its imposition upon the events which endow them with meaning.[73]

White said that each of these emplotments could be equally plausible and there was no recourse to logic to determine between different narratives about the past. Sometimes historians made statements in their writing which could not be based upon the reports of their research and this could be put down to compositional considerations.[74] In this regard, the moral, personal and political considerations of the historian are important.

White's work placed a new emphasis on the literary nature of history and, according to Ankersmit, his book *Metahistory* changed how historical theory was considered, even if he was not entirely in favour of this.[75] By focusing on the way narrative functions in history, White has suggested how stories are *constructed* about the past and that there is fundamentally no difference between fiction and history. Both history and fiction can be described as fictive; they are both authored and are imaginative constructions.[76] While the contents, the events, of historical works may be said to have happened, how they are combined together to give the past meaning is done in the same way as events in fictional stories. In both cases, how content is represented changes the meaning ascribed to it. Thus, how a story is told can construct different meanings and representations either about events of the past or imagined events. If content is a derivation of style – if the facts of the past are given meaning by the fashion in which they are written about and how they are emplotted – then what does this mean for history and its link to reality? To what extent can we say that history is really different to fiction?

While Ankersmit noted in 1989 that content was a derivation of style, he noted in 2001 that the use of literary theory in history had its limits. Though White's literary approach to history has yielded important ways to consider how history is written, Ankersmit suggests it does not provide a useful theory of history, of how history relates to the past. It provides too formal an approach to what historians can say.[77] While literary approaches can find new ways to read texts, which should be welcomed by historians (and I do), they do not actually give any criteria for saying whether the readings are historically plausible or not. Ankersmit sees this as the job of history and something which literary theories cannot help with.[78] There is a difference between what can be said and whether it is plausible or not. Ankersmit's summation suggests that there is a difference between fiction and history, despite similarities in their construction – that theories related to fiction cannot fully apply to historical works.

What the difference between history and fiction is will be explored in my histories. Some narratives may play with how time is represented; some may be linear, others more jumpy. Some will play with my place in telling the story; at times, I may be more visible than others. Some may play with the distinction between fact, fiction and history: just what is the border between fact and fiction, and why is this important to history?

Places and modes of production

> A social situation changes at once the mode of work and the type of discourse.[79]
>
> De Certeau, *The Writing of History*

Historical research is not purely a matter of finding archive material, reading it, placing it in a wider context and constructing a narrative around it; it is also influenced by wider personal, social, economic and institutional concerns which have a direct relation upon the final representation about the past.

Michel de Certeau emphasised how history was linked to the 'place' of the author within a wider social, economic and cultural network. The place of the historian was something which could limit the histories which could be produced. De Certeau suggested that a place was a 'recruitment, milieu, profession or business', which was 'ruled by constraints, bound to privileges, and rooted in a particular situation'.[80] The place was important in determining the methods, interests and organisation of research and was a key part of the production of a text.[81] De Certeau considered that history was an operation which linked the place of work to the wider discipline surrounding the research into the past by the writing of a text; one cannot erase the effects of the place or the discipline from the final text.[82]

The creation of knowledge does not arise solely from the interests of the author but does so within an institutional framework. Institutions, such as universities, academic societies or other bodies, are important in providing constraints on what is considered relevant within a certain field of research and how it can be represented. Institutions help define the rules of research and validate what is produced; they situate what is produced within a network of ideas accepted by peers as conforming to the rules of the discipline.[83] This work too has been 'peer reviewed' to make sure it fits within such criteria. De Certeau suggests that, in historical works, the text is bound more by the place of writing than by the reality of the past. A change in the place of the historian, in the social, economic or cultural ideas attached to their work, will cause a change in the discourse produced. He said that it was not a surprise that economic history became more important during the wars, or that cultural history in his own time of writing – the 1970s – had become more important as the socio-political importance of culture had grown.[84] My own work on sporting history can be placed against a growing interest in sport and the role it plays in contemporary society. Without an institutional acceptance that a topic is worth studying, without the acceptance by one's peers that one is following academic procedures and without the acceptance of a publisher that one's work is of interest, then a particular work of history will not appear. This is something which is independent of the reality of the past under investigation.

De Certeau linked the role of institutions to wider concerns about knowledge production and power; institutions shape what can be said and who can say it.[85] Foucault also noted that power relations and fields of knowledge were intimately linked; you could not have one without the other.[86] Further to this, he indicated how his own history of prisons in France was a 'history of the present', not only concerned with representing the past, but also in highlighting and changing present concerns.[87] The creation of knowledge is not immune to present concerns; it is intimately connected to dynamics of power, social institutions and wider academic interests. Knowledge is created rather than found. When historical knowledge is created, it is done so within a network of institutions, publishers, academic disciplines, existing works and the place of research. Situating work in the present is valuable: it makes history relevant and it enables us to think about ways to change the world we live within, although institutions may also limit the range, scope and type of histories produced. However, the role of place is yet another way in which historical representations are distanced from the past.

The mode of production, the form in which history is produced, influences what is said about the past. Munslow notes that, while most works of history are still produced in written form in articles, books or monographs, there is no reason why history cannot be represented in films, plays, television documentaries, novelisations or various digital forms.[88] He adds that history favours print media because this mode, with its footnotes, references and bibliography, still emphasises the idea of empirical research and the ability of others to test the author's statement. The supremacy of textual representations for history is being challenged with the newer modes of representation, but each of these different modes of production creates their own limitations and possibilities for how history can be represented.[89]

The method of production imposes limits on what can be said. In this work there are spatial constraints. I have had to make choices to fit in with the desires of the publisher, the editor and to fit with my own changing ideas. My decision to represent these histories as a written collection, rather than as a series of articles or films is based, in part, upon a professional consideration – if textual representation is prioritised in academia then I must take note of this. Within this work I have thought about how the parts fit together, how long each one is and how the sections will function. Irrespective of whether or not my choices have achieved what I wanted, all of these considerations are extraneous to the past but are important with regard to the effect the book has on the reader. This is not only true in written works but also in other works of history. What can be said about the past is constrained by the mode of representation, the place of production and the institutions concerned.

The historian and history

> Having knowledge of the past surely is one thing; but it is perhaps no less important to know what ethical and political values we should cherish.[90]
>
> Ankersmit, *Historical Representation*

I have, so far, focused on things which I might suggest are not in the control of the historian: the absence of the past; what has been kept or lost; the functioning of language; the role of narrative; the impositions of place, position and discipline. All these areas have an influence on what can be said about the past. But there are aspects which the historian does influence, even if this will not necessarily guarantee that their history is read in the way they want it to be. Personal desires, experiences, approaches, morals, political views and ability all have an important role to play in the construction of historical representations. This is another way in which present concerns shape the constructed representation about the past. I believe, along with Ankersmit, that it is not only unavoidable but also beneficial.

The idea that the historian should be objective, able to mediate the past to the reader through the text, was one of the basic assumptions of early disciplinary history in the nineteenth century. As Ankersmit notes, the idea of subjectivity was treated sceptically as it was thought that the subjective historian would add things to the object of the past which were not there in reality. In this way, the idea of the historian being able to put aside their own political or moral prejudices was seen as essential for any practicing historian.[91] The idea of the 'transcendental ego', the historian who is able to remove their own prejudices from their work, was linked to the belief that nothing of note happened in the process of creating a historical text and that historians could access the past by scouring the archive and objectively relating what they found. This view of history is no longer acceptable and I concur with Jenkins's view of the possibility of objective history. It is one to which many professional historians subscribe, at least to some extent: 'The idea of writing an objective, neutral, disinterested text, where explaining, describing and "introducing" something is done from a position that isn't ostensibly a position at all, is a naïve one.'[92]

The historian is a part of this process. It has always struck me as strange that historians are supposed to leave their political and moral beliefs to one side when they are constructing their work; are these not the same ideas and beliefs which drive a passion for research? This idea assumes that the historian can recognise their own thoughts and somehow step back from them when it comes to historical research; speaking only for myself, I certainly cannot do this. More than this, it assumes that the only choice a historian makes is whether to ignore their own beliefs or not and that, once this is done, we can assume the historian has had no effect on their work except for the artistic flourishes of the great author. This ignores that history is about choice all the way down. History is a practice that is concerned with choosing, with selecting what is researched (or not), what is included (or not), what is deemed important (or not), in what order traces are presented and in what form they are presented. Such selections are not given to the historian by the past; they require an interpretation and an interpretation which we cannot ask the past to judge.[93] Historians decide what agents in the past intended to do, what their 'voice' is. This is, in part, down to the traces, but also down to the presuppositions of the historian in terms of which traces they choose and how they view intentionality and agency.[94] Historians are not only prone to moral or political ideas but have interests in certain topics, are part of certain historical schools, have specific styles of writing and different capabilities. All of these variants influence how historians provide representations about the past.[95]

Yet, it seems that there is still some belief that historians should not allow their political and moral ideas to infiltrate their work – that in doing so the process of history is tainted and destroyed. Why is this? Of all the variables which historians may bring to their work, are political and moral ideas not those most connected to the past itself?[96] There is a deliberate attempt to ignore the fact that one's approach to history is morally informed, that when one talks of method or approach that this is informed by a view of the world and vice versa. The desire to eradicate subjectivity in history seems to stem from the (mistaken) belief that history is able to describe the past and that this is its primary purpose. The idea of the 'objective historian' is no longer plausible. To quote Gordon, 'the pose of objectivity is worse than explicit partisanship, because those who claim neutrality are misleading people about their actual positions'.[97] Once we accept that history is partial and subjective, we can be open to new suggestions about the role which history can play.

I believe that subjectivity is not only unavoidable but should be championed in historical work. For Ankersmit, history can become an 'experimental garden' where we try out different political and moral ideas before they are implemented in society; in this way, historians can be of use for the future and present.[98] His aesthetic proposal for evaluating history recommends that we search for the histories which are the riskiest, most hazardous and unlikely to be true, but which cannot be refuted by call to historical evidence. By finding out which values are prevalent in these texts, we can find a call for future action.[99] History becomes central to deciding which ideas and policies we should adopt. This requires that the historian is open about their interests and beliefs, their practices and choices. It requires honesty and self-criticism in order for the reader to be made aware of the gaps, limitations and areas of disagreement.

The histories I have constructed in this book are ones connected to the present. They are intended to stimulate new thoughts about how we live today, about ways in which we can change the world around us. These histories are not intended to be definitive but to open debate, to provoke opposition, criticism and new histories.

Jenkins is rightly sceptical about the continued need for the practice of History but I believe history can be important to society.[100] History's greatest purpose can be to provoke us to think about and to help clarify what we believe and what we should do – but for this to happen, historians need to be open about what they are doing and the limitations of their own work. For those of you who find my histories lacking, I would urge you to produce your own. History needs to be done by everybody if it is to fulfil its purpose as a way of decentring existing power structures and allowing more people to have a voice in how society operates. For my part, I am willing to risk that a greater number of histories will reduce the importance of my work and of professional historians. To slightly adapt the quote I used to open this section, knowledge of the past is one thing, but it is more important to know which values and ideas we cherish.

Discourses

The study of 'discourses' has become important for those interested in the link between language, power and the world around us. However, it is a term that is difficult to pin down. One of the most influential users of the concept, Foucault, noted that discourse was a term 'which I have used and abused in many different senses'.[101] And I will no doubt continue this tradition. Brown provides a useful outline of his own view of Foucauldian discourse. Discourse is seen as part of a wider system of links which permits a knowledge to exist in a cultural condition (episteme) and one which is intrinsically connected to power and language. Within the system are a number of other links which range from the small (the sign, mentioned earlier, comprising the signifier and the signified) to the very large (the episteme, a vast system of knowledge which shapes ways of thinking and understanding for millions of people in a specific time – such as 'modernity').[102] Brown envisages this system of links as follows: 'sign–statement–positivity–discourse (and its sites of exteriority)–discursive formation–episteme'.[103]

Signs require statements. These statements are not written by single authors but are a set of unwritten rules which define the possibility of the appearance of a sign; statements give authority to those that say them and are part of a wider network of statements which endure within society. Positivity puts the statements and the discourse which they make up into practice. It can consist of professional journals, or professional bodies, that reinforce which statements matter in society and make them into a discourse. Discourse in this system is a central link between language, knowledge and power. A discourse is a collection of statements which belong to a single formation, which imparts an obvious message, is encountered in everyday life and is viewed as a fact, rather than as a value or command. Discourses are seen as true, they have a 'truth effect' and operate next to other discourses in a positive/negative relationship. Thus, within every discourse, even where it is not made explicitly clear, is a sense of the 'other'. Individual discourses work with other discourses in a 'discursive formation' which forms a collection of mutually supportive messages. Discourses gain acceptance outside their initial field through 'sites of exteriority' such as newspapers, government reports or professions where they gain a sense of acceptance. These discursive formations unite to form a massive body of knowledge and understanding within an episteme. This body of knowledge is supported by networks of elites and other agencies which circulate mutually supportive specialist discourses. With the system of knowledge comes a system of political power. Brown explains that power is the practice of knowledge as a socially constructed system, within which elites circulate their discourses.[104]

Discourse forms a site where an explicit message is communicated and reproduced. As Brown notes, it 'sits in the middle of any system of knowledge' and it is where knowledge resides. But importantly, it is not a 'thing' but a practice, an activity or a norm. Discourse is about the power of the elite to shape and form how individuals in society behave – to transgress against the discourse is to become deviant.[105] Within the Foucauldian system, the connection of language–knowledge–power is the key to understanding society. As Brown summarises, the postmodern view of society suggests that it is not the physical control of the army or the police in which ultimate power resides, but the 'power vested in language that demands that every individual internalises it, and by which s/he becomes self-disciplined. The citizen becomes his/her own policeman through a language of discourses dominating their thoughts and activities'.[106]

The idea of increasing self-discipline and control of the body was central to Foucault's *Discipline and Punish,* in which he demonstrated how nineteenth-century French society changed from power being deployed in an overtly physical and external manner, to a more internalised form of self-discipline, promoted by families, communities and individuals themselves.[107] Foucault outlined how a new political anatomy emerged in which 'docile bodies' could be trained, improved and made more economically viable. In schools, hospitals and military locations (the architecture of each location also served to spread the discourse), the body was trained, measured, gradated, controlled, programmed and ranked, creating increasingly tighter discipline – the body could become more like a cog in a machine.[108] In this way, discourses did not purely reflect reality, but constructed social consciousness and cultural practices. Foucault noted that 'power' was something which was always in circulation, rather than in the hands of one individual or group of individuals. Individuals were never only the 'inert or consenting' targets of power, waiting to be crushed by it, but the sites of articulation and vehicles of power.[109] The body became a site where power was deployed and reproduced, it existed within and helped to produce discourses; it was the link between daily practice and large-scale power organisations.[110]

Booth suggests that '[a]t the heart of Foucauldian discourse analysis are variable and contested meanings and notions of truth and knowledge embroiled in struggles for power'.[111] These too are my concerns. The idea that discourse, or discourses, can shape how we understand the world, can give meaning to our experiences and can provide the limitations of what can be said and who can say it is an important part of this work. As Schirato summarises in *Sports Discourse*, discourses 'both naturalize a certain mediated version of the world, and simultaneously render anything else more or less unthinkable'.[112] To be explicit, when I use the term 'discourse' in this work I am referring to this view of the term. These concerns are more visible in some histories than others; however, the link between what can be said and who can say it remains fundamental to all of these histories.

The histories connected to space and the media are intimately concerned with how discourses of football reproduced and reinforced existing understandings of society, the body, and the wider world and how they were linked with authority. Bourdieu suggests that sport can be seen as a site where acceptable habits and manners become written into the body, where the player is, at one and the same time, free to move and perform but limited in what they can actually do.[113] I see sport as a practice in which ideas and concepts about the world, ideas of how one should behave, of how the world is organised, of what is 'right' and 'wrong', of what is 'acceptable' or 'not', can be made physical, can be written into the body or into a physical space. I consider that such discourses related to how one may use the body or behave can be seen as part of a wider 'discourse of values' linked to discourses about the body. The body or the buildings in which sport is practised may become a location for knowledge about what is permitted or not, for shaping perceptions of the world, for reproducing authorised action and for the contest over the 'values' which are said to represent these ideas. Part of this work will be aimed at representing how those within the sporting field promoted their own 'discourse of values' to those who were external to sport and to those within it.

But this work is also concerned with how historical works are linked to language, knowledge and power. The histories of Rotterdam and Amsterdam during the First World War, while not explicitly connected to representing the discourses of early twentieth-century Dutch football, are concerned with historical discourses. As I have noted, I see history as a powerful tool for shaping how we view the world around us, for making certain ideas thinkable or not, and for reinforcing or challenging ideas of identity. History is part of a powerful discourse which is used to tell us who 'we' are; it is a discourse which must always be assessed and challenged.

I advocate a more popular, democratic and anarchic form of history, where each individual has the opportunity to write their own history and contribute to a discussion of the past, future and present; where the authority to speak about the past, which currently resides within professional academic history, is challenged and reconsidered; and where history is viewed as a way of thinking about what 'we' want to do and who 'we' are, rather than as a simple reflection of where 'We', as a fixed group identity, have come from. It is popular in that it requires a multiplicity of different voices; it is democratic because it requires that all voices are listened to in a society of free speech; and it is anarchic because it requires that existing power structures are challenged and decentred. My hope is that, by constructing histories in this fashion, it will encourage everyone to think about how we construct the world around us, which stories we tell about it, who has the authority to tell them and, in turn, to challenge each of these.

Sport, early Dutch football and the four histories

Finally, I will turn to Dutch football. In recent years, there has been a growth in institutional and academic acceptance of sport as a field of study. In 1974, Stevenson noted that research into sport was a relatively new academic field, but today there are dedicated courses, degrees, departments and schools.[114] In Britain, Germany, France, the USA and Australia, among others, there are numerous institutions where sport is studied as a serious and relevant social, political, cultural and physical practice. With this has come a range of journals, associations, conferences and research projects looking to develop sporting research in new areas.

That institutions and academics take sporting research seriously today should come as no surprise when we consider the cultural proliferation of sport in today's world. The importance of sport as a business, with massive financial rewards from government and enterprise, could be a partial explanation for the rise in acceptance. High-profile corruption cases, drugs cheats, violence within or external to sporting matches and tragedies involving participants in sport or spectators have provided fertile ground for academics who wish to demonstrate sport's centrality to daily life. The idea that sport is unworthy of study partly because it is overtly masculine, or physical, has subsided in the face of media interest and an increase in popular culture in university departments.[115]

Thus sport has become an increasing concern for those attempting to represent how societies and individuals interact or have done so in the past. The first book I read that dealt with sport as a serious issue was Simon Kuper's *Football Against the Enemy*; I would heartily recommend anything he writes, particularly his work on Dutch football: *Ajax, the Dutch, the War.* Both this work and David Winner's *Brilliant Orange* have done much to publicise interest in football in the Netherlands to an Anglophone audience and to demonstrate that it is a serious concern.[116] Other popular works on German, Spanish and Italian football have emphasised that football is a topic worthy of serious study and one with popular appeal.[117] That sport is often seen as popular or enjoyable is not a reason to ignore it in academic study, but one of the primary reasons to think about it.

However, academic studies of sport have often been rather conservative in their historical approach. For all the recent work of a broadly postmodern nature, there remains a dearth of sporting histories which attempt to challenge the traditional notions of history.[118] As Douglas Booth highlights, the 'accepted and acceptable epistemology in mainstream academic sport history generally remains firmly anchored to a bedrock of empiricism and to an unshakeable belief that historians can recover the past, its realities and truths. Furthermore, most sport historians do not welcome or even tolerate alternatives'.[119] Perhaps it is unwise for such a new field of research, which has only just been accepted into the academy, to make too many waves; perhaps the same goes for individual researchers too. But there are a small but rising number of scholars who are trying to do things differently and who use alternative models. Booth highlights the work of Daniel Nathan, relating to the Chicago Black Sox scandal in baseball, in which the author explicitly notes the desire to highlight his own hand in the writing of the history and the competing and contrasting nature of the memories and representations of the scandal, as one of the few examples of deconstruction in sporting history writing.[120]

Booth shows the link between fiction and historical writing, noting that '[i]n both history and fiction, narratives and metaphors bring together the separate and the distant to create the new and the pertinent'.[121] In sport history, there has been a limited use of 'fictive' elements. Booth highlights the work of Eliot Asinof in *Eight Men Out*, where dialogues and conjectures of participants in the Chicago Black Sox scandal were 'reconstructed' and Lloyd Jones's *The Book of Fame*, about the 1905 British Lions rugby tour to New Zealand, in which the author interweaves fictitious accounts with authentic sources.[122] However, there have been novels and films based on sport which include historical elements, such as the 2000 Bollywood film *Lagaan*, a film about peasants in India during the colonial era, who form a cricket team and defeat a British XI. The film, according to Booth, demonstrated 'the power of fiction to disrupt dominant meanings and to rewrite the histories of subordinated and marginalised groups who are typically excluded from accounts of the past'.[123] Such an account, while perhaps considered outside of the field of academic history, can make us think about the nature of historiography, who is included or excluded from history and who can tell the story.[124]

Some sport historians have also researched cultural aspects of sport, investigating the link between discourses, language and meaning, and power relations. Grundy has looked into the area of discourses and investigated the relation between sporting and business languages, noting that there has been a fusion between the two, resulting in a blurring of the distinctions between athletics and society.[125] I hope that my histories can add to the field of experimental sporting histories.

In the following histories, I will focus on the cities of Rotterdam and Amsterdam between 1910 and 1920. My motivation for this choice is both historical and contemporary. While Haarlem and The Hague could lay greater claims to being the birthplace of early Dutch football, both having more successful and older clubs, the port-cities of Amsterdam and Rotterdam quickly grew into centres of sport and by 1910 were home to more football clubs than anywhere else in the Netherlands. Although the arrival of football in the Netherlands is often attributed to the anglophile Willem 'Pim' Mulier, who is said to have established the first club in Haarlem in 1879, Rotterdam and Amsterdam quickly overtook Haarlem in terms of the number of clubs and their quality.

Today, Rotterdam is the only city in the Netherlands with more than two professional teams – Feyenoord, Sparta and Excelsior.[126] In addition to professional clubs, both Amsterdam and Rotterdam are sporting cities which are home to a plethora of amateur football and other sporting clubs. The current rivalry between Feyenoord of Rotterdam (where, for the sake of full disclosure, I had a season ticket while living in the Netherlands) and Ajax of Amsterdam has also become one of more than just football. The cities are sometimes perceived as having different characteristics. Rotterdam is often considered as a city of industry, linked to the vast harbour on the river Maas, whereas Amsterdam is seen as a city of artisans, commerce and free-living. The rivalry between the two cities forms part of the identity of the two, in particular for the often negatively perceived Rotterdam. In terms of culture, Rotterdam is perceived to be the lesser partner; Rotterdam is the industrial centre, Amsterdam is the commercial and cultural centre.[127] The two cities are sometimes seen to represent a contrast in image and identity; how this identity was perceived in the period between 1910 and 1920 forms part of my interest in this subject.

Sport, as I have demonstrated, is a viable and important area for research and in the Netherlands it is no different. In 2014, a report noted that sport:

> for many people is a regular feature of their daily life. By doing sport themselves, by volunteering in one of the many sport clubs, by following our (top) Dutch sporting stars and encouraging them in their matches during the Olympic Games, Paralympic Games, at the European or World Championships. Or by encouraging their own children or family members in their weekly matches.[128]

In terms of numbers, there are more than 28,500 sports clubs in the Netherlands, of which around 2,750 are devoted to association football with an average of 425 members each.[129] Football, either amateur or professional, is the most popular sport in the Netherlands, with 62 per cent of all those who attend sporting events going to see football.[130] In addition to existing television broadcasters, new media broadcasters, such as *Fox Sports Eredivisie*, have ensured that football is never far from television screens. Between September and December 2013, they broadcasted 636 hours of football-related content.[131] The report also estimated that the income of football clubs was around €407 million and their costs around €401 million.[132] It is safe to say that football is an important part of modern Dutch culture. While it would be too simplistic to say that Amsterdam and Rotterdam are at its centre – and this would provoke a barrage of complaints from Eindhoven, Enschede, Alkmaar, Groningen, Heerenveen and other Dutch football cities – they are certainly very important within it.

Many of the sources I have used for these histories come from the decade between 1910 and 1920. As I noted above, the writing of history is in part influenced by external factors and for me these included the time available to research in the Netherlands and, crucially, the sources available. For the period between 1910 and 1920, there exists a much greater number of accessible sporting journals and articles in contrast to the period before; reports about football became more commonplace and extensive in the early twentieth century, and especially after 1910. Historically, the period around the First World War is one where many new clubs formed and the game seemed to gain popularity in a wider part of the population. Part of my research aims to examine why this development occurred, how it changed the physical space of the cities concerned and how it changed the reaction to the game itself. In addition, the period around the First World War provided me with the opportunity to research an area of Dutch cultural life which is often overlooked. While the Netherlands was officially neutral during the war, it had a dramatic impact on everyday life and I will use sport as an entry point to a wider consideration of Dutch society and culture.

This work is intended as a cultural history that focuses on sport, and I have used the term 'sporting history' as a shorthand for this. As Poster notes, 'cultural history' is itself a term which is not sharply delineated, but is often associated with 'new perspectives and new topics; they validate imaginative proposals and open the gates to heterodox formulations, tearing down the defences of disciplinary stability'.[133] I have chosen not to address specifically what 'cultural history' is, as opposed to other forms of history such as 'social history', 'economic history' or 'political history'. This is in part because of spatial concerns, but it is also because the style of postmodern history which I have advocated, as can be seen by Poster's words, overlaps with what is commonly referred to as 'cultural history'; I feel there is little point reiterating these ideas under a different moniker – especially as my primary concern in this introduction has been to address the practice of history as a whole and not to further divide it.

Each of the following histories offers a different constructed representation of early Dutch football culture. The first history focuses on spatial changes in Rotterdam and Amsterdam, especially with regard to the construction of new football fields and stadia. This chapter thinks about how spatial change can be a useful avenue for historical representations. I look at how stadia could be a key part, at least for some, of a 'discourse of values' and 'discourses of identity'. The chapter also thinks about the networks of power of those involved with building major stadia and suggests that football was part of a wider cultural, charitable, educational and political network of ideas about values and bodily use. The history suggests that discourses about what was acceptable or not did not go unchallenged and that tensions and conflicts about sport were as much about the 'correct' way of educating or controlling the young, or working men, as about the game itself.

In the second history, I think about differences between fiction and history. I provide a fictionalised narrative which places individuals at the centre of the historical story as a way to counter problems faced by historians when dealing with fragmented or missing traces of the past. The story is set in Rotterdam in the autumn of 1914, as fears about conflict in the rest of Europe grew. In this history, we take part in a conceptual, imagined journey through the city of Rotterdam, meeting members of Rotterdam football clubs: what did they do, where did they meet, how did the war change lives, what was happening in different parts of the city in August 1914 and how did football fit into this? This history poses questions about how we can represent the past and the power given to specific forms of writing about it. If the work had not been acknowledged as fictional would you have responded in the same way?

In the third history, I use media reports of football matches to represent the discourses connected to the game of football. Inspired by Foucault, I am critical of the role of football in society, outlining how the media reports of the time demonstrate that football was part of a disciplinary tactic to spread certain discourses more widely and deeply into society. The history also represents how various aspects of football culture – the players, administrators, referees and fans – were discussed in media reports and how the media themselves developed greater interest in the game. While different media outlets had different 'reality effects', and different perspectives on the game existed, by the start of the 1920s, the form of the game promoted by the *Nederlandsche Voetbalbond* (the Netherlands Football Association, *NVB*) had become the dominant discourse surrounding football and it was one which promoted order, discipline, measurement, rankings and regulation. If this view is accurate then what does this mean for the widespread participation and acceptance of sport and football today?

In the fourth history, I use the personal diary of C. J. K. van Aalst, a notable figure in Amsterdam football culture and Dutch business, to represent the personal interests of an individual connected to football culture and to give insights into wider Dutch culture and society. While Van Aalst was president of the company responsible for the largest football stadium in the Netherlands, *Het Nederlandsch Sportpark* (the Netherlands Sport Park, *Sportpark*) – the diaries suggest he only had a tangential interest in the game. This history looks at how Van Aalst represented his wartime experiences, and how I dealt with his distinct and often frustrating lack of interest in sport. While I question how useful Van Aalst's diaries are, they provide entry points to represent wider histories of Amsterdam during the First World War. There are suggestions of collusion, political disagreements and intrigue, insights into the lives of royalty, press freedoms, as well as insights into an often ignored rebellion in Amsterdam during the war and the place of sport within this. This history also reflects the tensions and emotions that exist within the historian and some of the problems which occur when producing a history and which will, no doubt, continue after its publication.

In this chapter, I have highlighted why I am sceptical about history, but also that I am hopeful that it can provide opportunities to create meaningful change. I hope that these histories can provoke further debate about how history and sport operate within society because, as I was when I was younger, I am someone who loves them both, even if I am not sure I always like them, or if they are good for us.

2

Physical Spaces of Football and their Construction

Rotterdam has changed a lot since my first visit there in 2007. In the five years since I lived in the Netherlands, when I would make the regular trip to the city on the banks of the Maas (often to watch Feyenoord), the numerous hoardings and scaffolds in various parts of the city have come down and been replaced by gleaming new structures. The station,

Fig 2.1 Rotterdam *Centraal Station,* 2016

which I remember as a crowded, hectic combination of container boxes, workmen, metal fences and signs promising a new building, has transformed into a new spacious structure, an impressive new entrance to the city for thousands of passengers each day.[2]

Elsewhere in the city, Blaak, a large open square flanked on one side by the distinctive building of the Rotterdam Library, has seen some bold architectural changes. The *Markthal*, an ambitious mix of food stalls, shops, flats and graphic design, accompanied by a set of revolving doors with the capacity to trap visitors at a moment's notice, has provided a new architectural, not to mention commercial, lure to the city. The centre of Rotterdam, which was almost entirely destroyed during the Second World War, has become an architectural playground, a location for new, different and quirky buildings, which are trying to say something about the city, its ambitions and its people.[3]

Something similar is happening on the southern side of the river Maas. In 2013, Koolhaas's enormous *De Rotterdam* building changed the city's skyline. Further south, next to the railway, is another iconic building: *Stadion Feijenoord*, home to one of the Netherlands' most popular and successful clubs, Feyenoord. Like the city around it, the 1936 stadium has seen changes – expansion, refurbishment and renovation. But it seems

Fig 2.2 Rotterdam *Markthal*, 2016

it is in need of further redevelopment. In 2008 discussions continued about the need for a new stadium, which would better serve the needs of the football club, the city and the people who live there. The discussions showed the sheer number of people involved in such a process. In addition to the football club, the Municipality had to consider how the plans would fit within the wider city context and transport agencies needed to consider access to the area. The press publicised the discussions, citizens had their say and businesses had to provide funding, sponsorship and support. By 2014, after extensive research, the plans had been finalised, demonstrating how lengthy such decision-making processes can be. The chosen option was to renovate the stadium to accommodate 70,000 spectators and to develop new training facilities. But this choice was not just about football. For one of those responsible for the choice, Wim van Sluis, it is about providing social benefits, and an impulse for further regeneration in southern Rotterdam.[4]

Space, even the most simple demarcation or building, is charged with ideas; it is the result of choices and decisions.[5] These choices and decisions are linked to discourses which construct how we interact with the world around us and how we interact with ourselves; they help construct, maintain and naturalise a view of the world.[6] The spaces we live

Fig 2.3 *De Rotterdam*, 2016

in and the discourses attached to them become an important part of how we can practise daily life, what we are permitted to do and what we are not. As Foucault notes, 'space is fundamental in any exercise of power'.[7]

This history is about how constructions in space are linked to wider discourses about the world. It is a history about how the physical spaces of football – pitches, grounds and stadia – were part of wider changes in Dutch urban centres and a contest to implement certain discourses. The construction of new facilities for sport can be seen as part of an attempt to spread discourses of order, discipline and civility in the city and crucially of promoting the 'correct' way to use these spaces. The development of new spaces and stadia in the early twentieth century demonstrates that football was becoming an increasingly important element of daily life, one which began to attract influential politicians and businessmen, as well as a wider public.

Urban change in Amsterdam and Rotterdam

While the plans for a modern stadium in Rotterdam promise to make it the largest in the Netherlands, this honour – if that is what it is – currently goes to the Amsterdam ArenA in the eastern suburbs of the country's capital. Amsterdam is the epitome of a one-club city. The city's museum even spells it out: 'Ajax is Amsterdam and Amsterdam is Ajax.'[8] As I can attest, the name resonates far beyond the leafy canals of the old city. A mention of my research into Dutch football can often see people light up talking about Ajax and the team's history, only to be slightly disappointed when I explain what it is my research involves.

There is good reason for this enthusiasm. Ajax was founded in 1900 and won its first national title in 1918, but it built its international reputation on the successful team of the 1970s with Dutch talent such as Cruijff, Rep, Neeskens, Haan and Krol, claiming three European Championships under the leadership of Michels and Kovács, with a style of football known as 'total football'. It is the club of Van Basten and Rijkaard, and of a younger group of stars, including Kluivert, Davids and Seedorf, which again rose to the top of European football. Along with some of Amsterdam's less salubrious offerings, Ajax is one of the first things people think about when they think of the Netherlands, or at least for those to whom I talk.

When Ajax play at home, the city's bars fill with supporters who move on to the stadium. Next to the ArenA is *De Toekomst* (The Future), a complex of training facilities and home to the famous youth academy. Around the stadium are numerous shopping facilities, restaurants,

Fig 2.4 The ArenA surrounded by houses, shops and offices, Amsterdam, 2016

cinemas and two large music venues, all linked by railway to the centre of the city and further afield. On match days, the ArenA sees a thronging, sprawling mass of people journey to the Bijlmer area of the city – a previously little-regarded neighbourhood and site of a disastrous 1992 plane crash.

For a hypothetical traveller to Amsterdam in the early part of the twentieth century, things were very different. The area where the ArenA now stands, in Bijlmermeer, was little more than pastureland and officially situated outside the boundaries of the city. Within the city of Amsterdam, citizens lived in the beating heart of Dutch commerce. Amsterdam was the financial centre of the Netherlands, home to many banks and commercial exchanges. Along the river IJ were a range of significant industries and important harbours. Goods from the Dutch colonies made Amsterdam one of Europe's leading market centres. Factories, diamond-polishing mills and shipyards all grew in the course of the nineteenth century.[9] Trade with the city was made easier by developments elsewhere. While there had been few spatial developments since the seventeenth century, the late nineteenth century saw a number of projects in and around the city.[10] In 1876, the opening of the *Noordzeekanaal* (North Sea Canal) gave Amsterdam a direct and easily navigable link to the North Sea at IJmuiden and two decades later the *Merwedekanaal* enabled more-efficient shipping between the city and the growing industries of the Ruhr. The expansion of the Suez Canal in 1869 also cut journey times between Amsterdam and the Dutch East Indies.[11]

While waterways were being reshaped by the cutting of canals in and around its borders, the construction of railways and stations also contributed a great deal to the new geography of the city. In 1889, the city received a new station, connecting eastern and western parts of the city with the Dutch hinterland. The *Centraal Station*, which today is still the first point of arrival for many tourists to Amsterdam, was built north of the historic Dam Square on a stretch of land between the docks. Prior to its construction, the idea was controversial, as the new structure, belching smoke, noise and people, would be the first man-made barrier between the heart of Amsterdam and the river IJ and its great ships. In Amsterdam, it was seen as a 'mistake', an 'attack on the beauty and glory of the capital' and it was only after pressure from the government in The Hague that the station was forced upon a reluctant city.[12] In 1869, after much debate, the Amsterdam *Gemeenteraad* (Municipal Chamber) accepted the need for a new station in the centre of the city and work finally began in 1882.[13]

In the last decades of the nineteenth century, and the first of the twentieth, developments in Amsterdam's industry, finance and infrastructure were so rapid that it became known as 'the small Golden Age' harking back to the glory days of Amsterdam's global financial power.[14] But some saw problems ahead. Entrepreneur Ernst Heldring was fearful that Rotterdam's growing port would cause problems for Amsterdam in the future.[15] While Amsterdam was a city that appeared to have a prosperous future, its physical expansion, accompanied by a massive influx from the Dutch countryside during the agrarian crises of the 1870s, caused concern about housing and employment.[16]

Baedeker's guide of 1910 notes that Amsterdam's concentric canals 'are flanked with avenues of elms and present a pleasant and at places handsome and picturesque appearance'.[17] But the central areas were no longer sufficient to serve the expanding city's needs. After 1870, the historical centre of Amsterdam was expanded upon with newer districts beyond the Singelgracht, permitting new houses to be built for the increasing population. New districts emerged in Dapperbuurt, de Pijp, de Klinkerbuurt and Staatsliedenbuurt and, in 1896, the borders of the Municipality were enlarged, taking in land from the surrounding areas with the possibility for new growth. Yet the new districts of Diemen, Nieuwer-Amstel and Sloten, still did not meet the need for housing.

As more people came to Amsterdam, the poorest found accommodation harder to find. Housing in the new districts was largely built using private money and charging high rents, which meant that many of Amsterdam's poorest residents lived in squalid, cramped housing; this no doubt aided the spread of an 1866 cholera outbreak, which claimed more than 1,000 lives. An 1893 report from the Health Commission showed that one in every thirteen people who lived in the city lived in cellar accommodation, greatly contributing to the rise in epidemics and health complaints.[18] In the second half of the nineteenth century, a growing hygiene movement emerged which played an important role in ensuring that Amsterdam, and other Dutch cities, received the benefits of sewerage systems and fresh water.[19]

In 1901, the *Gezondheidswet* (Public Health Law) and the *Woningwet* (Public Housing Law) attempted to deal with health and housing problems in the Netherlands, implementing a series of regulations to prevent substandard housing and improve the planning of Dutch cities. The *Woningwet* required that each city of more than 10,000 inhabitants, or which had more than 20 per cent growth over five years, produce an *Uitbreidingsplan* (Expansion Plan). The accompanying *Gezondheidswet* required that cities establish health commissions comprised of doctors, architects and planning experts to verify the efficacy of the plans.[20] In line with Foucault's suggestion, space, and how it was planned, began to play an increasingly important role in power and political life. The city was seen as the state in microcosm and a model for rational government.[21] If the city could be planned and ordered properly, then so could the state and the people.

After 1900, the Amsterdam *Gemeente* (Municipality) also passed legislation. In 1902, it became the first Dutch city to enact a law regulating basic standards for accommodation, yet a lack of public financing meant that in the first decade of the century, housing was still largely built by private companies and beyond the reach of the poor. Charities, societies and organisations which aimed to solve these problems became increasingly numerous, but housing production still fell short of what was needed.[22] Such philanthropic societies and charities were a part of the rapid increase in voluntary organisations in the Netherlands between 1870 and 1900, many of which aimed to spread a specific set of values throughout Dutch urban society, providing a form of paternalistic 'civilization offensive'.[23]

Societies were not only limited to philanthropic endeavours. A number of cultural organisations and societies played a part in Amsterdam life towards the end of the nineteenth century. By the turn of the century, the society or club had become a widespread phenomenon in the Netherlands, particularly among industrialists and businessmen.[24] Many societies and individuals helped in the building of new spaces. In 1888, the Concertgebouw theatre opened and became the home of the *Koninklijke Concertgebouworkest* (Royal Concertgebouw Orchestra). Constructing the venue took seven years and involved the financial participation of a number of wealthy Amsterdammers who seemed to agree with the *Amsterdammer* newspaper when it suggested that Amsterdam needed a concert hall, like so many of the world's great cities.[25] The links between space, power and prestige were also important in the construction of sporting space in the early twentieth century.

In other parts of the city, Amsterdam boasted the exhibition halls of the *Paleis voor Volksvlijt* of 1864 and the galleries of the *Rijksmuseum* from 1885. Amsterdam received its first great park in 1865. The Vondelpark, like many other parks and cultural buildings across the Netherlands, was aided by private money.[26] It was also intended to have a social purpose. Parks like the Vondelpark could provide space for Amsterdammers to unwind after their demanding jobs and provide greenery for the many who lived in cramped accommodation.[27] Other parks were proposed by city architect Van Niftrik, but of these only three were built by the early twentieth century – the Westerpark, the Oosterpark and the Sarphatipark.[28] Transforming plans into physical reality was not an easy task. The ambitious plans of Van Niftrik were largely rejected when Kalff took the role of city architect and introduced more practical and financially viable plans.

Amsterdam's political culture was changing at the same time as the development of its physical space. In 1888, Amsterdam gained its first radical liberal municipal member.[29] In 1894, the *Sociaal-Democratische Arbeiderspartij* (Social Democratic Workers Party, *SDAP*) was formed in Amsterdam; in 1903, they organised a number of railway strikes in the Netherlands. While the *SDAP* began to attract an increasing number of votes, it received a relatively small number of seats, owing to the geographical divisions of the city's *Gemeenteraad*, although some members did become important in local committees.[30] For some, the *SDAP* was not radical enough and in 1909, the more radical Marxist members, under David Wijnkoop, formed the *Sociaal-Democratische Partij* (Social Democratic Party, *SDP*).[31] The municipal elections of 1909 showed that liberals were still the most dominant force in local politics, however, the *SDAP* were not far behind, along with denominational parties, particularly the *Anti-Revolutionaire Partij* (Anti-Revolutionary Party, *ARP*) of Abraham Kuyper.[32] Organisations and clubs were also beginning to take on more of a politico-religious nature towards the end of the nineteenth century.[33]

In Rotterdam, liberals also held the balance of power. However, there were often factions and splits within liberal groups. While the *Liberale Unie* (Liberal Union) dominated national politics between 1885 and 1901, some of its more socially progressive members left to form a new party, the *Vrijzinnig-Democratische Bond* (Free-thinking Democratic Association, *VDB*).[34] After 1900, liberal support began to cool. In 1897, almost 80 per cent of the Rotterdam chamber consisted of various liberal politicians, but by 1910, it was around 30 per cent. Socialists and denominational politicians gained where liberal politicians lost, although, as in Amsterdam, voting limitations meant socialist members were not prominent in the chamber.[35]

In Rotterdam, the second half of the nineteenth century saw a massive growth in population from nearly 92,000 in 1852 to over 332,000 in 1900.[36] Much of this was connected to the growth in the harbours, which had expanded in the late nineteenth century. Rotterdam had changed from a merchant city, with the second-largest port in the Netherlands, into a centre for international trade, with the second-largest port in Continental Europe. By 1913, more than half of those employed in Rotterdam had jobs in or around the harbours.[37] As Van de Laar comments, Rotterdam 'was a water city, where even the dead were ferried to their last location by boat'.[38] The great docks which emerged to deal with the increase in trade were largely located on the southern side of the Maas. Here shipyards, machine works, distilleries as well as cocoa, tobacco and margarine factories provided much of the city's income and employment. To the north of the river, the city centre was entwined with canals giving a 'characteristic air', all served by international steamer boats and various train stations.[39]

The physical geography of the city changed with the increase in population. From 1854, under the stewardship of Rose, new boulevards were designed to ease congestion and help alleviate the city's growing sanitation problems.[40] In 1879, De Jongh took over the *Gemeentewerken* (Department of Municipal Works) and set about turning Rotterdam into one of the world's greatest metropolises. Land in neighbouring municipalities was incorporated into an ever-growing Rotterdam: in 1886, Delfshaven and, in 1895, Charlois, Overschie and Kralingen. After 1890, 'Rotterdam grew faster than any other city in the Netherlands', a growth fuelled by the development of the massive harbours.[41]

What marked De Jongh's tenure at the helm of Rotterdam's city planning was the scale of the proposals made. In 1887, the Rijnhaven opened, in 1905 the Maashaven was completed and on the north banks smaller docks emerged. Rotterdam's first electric power plants were established in 1891 to power the cranes and machinery in the port. De Jongh's ruthless focus on the development of the harbours also saw railway lines cut through working-class areas south of the river to get to the new quays. Under De Jongh, Rotterdam experienced its most turbulent period of growth and much of the city's current character can be attributed to him.[42]

In 1910, a new director, Burgdorffer, took over the *Uitbreidingsplan* which De Jongh had created in 1903. *Uitbreidingsplans* contained provisions for worker housing, transport links, municipal buildings and for green spaces to provide the city with areas to relax and exercise. In Rotterdam, schools, gymnastic and swimming lessons were promoted and in 1907 a swimming school opened to the northern banks of the river Maas. The Municipality was often not involved in running these organisations and many swimming classes were organised privately or by swimming associations.[43] In 1911, the first complex of *volkstuinen* (allotments) in Rotterdam appeared in Kralingen, numbering 154 plots. This development was made possible by *Maatschappij tot Nut van 't Algemeen* (Society of Public Welfare, *MNvA*) with the involvement of the *Departement van Nut* (Department of Welfare) – indicating links between governmental organisations and private societies. In 1914, 132 allotments opened on the Spangen Polder in the west of the city, a site that would later see the development of the Sparta Stadium, also known as *Het Kasteel* (the Castle).[44]

Allotments, gymnastics and swimming were not the only things available for recreation-minded Rotterdammers. In the mid-nineteenth century, Rotterdam gained its own park on the banks of the Maas, but public greenery remained a low political priority until the turn of the century.[45] The growing urbanisation of the city around 1900 saw a move from a number of intellectuals to encourage the public to take part in walks and, in around 1911, school trips to the coast.[46] In 1904, the Rotterdam *Bond voor Lichamelijke Opvoeding* (Association for Physical Exercise, *BvLO*) was established with the aim of promoting physical activity in the city and finding space to do this.[47] Thus, recreational space in cities in the early twentieth century was becoming an increasingly important part of the discussion about urban planning. Space was wanted for parks, allotments, school fields, daily worker exercise, gymnastics and sporting exercise; each of these different activities were competing for a limited amount of space and saw different organisations trying to assert why their needs were greater, or would be more beneficial for the population. Discourses of values became increasingly attached to the development of urban space. In the early twentieth century, football pitches, grounds and stadia were not special cases but were a contestable part of the wider urban plan and the discourses of values in society.

Spaces for football in 1910 Amsterdam and Rotterdam

For a hypothetical traveller to the Netherlands in January 1910, there were many opportunities to watch football matches. Arriving in the harbours of Rotterdam, with a copy of the 1909/10 *Voetbal-Jaarboekje* (Football Yearbook) to hand, the visitor could plan a trip across the Netherlands. Within the guide, they would find contact details, club addresses and a series of articles on the positive aspects of football to pass the time between matches.

The guide was compiled and distributed by the *NVB,* which had been established in 1889 under the initiative of Willem 'Pim' Mulier. He was credited with founding the first organised football club in the Netherlands when, in 1879, he established the Haarlemsche Football Club (HFC) with some of his young friends, and early clubs in the Netherlands were largely a mixture of young students from what Miermans describes as the 'so-called better milieus'.[48] These clubs, like other organisations, functioned as a location for predominantly young men to get together and discuss the world. Next to the pitch in Haarlem, men like Van Eeden, Gorter and Roland Holst would lie and discuss literature and sociology while watching the others.[49] The game itself was a casual affair, rather than part of an organised or regulated system. But this brought problems with it; matches were difficult to organise, locations were hard to find, and arranging kick-off times and ensuring that both teams had enough players were no easy tasks. The establishment of the *NVB,* which created a network of clubs and, with this, the first steps towards a regulated league system, made such organisational matters easier. It also moved the game of football from play towards something more structured, towards a sport.[50]

The *NVB* was neither the only nor the first sporting organisation in the Netherlands. The structuring of physical activity within an organisational framework became increasingly common towards the end of the nineteenth century. Physical activities, which had been common in the Netherlands before the nineteenth century, such as sailing and skating, underwent, for want of a better term, a 'sportification', becoming more regulated and organised. A number of activities gained some organisational structure before football and athletics: sailing and rowing in 1847; gymnastics in 1868; yachting in 1874; trotting and horse racing around 1880; skating in 1882; cricket, cycling and student rowing in 1883; the game of kolven in 1885; and swimming in 1888.[51] Physical activity was also helped by other organisations and the *MNvA* was instrumental in providing training for teachers in gymnastics from 1847, and other associations promoted the need for exercise and exercise spaces.[52] By the late nineteenth century, organised exercise and sport became an increasingly important part of the discussion about constructing society. By the turn of the century, there were around 30,000 members of sporting clubs in the Netherlands, and by 1910 this had more than doubled.[53]

While the name '*NVB*' suggests a nationwide organisation, this is a little misleading. Initially, it was based in the urban centres of the western Netherlands. The clubs that were involved in establishing the *NVB*, in 1889, came from Amsterdam, Rotterdam, The Hague, Haarlem, Delft and, to slightly disrupt this narrative, from the city of Wageningen near Arnhem.[54] Early leagues were formed from a selection of clubs from this area. In the period before 1900, there were sometimes as few as five teams in the highest division. This is not to say that these were the only football clubs in the Netherlands. Although football was not a mass sport in the Netherlands, there were clubs who did not take part in competitions or join the nascent *NVB*; football clubs emerged around the whole of the Netherlands in the period around the turn of the century.[55] After 1889, regional associations emerged across the country and these began to organise their own competitions.[56] One of the key functions of the *NVB* was to promote the sport of football across the Netherlands, to change it from an elite game in the west of the Netherlands into a popular practice accepted across the country. After 1900, football, along with cycling, had clubs which were open to most parts of society, in contrast to many sporting organisations which were socially exclusive.[57] That the *NVB* discouraged the adoption of a motion in 1913, which proposed that organisation of competitions should take no notice of the social status of teams, suggests that football was not inured from such tensions.[58]

At the end of the nineteenth century, football was an activity that was not universally liked. The sport faced challenges from parents and teachers, who saw it as a waste of time; from medics, who were worried about its physical nature; from others, particularly those in gymnastic circles, who saw that increasing competition in sport would have a negative influence on the young of the Netherlands; and from some religious preachers and politicians.[59] Such criticisms did not entirely disappear and were evident in the debate about stadia in the second decade of the twentieth century.

By the 1909/10 season, ninety-six clubs had affiliated to the *NVB* and between them they could field 131 sides.[60] For the first time since the establishment of the *NVB* leagues, Rotterdam was home to a champion.[61] Sparta Rotterdam had won the national championship for the 1908/09 season after winning both legs of the championship play-off against Wilhelmina, from den Bosch. This win had brought an end to nine seasons of dominance for teams from The Hague. Sparta played their home games at the Prinsenlaan ground to the north-east of the city centre in Crooswijk. This space was rented from the Municipality and was secured after consultation with the Rotterdam *BvLO*. The initial rent was set at 225 guilders per year.[62] Although this shows that clubs could find space to play, it also indicates that their needs were dependent on the future plans of the Municipality and plans to expand the city. This would be one of the driving factors in necessitating Sparta's move to a new stadium in 1916.

Sparta was not the only team that played in Crooswijk. On the Schuttersveld, not far from the Prinsenlaan, three other teams played their home games: Achilles, Door Vereeniging Sterker (DVS), and one of Rotterdam's best teams, Volharding Olympia Combinatie (VOC), born from a fusion between Volharding and Olympia on 1 January 1904. To the east of the centre, in Kralingen, was the Woudestein, which was where Excelsior Rotterdam and Leonidas played. In the west of the city, near the park, was the Heuvelterrein which was home to Neptunus and Unitas Saturnus Combinatie (USC), while Xerxes and Rotterdamsche Football Club (RFC) played slightly further away from the centre, on the Boschpolder, in the less developed parts of the city.[63] A number of other clubs played in the local leagues of the *Rotterdamsche Voetbalbond* (Rotterdam Football Association, *RVB*) against reserve teams from Rotterdam's larger clubs. Unfortunately, many of their pitch locations do not appear in the *Voetbal-Jaarboekje*.[64] Of these smaller clubs, Celeritas played their home matches on the large Afrikaanderplein, on the southern side of the river. This team, founded in the *Vereeniging* café in 1908, as Wilhelmina, joined the *NVB* leagues in 1912 and later changed their name to Feyenoord.

The situation in Amsterdam was different. As Sparta were celebrating their first victory, football lovers in Amsterdam were desperately looking around for any signs of hope. The last club from the city to participate in the highest division of Dutch football was RUN Amstels Progress (RAP), in the 1904/05 season. When the 1909/10 Western First Division began, Rotterdam was represented by two clubs, The Hague by three, Haarlem by two, with Utrecht, Leiden and Dordrecht each having one club. However, the highest-placed league teams in Amsterdam were to be found in the Second Division of the Western leagues. Arguably the best of Amsterdam's clubs in 1910 was the Amsterdamsche Football Club (AFC). This team had finished top of the Western Second Division B in 1910, but had failed to be promoted after losing a play-off. Amsterdam's most successful club was RAP. They had won the national championship on five occasions, in 1892, 1894, 1897, 1898 and 1899. By 1910, only the Haagsche Voetbal Vereeniging (HVV), of The Hague, had won more championship titles, with seven. But like AFC, RAP found themselves in the Western Second Division. The modern giants of Dutch football, Ajax, were not only not Amsterdam's best team, they were not even the best team with the name 'Ajax'. This honour belonged to the Leiden-based Ajax, who were in the First Division, until the end of the 1909/10 season, while Amsterdam's Ajax were in the Second Division B – they would experience several promotions and relegations before 1918.

In addition to clubs that were members of the *NVB* and the *Amsterdamsche Voetbalbond* (Amsterdam Football Association, *AVB*), there was another form of football in Amsterdam. The *Amsterdamsch Volks Voetbalbond* (Amsterdam People's Football Association, *AVVB*), founded in 1904, was a form of protest association for poorer clubs who could not afford the increasing costs of joining the *NVB* or for equipment. Formed from what are often termed '*volksvoetbal*' clubs (people's football clubs), there was a difficult relationship between the *AVVB* and the *AVB*, which contained the older, more established clubs. Despite joining the *NVB* in 1906, there remained some considerable tension between the *AVVB* and other organisations.[65] After 1906, Amsterdam had the rather strange situation of having multiple forms of football, with different participants and motives, organised under one authority. An additional organisation, for those who wanted to play football with their colleagues, called the *Kantoor Voetbalbond* (Office Football Association), provided yet another form of sport; this would also unite with the *NVB* in 1911.

The geographical position of the clubs in Amsterdam was also peculiar. The majority of Amsterdam teams played their matches on, or near, the Middenweg in the Watergraafsmeer. In 1910, this included at least nine clubs affiliated to the *NVB*: Ajax Amsterdam and AFC played near a farm north of the Middenweg, while Amstel, Amsterdamsche Voetbal Vereeniging (AVV), Voetbal Vereeniging Amsterdam (VVA) and Door Eendracht Verbonden – Eendracht Combinatie (DEC), played near a different farm to the south. Around the corner, RAP played on the Oud-Roosenburgh pitch, while Door Oefening Steeds Beter and Volharding had a ground on the Kruislaan.[66] Today this land is part of the western suburbs of Amsterdam, but in 1910 it was not part of the Amsterdam Municipality – the Watergraafsmeer remained a separate administrative body until 1921. Another Amsterdam team, Blauw-Wit, also played some distance from the centre of the city, near the Hembrug in the east, which connected the railway line across the *Noordzeekanaal* to Zaandam. The clubs closest to the centre of the city were the relatively small clubs of Neerlandia and SDE; both these clubs played in the west, near the St Barbara Kerkhof in Sloterdijk.[67] So, while Amsterdam had provided one of the most successful teams of the late nineteenth century, in 1910, the city had no teams in the First Division, no substantial football grounds in the city and its best teams played in a neighbouring municipality.

Stadium crisis in Amsterdam

The lack of success weighed heavily on the minds of some Amsterdammers. The first month of 1909 saw a provisional committee established whose task was to establish whether the construction of a new sporting stadium was desirable and viable. The committee had taken note of the negative depiction of Amsterdam's sporting grounds in the press and the poor status of its sporting teams. It painted the current situation in stark and sombre tones:

> It is, we trust, not unknown, that for many years now, the sporting spirit in Amsterdam amongst the upcoming generation has been on the wane, mainly caused by a lack of concentration. To support this we only cite the lamentable state of the Amsterdam Velodrome; the fact that the capital of the Empire, despite its many football clubs, has for many years been unable to field a First Division team; that here much less is done in Turnen and other physical activity than in e.g. Germany. These examples could be still multiplied.[68]

Lack of adequate sporting space was having a detrimental effect on young Amsterdammers and on the city's image. That Amsterdam did not have adequate sporting space was not just a problem in terms of sport, but it was a problem that reflected badly on the city, the country and was a reflection of a moral problem. Sporting facilities were being connected to wider discourses in society. These discourses were about what people should do and where they should do it and became linked to identities. Sporting space was seen as a symbolic representation of a wider moral problem, a problem of how young Dutch men were being educated and raised. A new stadium would rectify this problem and it was something that would help spread the 'correct' set of values in society.

However, ensuring that such values could be spread was not always straightforward. Just months before the establishment of a committee to look into a new stadium in Amsterdam, a previous attempt to construct such sporting space had failed. Under the auspices of the *Werkloozen Comité* (Commission for the Unemployed), an attempt had been made to finance the building of a new stadium. In newspapers and committee circulars, the case in favour of the new stadium was clear and consisted of two key points. First, Amsterdam needed a new sporting stadium to add to the existing parks and recreational space. Secondly, the stadium could provide work for the unemployed; new workers would ensure that the land was raised and prepared correctly before more qualified builders took over.[69] Thus, sporting space would serve a dual role. It would provide entertainment for Amsterdammers and would serve a social good. For those establishing sporting space in the city, this duality would become the basis for future projects.

The stadium, like other spaces, was to be funded by a mix of public and private money. Providing that those behind the proposal could find at least 100,000 guilders of private capital, the Municipality would match this sum. Despite being backed by political members, bankers and businessmen, the project could only raise two-thirds of what was required. By December 1908, it was clear this attempt had failed.[70] The later attempt of 1909 shifted the focus somewhat, from providing jobs and entertainment to giving a sense of pride to the city, the country and playing a role in the formation of the young – but it retained the dual ideas of entertainment and social good. The groundwork had been laid to make a sporting stadium not just socially useful but morally imperative.

Calls for a new stadium received a large boost in April 1911. On Monday 17 April, the Dutch national team played a match against a touring English Amateur XI in Amsterdam, on RAP's Oud-Roosenburgh pitch. Demand for tickets had been high, perhaps too high. As Verkamman outlines, the stands were packed and tickets had been sold on the black market. In a stadium officially permitted to hold 11,000 people it seemed that many more had managed to enter the ground.[71] Newspaper reports suggest that there were not enough police to maintain order and that, before kick-off, around 20,000 were in attendance. Suddenly, at around half-past midday, one of the stands along the Middenweg side of the ground dropped. Fortunately, only around 250 spectators were in the stand and of those involved most had only minor injuries. One man from Delft suffered injuries to his back and ribs but remained to watch the game, being taken to the *Centraal Station* by ambulance afterwards. The stand itself was newly built and had been approved for use the previous evening by the Watergraafsmeer municipal architect. It seems that the nails holding the wooden planks together had collapsed under the weight and caused the stand to collapse.[72]

The incident overshadowed a creditable 1–0 loss for the Netherlands and saw calls for change. In *De Revue der Sporten*, which had many important members of the *NVB* as contributors, perhaps unsurprisingly, both the *NVB* and RAP boards were absolved of blame. Rather, it was the 'lame building regulators' and 'the unscrupulous constructor of the stands' who attracted criticism.[73] This incident was a warning and what was needed, according to the editor, was a new stadium, one that could hold 50,000. What was more, there was a need for order and regulation. The behaviour of many of those in attendance called into question the 'national character': 'Gentlemen stood right in front of your nose, ladies sat straight on your press-seat, and the dregs slung clods of earth and apple remains.'[74] To combat this, the editor suggested a handful of police and a stadium where there was space to take a corner, otherwise, he warned, the English team may not return.[75] A letter to the *Algemeen Handelsblad* from a Haarlem gentleman in attendance at the match reinforced the scene of disorder. Suggesting that descriptions of views of the match being 'somewhat' hindered were something of an understatement, he noted that thousands of people could see almost nothing of the game. He had paid 2.50 guilders for a seat on the first row, but could see little thanks to the throng of standing supporters. The supporter criticised the organising commission for their lack of proper regulation and pointedly asked: 'Do the regulations committee not now know that the cooperation of the public cannot be counted upon?'[76] The public, it seemed, needed to be disciplined; and they needed a stadium, which could train them to behave.

By late 1911, the calls for a new stadium had progressed significantly. The Municipality had agreed to put aside a 10-hectare piece of land to the south-east of the city on the Amstelveenscheweg to build a stadium. The land had formed part of numerous plans to expand Amsterdam since 1860. In 1904, noted architect H. P. Berlage had developed an extensive plan which incorporated parks, walkways and villas; however, this had been rejected by the Municipality.[77] Nevertheless, the executive board of the Municipality were glowing in their support of the scheme for the stadium, outlining that even if it were to be financially costly, it would further the aims of the Municipality and might encourage international matches to be held in the city as a result.[78] The *Maatschappij tot Exploitatie van het Nederlandsch Sportpark te Amsterdam* (Society for the Development of the Netherlands Sport Park, *MENS*) was charged with assessing the feasibility of the proposals and securing finance for the stadium. In the following months, they undertook feasibility studies for the project, including trips to London, Liverpool and Manchester and communications with the FA in London.[79]

A major hurdle was passed when the scheme was approved in the *Gemeenteraad* meeting of 28 February 1912, with only one vote against. Some had complained about the lack of influence the Municipality would have in the finished stadium and others had questioned whether the private shareholders would profit too much from public money.[80] However, the *Gemeenteraad* agreed to provide a sum of 175,000 guilders for the raising of the ground and had also agreed to give the land for the stadium rent-free for twenty-five years, on the proviso that 300,000 guilders of private capital could be secured by 28 May 1912.[81] Those behind the project used newspapers to emphasise the positive aspects of the construction. It would, they said, promote the 'flourishing of Amsterdam' by bringing thousands of new visitors to the city; it would provide entertainment to thousands of individuals as part of a healthy balance between body and mind; and it would appeal to young and old and to all classes of society.[82] It is safe to say that they were not aiming low.

Despite consensus in the *Gemeenteraad*, the agreement to build the *Sportpark* illustrated wider tensions between political groups. With only one dissenter, the vote on the construction of the new *Sportpark* suggested that local politicians liked the prospect of what the stadium would bring: prestige, unity, civic pride and public enjoyment. However, a sarcastic report in the *SDAP* daily newspaper, *Het Volk*, on 2 March 1912, demonstrated that things were more complex. The report focused on a 'notable incident' in the midst of the debate, which served to underline the 'hypocrisy' of the *ARP*.[83] The report noted that the *ARP* had always been opposed to the practice of football on a Sunday, but four of its members had voted for the establishment of a stadium where this would take place. This, according to *Het Volk*, was a further illustration of the hypocrisy of the religious political party where they 'were allowed to do what a normal Calvinist citizen and worker could not'.[84]

The portrayal of religious attitudes towards football in *Het Volk* masked a more nuanced picture. In areas of the Netherlands with strong orthodox Protestant influence – particularly in the countryside – football was not often played. Some in the Catholic Church saw it as a distraction from more spiritual pursuits and many early socialists thought that the antagonistic elements of competition would be inimical to the workers' struggle. However, there was not a uniform position on sport within these groups; for example, Catholic priest W. J. C. Binck was instrumental in promoting football and establishing Catholic organisations in Brabant. The first clubs organised along Catholic lines began to emerge around 1900 and were permitted into the *NVB*. However, such clubs were viewed with scepticism and seen as unnecessary by the national body.[85] In Rotterdam, Leonidas, who were formed along Catholic lines, were admitted into the *NVB* but were intially refused entry into the *RVB* because of their Catholic allegiance.[86]

With the establishment of five Catholic diocese organisations in 1915, tensions between the *NVB* and Catholic football grew. However, by 1917, both sides had come to an agreement which would see each retain a certain sphere of influence; the *NVB* retained responsibility for representing the Netherlands in international matters, while Catholic associations could promote the game amongst Catholic congregations. Before the First World War, *verzuiling* (pillarisation) was not a prominent part of Dutch football. However, by the 1920s, clubs were increasingly formed along such lines, especially in Catholic circles. By the late 1920s, socialist and Christian associations became more organised.[87]

The initial scepticism of religious practitioners, socialists and others towards the game suggests that, within society, football did not occupy a single position within the discourse of values. The failure to build a stadium in Amsterdam in 1908 suggests that at this time there also remained significant parts of Dutch society which were not behind the growth of football. However, the establishment of confessional organisations and clubs by the 1920s demonstrates that by this time football had become more accepted in various parts of society. Importantly, the increasing acceptance of the role of football in society demonstrated an awareness that football could play a part in the spread of discourses of values. While the establishment of different organisations may seem like a challenge to the authority of the *NVB*, it highlights that one of the initial aims of the *NVB* – to demonstrate the social and moral importance of football – had achieved remarkable success by the 1920s. The votes of the *ARP* can perhaps be seen in this light. By 1914, it was generally accepted that sporting space could construct and shape discourses about the world but there was still a tension about which discourses would be attached to this space, and whether these were entirely desirable.

Rotterdam innovations

In Rotterdam, the motivation to build a new stadium in 1913 was anything but sporting failure. Sparta Rotterdam had followed up their first championship of 1908/09 with three successive victories between 1910/11 and 1912/13. In the period before their first championship win, they were innovators, not only in Rotterdam but in Dutch football as a whole. While Concordia Rotterdam had played the first match against a team from abroad, beating FC Antwerp 1–0 in March 1890, their local rivals Sparta became the first Dutch club to play against an English team. In 1893, they played the amateur team Harwich & Parkeston FC, losing 8–0 in Rotterdam.[88] In the same year, Sparta made their first tour to England, playing the same opposition. By 1910, Sparta had played numerous teams from Prague and Vienna to Kings Lynn and Hastings.[89] In 1906, they recorded a 2–0 victory away at Chelsea, although this was marred somewhat by the feeling that Chelsea had not fielded their strongest team.[90]

But, for all of their qualities, Sparta's ground on the Prinsenlaan was causing problems. After heavy rain, the pitch was liable to flooding, meaning volunteers would have to spend Saturday afternoon and Sunday morning preparing the pitch for play.[91] In addition, the new stadium in Amsterdam had made those in charge of this ambitious club think about the possibilities offered by a larger and better ground.[92] No international matches had been played in Rotterdam since 1909, when Belgium played on the Prinsenlaan. To make matters worse, internationals had been played in Haarlem, Dordrecht, Arnhem, Zwolle and Amsterdam. A new ground, it was thought, would be good for the club and the city.

Like many teams in the Netherlands, Sparta rented their land from the local Municipality and, in 1913, it was decided that this land was needed as part of a future expansion. In 1913, Burgdorffer had become increasingly concerned at the poorly built, piecemeal developments on the edge of Rotterdam and to resolve this problem he set out to create a new development where a large number of new houses could be built. To the west of the city, the Spangen Polder was earmarked as the cheapest and most practical location.[93] As part of the plan, Sparta had submitted a sketch, which they were told would receive consideration within the general development.[94] By mid-December, Burgdorffer had entrusted Verhagen, Rotterdam's city planner, to draw up plans and they were ready for further consideration before the *Gemeenteraad*.[95] What was presented was a comprehensive plan for the area, consisting of affordable housing, public amenities, schools and places for recreation, as well as a detailed financial breakdown for pumping water and temporary bridges.[96]

Not everyone was convinced. Speikman, from the *SDAP*, was enthusiastic about the development, particularly the plans for worker housing, but he felt the future had not been given enough thought; how could workers make it to and from the area when no provision had been made for their transport? Member Vlug, of the *VDB*, questioned how Spangen had become the location for development; why had it not been taken into account in the earlier *Uitbreidingsplan*? If this had been done, he said, a number of costs could have been saved. His attention then turned to the recreational space in the plan. A concerned Vlug wondered what effect a recreational space at the edge of a worker district would have.[97] Even though recreation was freely available for Rotterdam's workers, as some other members kindly pointed out, would not it prove to be just too big a distraction?

Sporting space was the site of a moral quandary. Just as football had been questioned by parents and teachers in the late nineteenth century, for workers in the early twentieth century recreational space was seen by some as a danger and as a path toward moral degeneration. Again sporting space had been connected to discourses of values and particularly to the values of the young and workers, namely those in society who could be, or perhaps needed to be, educated and shaped.[98] These paternalistic discussions about sporting space placed sporting discourses firmly at the heart of discussions about authority, space and the construction of a specific form of society. But although sporting space was contested, its potential importance, either positive or negative was increasingly accepted.

Despite the disagreement, the plan for the Spangen development was eventually passed in the *Gemeenteraad* and sport would be part of it.[99] Over the next two years, negotiations occurred between representatives of Sparta and the Rotterdam Municipality. A rental price had been suggested by the Municipality of 5,000 guilders per year in 1914, which was already a substantial decrease on their initial demand. However,

Sparta were keen to point out that this was based upon out-of-date financial projections. The outbreak of war in late 1914 threw much of Rotterdam life into a state of confusion and Sparta noted this concern, stating that: 'The present conditions do not work with us to reinforce our financial position [...] the repercussions from the current crisis will be clearly seen in the budget in the forthcoming year.'[100] Fears of a prolonged conflict saw the prospect of prestigious international matches, and the income attached to them, dwindle. After lengthy negotiations, an incremental agreement was reached with the Municipality in line with Sparta's wishes. Club president M. J. Overeijnder gleefully welcomed the final agreement, noting how they had the opportunity to build a stadium without equal in the Netherlands.[101]

Money was a key part of the negotiations between the club and Municipality, but so too were other factors, which illustrate the wider significance of sporting space in the local area. The Municipality wanted to use the space for school matches and for festivals on special occasions. However, this posed a potential problem for Sparta, as they wanted to have access to the pitches during the weekend to prepare for matches and also so they could rent the pitches to office teams on Saturday afternoons. Sporting space was playing an increasingly important role in the practice of everyday life, not only for Sparta and their supporters but also in Rotterdam's education, leisure and working life. Football, while still an arena for conflict, was becoming increasingly normalised in culture and was beginning to attract significant financial, political and cultural support. This would continue to spread the discourses of the game further and deeper into society.

Finance

The change in the wider acceptance of sport is further illustrated by the success of both the *Sportpark* and Sparta Stadium in raising capital. In 1908, the proposed Amsterdam stadium failed to raise 100,000 guilders; however, the 1912 effort raised three times as much in just four weeks. By 27 March 1912, the option to invest in shares for the *Sportpark* had been closed.[102] In Rotterdam, the Sparta Stadium raised 125,000 guilders in 1915, despite other building projects failing to raise funds. In the case of both stadia, the financiers were some of the most famous names in finance, business, trade, industry and politics. Football was not only widely accepted in the city but was something that influential people wanted to support and develop.

For those behind the investment, football was just one area of city life which needed support. Many investors participated in other organisations and associations both before and after their investment in the stadia. The investors formed powerful networks in each city; many worked with each other, sat on the same committees and boards or had personal relationships. In this sense, investment in the stadia did not so much represent a passionate interest in sport or football, although this may have been important for some, but was part of a wider attempt at shaping the future of the cities, in the same way that other clubs, societies and charities had been in the late nineteenth and early twentieth centuries.

Those who invested in the *Sportpark* were able to take advantage of a number of benefits. Anyone who gave 250 guilders by 15 March 1912 would be rewarded with free entry to the stadium on its completion and an option to reserve three more seats. Keener investors, of 1,000 guilders, would gain a seat in the grandstand and up to five extra places. Those who gave the maximum 5,000 guilders would receive six free tickets and the ability to reserve a further six places. As the share issue made clear, they would not only receive these benefits but would also be taking part in a project which would bring thousands to Amsterdam and create a blossoming of the city.[103] A provisional list of investors was drawn up in early March for presentation to the *MENS*. On this provisional list were thirty-seven typed names and numerous handwritten ones, of whom fourteen individuals had pledged the full 5,000 guilders.[104]

The first name on the list was Jacob Cremer, who came from a banking family in Gelderland and who by 1912 was influential in Amsterdam business and cultural life. Cremer was a member, and later president, of the *Nederlandsche Handel-Maatschappij* (the Netherlands Trading Society, *NHM*) and was deeply involved with business in the Dutch East Indies in the latter part of the nineteenth century. Cremer was also an active politician and was Minister for Colonies in the Liberal Union dominated Cabinet of 1897; he was a member of the *Tweede Kamer* (Second Chamber, the Lower House of the Dutch Parliament) for Amsterdam from 1884 to 1897 and 1902 to 1905; in 1912 he became a member of the *Eerste Kamer* (First Chamber, the Upper House of the Dutch Parliament).[105] Links between business and politics were not unusual amongst investors. Samuel van Eeghen was part of a prominent business family and was also a senior member of the *NHM*. In 1904, he was elected as a member to the Provincial States for North Holland where he would serve until 1919 promoting liberal ideas. As a businessman, he sat on a range of committees and was a board member of a school for seafaring. He was also brother-in-law to W. H. van Loon, who had given 5,000 guilders to the project. Together, they were said to have held Amsterdam's business and financial life in their hands, with Van Eeghen's numerous committee appointments and Van Loon's role at the stock exchange.[106]

The *NHM* featured prominently in the lives of many investors. In addition to Cremer and Van Eeghen, Abn. Muller was a director there, and Van Aalst was a key figure. Both Muller and Van Aalst committed 5,000 guilders to the project. Van Aalst was also the director of *MENS* throughout the initial period. In 1913, he followed Cremer as president of the *NHM*. In 1902, Van Aalst was successfully recommended for a senior post in the Amsterdam office of the *NHM* by Ernst Heldring, whose father was president at the time.[107] Heldring invested 1,000 guilders in building the *Sportpark* and was an influential figure in Dutch shipping, the Amsterdam *Kamer van Koophandel* (Chamber of Commerce) and in other economic, cultural, social and political areas.[108] Adam Roelvink – who, together with his brother, invested 5,000 guilders – was known for his work for the *Twentsche Bank* in Amsterdam.[109] Baron George Rosenthal, who invested 5,000 guilders, was the son of a great banker who established the *Lippman, Rosenthal and Co.* bank, and he also worked there. So too did Amandus May, who gave 3,000 guilders to the projects. May was also Rosenthal's uncle.

Mari Paul Voûte was connected to banking and trade with the Dutch East Indies and was active in other Amsterdam circles. In 1912, he became the president of the *Vereeniging Rembrandt* and would become heavily involved in art trading and other artistic committees.[110] Likewise, Charles Ernest Henri Boissevain, who invested 1,000 guilders, was part of business and artistic networks. He was on the board of the Concertgebouw at various times after 1897, a member of the board of the Society for Music from 1910 to 1917 and a director at the *Algemeen Handelsblad* newspaper. He too was a member of the Amsterdam *Gemeenteraad* and the Provincial States of North Holland.[111] J. W. Edwin vom Rath was a board member at the Concertgebouw and deeply connected to the Amsterdam art scene, as well as providing 1,000 guilders for the *Sportpark*.[112] Such similarities and points of interaction occur throughout the list of investors in the *Sportpark*; these people were not only investors in sport, in a stadium, but formed a significant network of wealthy and powerful Amsterdam individuals.

The twenty-seven investors in the Spangen development formed a different, but equally prestigious network in Rotterdam. In addition to the Sparta president, M. J. Overeijnder, who invested 13,000 guilders, two men invested 25,000 guilders in the new Sparta ground. The first on the list was Willem Simon Burger, a Rotterdam local and leading member of the *Boutmy & Co.* trading company. In the years before 1914 he had been a prolific investor in local projects and had given 25,000 guilders to help establish the *Nederlandsche Handels-Hoogeschool* (the Netherlands Business School, *NHH*) a precursor to the Erasmus University. He also invested 20,000 guilders in the *Rotterdam Tuindorp* housing development. After his death, he left the majority of his inheritance to an organisation aimed at the promotion of spiritual and physical well-being for the poor.[113] The second 25,000-guilder investor was J. van Hoboken. In total, members of the Van Hoboken family, all called Jacobus, invested 31,000 guilders in the development. The Van Hobokens were one of Rotterdam's most prominent trading families and partners in *Hoboken & Co.* The firm had a long history in international trade, specialising in goods from the Dutch East Indies.[114]

Burger was not the only investor connected to the new ground in Rotterdam who had given money to establish the *NHH*. D. P. Hoijer, Anton Kröller, Wijnand Mees and Philippus van Ommeren had all invested in both.[115] Kröller was a major trader and with his wife he became an important member of the Netherlands artistic landscape. In the 1920s, the couple established the Kröller-Müller Foundation, which in the 1930s was behind the development of the Kröller-Müller Museum. But art was not his only interest. In 1904, he helped to fund a hockey team in The Hague.[116] Wijnand Mees took part in the *Rotterdam Tuindorp* development, was a director of the *Mees & Zoonen* bank and involved in public housing initiatives.[117] Among other things, Van Ommeren was responsible for one of the largest shipping firms in Netherlands and took part in the development of the Rotterdam harbour.[118] Hoijer was a director in the local *Oranjeboom* brewery, a politically liberal member of the Rotterdam *Gemeenteraad* and heavily involved in social housing.[119]

In Rotterdam, politics and business were never far away. Sam van den Bergh was a prominent margarine manufacturer and had been a member of the Rotterdam *Gemeenteraad* between 1897 and 1906, as well as a Liberal Union member of the *Tweede Kamer* between 1905 and 1909.[120] George Hermann Hintzen had business connections with the Mees family and was one of Rotterdam's most influential men. He was a banker, businessman and staunch liberal and had been a member of the *Tweede Kamer* at the end of the nineteenth century; he was involved in numerous other associations and poor-help societies.[121] Other investors in the stadium were connected to Rotterdam's expanding industries and business, which revolved around the harbours and banks. Those who had financed the new Sparta ground were highly influential and formed a strong network with deep personal and professional ties.

Table 2.1 Investors in the Sparta Stadium*

	Name	*Contact address (Rotterdam unless stated)*	*Amount (guilders)*
1	W. S. Burger	Firma Boutmy & Co.	25,000
2	J. van Hoboken	Parklaan 13	25,000
3	M. J. Overeijnder	Esschenlaan 18	13,000
4	S. v.d. Bergh Jr	Westerlaan 1	10,000
5	Herm. de Jongh	Willemsplein 6	10,000
6	A. van Driel	Maaskade 168	5,000
7	Mr J. van Hoboken	Parklaan 13	5,000
8	B. E. Ruijs	Westerkade 7	5,000
9	G. L. M. van Es	Westplein 11	2,000
10	J. van 't Hoff	Veerhaven 15a	2,000
11	Dr D. P. Hoijer	Parklaan 44	2,000
12	A v. d. Leeuw	Firma Wed.J van Nelle	2,000
13	W. A. Mees	Parklaan 9	2,000
14	Ph. van Ommeren	Westersingel 64	2,000
15	C. J. van Schaardenburg	Westerlaan 8	2,000
16	C. A. P. van Stolk	Javastraat 6	2,000
17	W. Westerman	Boompjes 78	2,000
18	D. G. van Beuningen	Parklaan 46	1,000
19	W. Dekking	Kon. Emmaplein 8	1,000
20	A. J. M. Goudriaan	Hoflaan 71	1,000
21	G. H. Hintzen	Javastraat 4	1,000
22	J. v. Hoboken Azn [Abrahamszoon]	Parklaan	1,000
23	W. [T.] Klaare	Van Vellenhovenstraat 29	1,000
24	A. G. Kröller	Firma Wm. H. Müller & Co., The Hague	1,000
25	A. La Verge	Koch & Co., Middensteiger 20	1,000

	Name	*Contact address (Rotterdam unless stated)*	*Amount (guilders)*
26	J. Rijpperda Wierdsma	Calandstraat 23	1,000
27	N. Haas	Heemraadsingel 194	5,000

* This table represents a version of the typed list of names of those who had given an interest-free loan for the stadium. The original, including many additional scribbled notations not represented here, can be found in *SAR*, Archive 257, Stukken betrefende geldleningen ten laste van Sparta (Part 208), document entitled 'Rentelooze leening 1915'.

The investment in the two stadia, by many of the two cities' most influential and wealthy citizens, was important for the establishment and credibility of the ventures. However, these individuals could be said to form part of a broadly similar and fairly limited part of society. Almost all of the investors were wealthy businessmen, bankers or industrialists, and those actively involved in politics were all broadly liberal in nature – perhaps further exacerbating the tensions towards football from some other quarters. The investors also shared another common link: the stadia were only one part of their wider involvement in societies and organisations. The investors in stadia also invested in artistic ventures, in charities and in schools. By investing in football and sporting stadia they had a financial incentive to ensure that the stadia were a success, but they also had a wider incentive not necessarily connected to finance. These individuals were taking part in projects which were intimately connected to wider discourses of values and identity in society, projects which were founded on the belief that sport – just like business, education and charity – could construct a better society and that through its promotion the city and society in which they lived could be improved. They were involved in projects that promoted discourses of civic pride, entrepreneurship, order, civilisation and respect.

Order and civilisation in the new functional stadium

How exactly did stadia help construct and reinforce certain discourses? Foucault outlines how enclosure – the use of specific places for specific tasks, such as factories and prisons – was an intrinsic part of the imposition of discipline on a wide number of people from the late eighteenth century onwards. Architecture begins to code spaces; it segments, maps and measures the individual in the group and increases a certain form of productivity. The first operation of this coding is to transfer the confusing multitude to an ordered construct.[122]

One can see in the development of increasingly functional sporting stadia an accompanying attempt to spread discourses which valued efficiency, order and discipline. The increasing popularity and acceptance of sport and the accompanying development of sporting space offered the opportunity for such discourses to become embodied in a great number of people. The discourses attached to sport could be attached to space and could become naturalised, from the player to the spectator, the tangential observer and onlooker. Sporting space became another way to reproduce discourses in everyday practice and made these discourses seem natural and unquestionable.

Precise measurement for certain tasks was crucial to the design of the stadium. In Amsterdam, the Municipality had arranged for a specific portion of land to the east of the Amstelveenscheweg to be set aside for the *Sportpark*. It was decided that 240 × 125 metres were to be given to the stadium, with the rest of the land dedicated to a variety of other sports pitches. On 11 May 1912, a competition was announced in a series of Amsterdam architectural weekly publications requesting designs for the new ground. The panel of judges would include H. P. Berlage, who had designed the Amsterdam stock exchange; Dutch Olympic Committee president F. W. Baron van Tuyll van Serooskerken; and J. Warner, president of the *NVB*. The successful winner would receive 4,500 guilders, but there were limits. First, the designer had to be Dutch, injecting an element of national identity into the discourse surrounding the building, and, secondly, they had to consider thirteen precise requirements.[123] These requirements started to code the space of the stadium with certain concepts before it had even been built.

The proposed 30,000 spectators would be divided into different areas, with a range of facilities. There would be covered stands for those who paid more, and a larger uncovered section for the rest of the general public. The covered stands would be situated so that the spectators would not get the sun in their eyes and would have a covered walking area in front. Numerous other spatial requirements were made. The size of the pitch was to be 110 × 74 metres, the sizes of the changing rooms, bathrooms, doctor's room, police post, fire post, restaurant, buffet room and committee rooms were predetermined. So too was the size of the pressroom and a hall with ten telephones for the use of the press. For spectators, there would be bars, cafés, food stalls and toilets; there would be smaller changing rooms for teams using external pitches and a lodging for the head of the restaurant and the concierge.[124] The Netherlands first great stadium was not going to be lacking in facilities, but they were being coded with specific functions, from the stands to the walkways, to the changing rooms and the bars. Space was being measured, regulated and ordered. The possible uses of a space were being limited and those that would use them were being directed to do so in a certain way – a way which, in time, would become embodied and appear natural. As Bale has noted, the story of the football stadium in modernity is one of a 'great confinement', where barriers between different groups have become increasingly fixed and etched in its architecture.[125]

The winning design was submitted by Harry Elte, a former pupil of Berlage.[126] The judging panel noted that Elte's design was the most succinct, well-ordered and simple solution which kept to the firm rules laid down. It was 'sober, yet civilised and – despite its somewhat great size – of a fitting character'.[127] Ordered, sober and civilised, keeping to the rules and the budget. Yes, this was a description of the design, but it was also how the judging panel and those promoting the stadium wanted the space to be used and people to behave within it. The sporting space was measured, regulated and ordered, and this was the discourse which would be spread to those who interacted with it. It was a vision for a stadium, but it was also a vision for society.

Pride in the city – what I will call 'civic pride' – was an important element of the discourse of the stadium. During the construction of the *Sportpark*, an article appeared in *De Revue der Sporten* which reassured the reader that work was on schedule and that the new ground on the Amstelveenscheweg would be an outstanding location. The lack of a velodrome, which had been part of the initial plan, was mentioned, but it was noted that the crowd would be closer to the pitch, unlike at the stadium in Berlin. The stadium would boast great facilities, which would be a benefit to Amsterdam sport and a source of national pride.[128] When the stadium was finished the *Nieuwe Rotterdamsche Courant* (*NRC*) noted that, while The Hague and Rotterdam had stadia, the new stadium in Amsterdam would make citizens there jealous and would be needed if Amsterdam had designs to host the 1920 Olympic Games.[129] Similar sentiments were stated upon the opening of the new Sparta Stadium, when, on 15 October 1916, both Mayor Zimmerman and Sparta president Overeijnder emphasised that the new stadium would be a benefit for the whole of Rotterdam and not just for Sparta.[130] The newly functional and ordered sporting stadium was firmly positioned within a discourse of identity. It was something to be proud of, something which set one's own city apart from others – even if they had one too.

The new functional stadium was also something to be used correctly. Press reports of the first match played at the *Sportpark* illustrate how the discourses of values connected to order, discipline, civic identity and entrepreneurship were reproduced. The match between the Netherlands and Germany, on 5 April 1914, was eagerly anticipated in the Amsterdam press. On the day before the game, the *Algemeen Handelsblad* printed a diagram of the stadium showing how the public could arrive at their seats in an orderly fashion.[131] Order extended to the use of the wider city during the day of the match. *De Courant* noticed that visitors to Amsterdam's shopping streets had greatly increased; around the Weesperpoort station, the trains arriving from across the country were constantly adding to the pleasant atmosphere. From the station, people were directed to trams which would take them to the stadium in the southern part of the city.[132]

Once they arrived at the Amstelveenscheweg, plans had been made to regulate the great masses of people:

> The traffic regulations designed by the Traffic Department appeared, in practice, to be sufficient. It goes without saying that the police operated in unusually large numbers. No less than 300 agents were detached to the stadium and its vicinity. They did their duty excellently, but, what would these hundreds [of police agents] have accomplished, if the cooperation of the thousands of those who visited the match was lacking? The public conducted themselves in an exemplary manner for this first match and greatly contributed to the outstanding running of affairs.[133]

Reports in the *Algemeen Handelsblad* and *Het Volk* noted that the areas around the entrances to the stadium were unfinished and needed work.[134] However, in *De Courant*, they focused on the positive:

> People wandered very calmly along the Amstelveenscheweg, heading from the open sections through the 'funnel', a small area in front of the Sportpark, the square and to the turnstiles. 'Make your tickets visible, ladies and gentlemen!' sounded from the mouth of the officer on duty and then they emerged, the tickets, in green, brown, white, red or orange tint, harmonised with the coloured signs, which indicated to everyone the way to their designated turnstile.[135]

The role of authority was also indicated:

> At the centre of the partitions stood one of the head-conductors of traffic, inspector C. Bakker who, with a hand gesture and a friendly word, an individual in the place of ten thousand, calmly, kept the masses going in the right direction, and the stream of people moved ever forward.
>
> [...]
>
> People know, from the messages we have published, that there were also specific measures for wheeled transport. Under the experienced leadership of the chief inspector, W. E. van Kervel, the police ensured that no vehicle, in any shape or form, could come further than the Lomanstraat.[136]

The completion of the stadium and the arrival of a major sporting event had transformed the physical space of Amsterdam, but it also served to reproduce discourses of order within the city and within the individual. Those in attendance were to be ordered, regulated and respectful of authority; they should follow the signs, go to the allotted space and do so at the right time. Police numbers were increased to 300 but this was more symbolic than an imposition of physical force. Physical force, after all, was not needed because the discourse of values, of how to use the city, had already been embodied, been internalised, by those who used the stadium. While the stadium may have represented a new building, its discourses were not new, they were part of an existing set of discourses in society which favoured order, discipline and regulations; the same discourses which saw numerous voluntary societies set up in the nineteenth century; the same discourses which saw the city become the location of the great planning experiment; the same discourses favoured by those in positions of influence. The new functional stadium was merely a new, impressive and efficient way to demonstrate this.[137]

In addition to reproducing discourses of order and discipline, the stadium further reproduced discourses of capital and entrepreneurship. In the streets around the stadium, space was dedicated to vendors of various types and new advertising. Spaces to sell goods on the day of the game had been purchased in advance. In addition to the fruit, chocolate and flower sellers:

> More wealthy entrepreneurs had, in the literal meaning of the term, pitched their tents in the pastures bordering the Stadium,

> selling food and drink. The bread rolls, with or without meat, lay highly stacked and even the well-known doughnut stall of old was not absent from this modern sporting event.[138]

Football was not new to entrepreneurship. Throughout the early twentieth century, numerous companies and businesses used images of football and footballers to sell their products. Although players were strictly amateur, football clubs themselves were aware of business opportunities. When the new Sparta ground was complete in 1916, they negotiated a contract with a Rotterdam chocolate firm. This contract granted A. Driessen the exclusive rights to sell their products in the stadium for a sum of 500 guilders per year. Included in this agreement was the right of the company to select two vending locations within the stadium.[139] Sporting space became a valuable resource for clubs and businesses, and the new functional stadium reproduced a discourse that linked the space of the city and the space of football with finance, capital and entrepreneurship from an early period. Those who invested in the stadium saw the opportunity to spread these discourses into new areas because the values of entrepreneurship and capital were an intrinsic part of their own discourses of values: finance and prosperity were essential parts of constructing a better society.

The opening of the Sparta ground saw a series of dignitaries praise the new development, while the Mayor presented a portrait of the Queen to be placed in the boardroom.[140] But for those looking out from the stadium to the area around, it would have been clear that the plan for the new grounds to be at the heart of a new district had not come to fruition. Poor financial conditions connected to the conflict outside the Netherlands and a lack of private funding meant that the Sparta Stadium was one of the few buildings on the Spangen Polder. The first inhabitants did not move into the area until the 1920s.[141]

While Sparta had an impressive stadium, access to the ground was less impressive and spectators had to use temporary bridges to reach the area until the Mathenesserbrug was fully completed.[142] The large-scale housing blocks, which were intended to fill the area, were difficult to achieve and this was in part down to the initial design of Verhagen's plan. While Spangen developed into a site for experimentation in social housing, architects found that the numerous curves within the original plan made affordable and practical buildings more difficult to design. One of the lessons of the Spangen Polder was that large, standardised, cheap housing required perpendicular corners and straight lines.[143] This is perhaps another reminder of how discourses – in this case of efficiency, economy and regularity – can make certain spatial configurations preferable.

Other sporting spaces

The construction of the *Sportpark* and the Sparta Stadium are just two examples of where football, its spaces and its discourses became more important within the urban landscape in the early twentieth century. Other stadia and grounds were also constructed, reproducing the discourses of values and identity in other parts of the cities. One of Rotterdam's largest clubs, VOC, moved twice in a short period of time. Between 1904 and September 1910, they played their games on the Schuttersveld, not far from Sparta's Prinsenlaan ground. The pitches of the Schuttersveld were home to other local clubs throughout the early decades of the twentieth century – Achilles, DVS and USC all played matches there during this period. VOC moved to the Pelgrimsstraat, where RFC also played, and shortly afterwards, in 1912, to a more permanent home on the Schieweg in the northern suburbs of the city. Facilities at this ground, which had three pitches, no gas or electricity and cost 900 guilders a year, were a far cry from those of the newer stadia, although they improved over time. VOC would stay on the Schieweg until 1925.[144]

In the south, the quickly improving Feyenoord also had to move grounds following a successful promotion campaign to the First Division B in 1916/17, where the play-off matches were held on the ground of Xerxes. In 1916, Feyenoord merged with another local team, Door Combinatie Sterk, who played in the local leagues outside the *NVB*; both teams played on the Afrikaanderplein. This vast green space was the location for matches of many of south Rotterdam's football clubs, but in 1917, as the conflict continued outside the Netherlands, it was developed into allotments, again demonstrating a contest for the use of municipal space.[145] As the Afrikaanderplein was a public space owned by the Municipality, clubs could not charge for entry. In response, Feyenoord moved to a location a few kilometres to the south-west on the Kromme Zandweg.[146] The new grounds, with a stand and changing facilities, were celebrated in the official Feyenoord publication. In the 25 August edition, the editor, J. D. van Bennekum, excitedly exclaimed: 'Next Sunday it will happen.'[147] The ground was to be opened with a match against 'Be Quick' of Zutphen, but the week before, many members had taken the opportunity to examine the new facilities. According to the magazine, 'they had walked across our marvellous facilities in satisfaction without having the need to think in a melancholy manner about the old "battle-field", the Afrikaanderplein. How many teams there did not fall victim to our lads.'[148] Journalists from the local press had also come to inspect the grounds and in the *NRC* it was said to be a better stadium than many of those of clubs in the top division. This was a stadium to be proud of.[149]

The opening-day events were promoted in the club journal, but again regulations and values were not far away. Members were urged to arrive on time for the game; they were instructed that those who had not paid the 2.5 guilders for a demarcated place in the stand would have the opportunity to take a place in the first row of the stands and there was also a covered section; space was coded with ideas of status, segregation and capital. Van Bennekum pleaded with members not to enter the field of play at any time. Although this was usually acceptable, on this occasion they did not want to give a chaotic impression to the 'outsiders' in attendance. Finally, members were urged not to go into the changing rooms, especially in wet weather, as they had to remain clean.[150] The opening of a new stadium was a celebration of the growth of Feyenoord, of the success they had claimed in the years before, but it was also something which necessitated a change in behaviour. The board wanted to project a positive, ordered and civilised impression to those who were coming for

Fig 2.5 *Stadion Feijenoord,* Rotterdam, 2016

the first time, and there were new ways to use the new space; with new space came new regulations and new coding. Feyenoord would remain on the Kromme Zandweg until 1937 when they would move to their present home; they claimed three national championships in this period in 1923/24, 1927/28 and 1935/36.

Moving to enclosed space also gave clubs the chance to protect their own income. In the Rotterdam suburb of Charlois, Charlois Voetbal Vereeniging (CVV) played on land near the church. The openness of the ground meant that they could not charge for admission to their home matches. In 1918, it was announced that they would move and from 1919 they played at a new ground which could better protect their financial outlook.[151] Other clubs moved location too. RFC moved from the Delfshaven to the Heuvelterrein nearer the centre of the park; USC moved north from the Heuvelterrein to the Schuttersveld; by 1913, DVS had moved from the Schuttersveld to the Kethelweg near Vlaardingen and in 1919 merged with Schiedam-based Hermes.[152] In 1917, the redesignation of the Afrikaanderplein also meant that Transvalia had to move to new premises on the Sluisjesdijk and then, in 1919, to the Vreewijk.[153] The Woudestein saw UDI, Leonidas, Groen-Wit and Het Noorden play, in addition to Excelsior. The numerous moves of location demonstrated the continued need to re-evaluate the use of space within the city, either by the clubs or other bodies. As cities expanded, space needed to be found for the growing number of football clubs who wanted to play, as well as other uses. One side-effect of a growing number of supporters and members at various clubs was a desire for stands and more concrete facilities; this not only recoded the spaces of football but more firmly cemented football, and its discourses, into urban space.

In Amsterdam, the *Sportpark* became the location for many sporting clubs. Following the thrilling 4–4 match between the Netherlands and Germany, the stadium was officially opened with a match between a Dutch representative Zwaluwen side and a touring Reading team. The Dutch side lost 10–2 in front of a capacity crowd.[154] The *Sportpark* became the location for regular football after the merger of two of Amsterdam's oldest clubs in July 1914: RAP and Volharding joined to form Volharding RAP Combination (VRC). The merger itself had been initiated by the secretary of the stadium, J. M. Coucke, in collaboration with the clubs and was intended to create a multi-sport super-club to play in Amsterdam's new stadium. The new club would play its Western Second Division football matches in the *Sportpark*. They would be joined by the Amsterdam Hockey Club and the Amsterdam Cricket Club, who would use the pitches behind the new stadium with athletics events being held in the summer.[155] In this case, the stadium had changed how clubs would operate and was instrumental in creating new associations and networks. Sporting space had changed practice and constructed new elements of everyday life.

However, the same day that the merger of RAP and Volharding was announced in the *NRC*, a report indicated that not all involved in Dutch football were benefiting from the support which was given to those at the *Sportpark*. It was noted that space further along the Amstelveenscheweg, temporarily designated for teams in the *AVVB*, was unsuitable for play. There were no cafés, bars or telephone rooms here. In fact, players could not even get to the pitches. While the Municipality promised 1,600 guilders to rectify the situation, the difference between the giant venture of the *Sportpark* and those of the *AVVB* was clear. This organisation, while accepted within the *NVB*, could not rely on wealthy investors, but had to be content with poor pitches separated from changing facilities by an impassable ditch.[156] Space was coding how sport was viewed, and it was perhaps a metaphor for the relative finance and power of the organisations: new functional stadia for the *NVB* teams compared to the potholed turf of the *AVVB*.

The outbreak of war, just after the opening of the stadium, put a halt to international football matches in the Netherlands for almost five years. The first post-war match in the *Sportpark* saw a 3–1 victory against Sweden in 1919; the excitement of the return of football to the city was so great that the *NRC* described the scene at the *Centraal Station* where thousands of people had turned up to greet the Swedish team off the train.[157] The lack of a major source of income was a serious problem. In December 1914, the *NRC* reported that because raising the ground had cost 21,000 guilders more than expected and other costs had increased, combined with the lack of income from international matches, the first rental payment would only be made in 1919.[158] To supplement the loss of income, the stadium became host to other artistic and sporting ventures. A singing club was formed, cycling races ended at the stadium, korfball demonstrations took place, as did a concert of over 1,600 trumpeters and military marching bands. VRC's income was also erratic, varying between 16.60 guilders and 221.45 guilders in 1915. They recorded a loss of 30 guilders against Haarlem. In 1916, VRC abandoned playing football and continued purely as a cricket club, but newly promoted Blauw-Wit took their place after moving from the Watergraafsmeer. As a result, Amsterdam finally had a world-class stadium and a First Division football team to play in it. But Blauw-Wit's attendances were little better than VRC's, and they attracted an average of 1,750 paying spectators in

1916/17.[159] In a stadium built for 30,000, home matches, with the exception of nearly 10,000 who saw a match against Ajax in 1917/18, must have been somewhat sombre.

Ajax, who in 1917/18 finally brought the national championship back to the city on the IJ, also changed their ground. In 1911, a wooden stand was erected in response to their promotion to the First Division. The *Houten Stadion* (Wooden Stadium) would remain their home until 1934.[160] Unlike Blauw-Wit, Ajax could fill the stadium, but there were still problems. In 1918, in a match between Ajax and Blauw-Wit, *Het Volk* criticised the police handling of the game, which saw 'many people roughly forced against the fence'.[161] What was needed was more order and a change in space; the reporter suggested a simple solution: expand the entrance and start cordoning the crowd on the street beforehand.[162] The use of space as a technique for order and discipline was something which needed to be perfected.

Between 1910 and 1920, AFC also built a new stand for their ground. At the beginning of the 1920s, Amsterdam had gone from being a city lacking adequate sporting facilities and with no great football teams, to one that had a stadium hosting international football, regular fixtures in a variety of sports, with three Western First Division clubs. In the area around the stadium, architect Berlage, who had been instrumental in choosing the stadium's design, saw his *Plan Zuid* for the southern expansion accepted in 1917. In the immediate vicinity of the *Sportpark*, architects from the Amsterdam School set about designing and constructing new homes, schools and facilities alongside the broad and lengthy streets.[163] Today the *Sportpark* no longer exists; the only remaining part is the first ceremonial stone laid by Van Aalst's son in 1913. This stone sits in the grounds of the *Olympisch Stadion*, which was built adjacent to the *Sportpark* for the 1928 Games, a tournament in which the *Sportpark* hosted hockey matches. Although the stadium is gone, the discourses of order, regulation and discipline are still part of sporting life and the life of the city.

Summary: the rise of the new functional stadia

The development of football stadia in the second decade of the twentieth century was part of wider urban developments aimed at providing order and regulation in the city. That stadia became needed, wanted and built in this period demonstrates that football had become normalised in society; it was no longer just a game for the few, but was increasingly viewed as a game that could be beneficial for all in Dutch society. However, football was not treated as a special case. As the developments in Amsterdam and Rotterdam show, plans were contested as parts of the wider development strategy of cities and were sites for political and religious conflict, even if this was not always uniform in its nature. Stadia, like other building developments, needed finance and in this respect football stadia, unlike many other projects, demonstrated the ability to attract large amounts of capital relatively quickly.

That stadia could attract such capital so quickly was because discourses of football, the aspects of the of the game which emphasised the positive role of the game within society, both chimed with other discourses in society and became more widely accepted within the Netherlands. Football organisations, such as the *NVB*, were established to promote a specific discourse of values, just as other clubs, societies and organisations did around the turn of the century. These discourses of values portrayed football as a game that could help educate those in society who were in need of guidance, especially the young and this was attractive to many in politics and business who were already involved in a variety of similar organisations. Football became portrayed as a social necessity and a moral imperative and as such could obtain support from those with power, capital or often both.

In both cities, support and money for the new functional stadia came from the most influential and wealthiest in society. The networks involved in building the stadia demonstrate that football was anything but an outsider and that from an early period, popularisation was linked to power and capital. The investors in the stadia were wealthy, largely politically liberal, and saw sport as another way to spread their discourses of values to wider society. From schools to housing developments and from concert halls to hockey clubs, investors took opportunities to establish new organisations and, crucially, to construct new buildings in the city landscape. The new functional stadium was another way to cement what were believed to be socially beneficial discourses into the fabric of the city.

The new functional stadium operated on a symbolic and practical level. Symbolically, the stadium was shown to demonstrate ambition, ability and forward thinking. It was said, by those involved at least, to be a representation of the best of a city, a region or country. The new functional stadium allowed cities to measure and compare themselves with each other, and to stage prestigious events and shows. But the new functional stadium was also linked to discourses that favoured order, regulation and measurement; the appearance of stadia did not create such discourses in urban planning, but gave a new way to implement them. With the emergence of the new functional stadium came new practical ways to regulate movement in the city, new possibilities for business and commerce, and new, massive locations to reproduce the discourses of values. The new functional stadia demonstrated that football was not only important, and popular, but that it was actively involved in reproducing these discourses within society. The emergence of new functional stadia represents a period when football, business and politics entered into a close symbiotic relationship which was cemented into the streets around us. This has not changed.

In the six years since the failed attempt in Amsterdam to create a new sporting space, the construction of stadia went from ignored to essential; disasters, disorder and the relentless need to plan were important in this change. In both Amsterdam and Rotterdam, the stadia were among the first buildings to be constructed in areas earmarked for other uses; the new stadia were not only functional in operation but, compared to other buildings, could be built quickly and with private support. In both cities, the *Sportpark* and the Sparta Stadium changed how the spaces around them could be built. They became the focal point of new areas, reproducing their discourses in daily life. They brought new ways to code the space of the city and how the body of the individual could use it. By coding space, the stadia helped to code the body too. Looking at the new buildings in Rotterdam, I wonder how they will continue to shape the city around them and the people who live there. And I wonder how much I have been coded by the sporting spaces I have used.

3

Football Club Members in Rotterdam: History and Fiction

What is the difference between history and fiction? As Southgate notes, the two have often been seen as 'mutually exclusive opposites. From the earliest times, historians have defined their subject by direct reference to its absolute distinction from fiction: history is history precisely because it is *not* fiction, but aspires rather to supplant fiction with *fact*.'[1] Around the borders of the historical 'true', a secure fence seems to have been erected to ensure that any of the pesky creativity of 'fiction' does not infiltrate or cheapen the product of the historian's research. De Certeau noted this practice in historiography when he said fictional elements were considered 'shameful and illegitimate'.[2] Fiction is the erroneous 'other' of history, which is 'deported to the land of the unreal'.[3] The dichotomy between 'fact' and 'fiction' seems to be engrained in our language, with 'fact' being a virtuous, solid, reality and 'fiction' a rather fanciful, duplicitous set of ideas removed from reality. If this is the case, then there is no wonder historians might eschew any connection with fiction. But is the distinction between history and fiction really so vast? Is history really so removed from fiction?

Previously, I outlined the ideas of White, Munslow and de Certeau who suggested that history and fiction were intimately connected and that important narrative structures and processes were engrained in the production of history. Rather than being polar opposites, historical accounts and fictional accounts were part of a storytelling genus, which intended to provide meaningful ways of thinking about and representing the world. Mink considered that this was a valuable means of comprehending the world, just as scientific and philosophical methods were. In the process of writing, the historian is constructing a story about the past in which how the 'facts' are placed within a narrative is just as important as which 'facts' are selected. In any event, there remain questions about the distinction between 'fact' and 'fiction'. Can we really be so sure that the two do not overlap? As Munslow outlines, Hayden White is clear that history is a process of turning 'facts' into 'fiction' by use of narrative. In such accounts 'fact' and 'fiction' are not at odds, but co-dependent bedfellows.[4]

The distinction between history and fiction has become a growing part of historical debate in recent years, as fictional histories, historical fictions and plain old histories are evaluated for their ability to give us meaning about the world. A double issue of *Rethinking History* was published in 2005 where the relationship between history and fiction was discussed. Hayden White noted that the key difference, which has driven the distinction between the two, is a matter of intention; for historical discourse everything is staked on the 'true' while for fictional discourse it is about the 'real', the imaginable and the possible. White suggests that the professionalising of history in the nineteenth century and the desire for it to be seen as scientific was responsible for the widening gap between fact and fiction. Citing the work of Levi, White suggests that the power of representation lies not purely in the 'truthfulness' of what is said, but in the artistry and relation to sensations of the real. White suggests that the value of Levi's work lies not in its factual statements but in how the author weaves them artistically within the narrative to give wider meanings broaching the truth–reality dichotomy.[5] Orr showed how her own work benefited from the inclusion of fictional sections while Slotkin has used novels as a way of expanding on his own historical output.[6] Those involved in this kind of writing operate on the borderland between history and fiction, where clear distinctions are not always possible, where 'fact' and 'fiction' merge to varying degrees and where stories can be said to be neither 'true' nor 'false' but, hopefully, coherent, plausible and challenging.

This history is an experiment within these borderlands. I have noted my belief that once historians are freed from the idea of having to recreate, reflect or describe the past reality then they can attempt to provide new representations, new imaginaries about the past which may help us think about the present. As Orr's recollection of her own experiences in this borderland shows, it is not always easy for historians to experiment with fiction.[7] Despite my own approach, this experimentation has been a difficult enterprise; I present it with trepidation and a sense that I may invite criticism of my work as both bad history and bad literature. But as Orr rightly says, 'Historians/we do not skirt mortal danger, total confusion, vertigo or madness by coming too close to fiction, by asking ourselves about writing and form, about our own narrative status'.[8] Or perhaps sometimes we come closer than we would like.

The motivation for this history comes from my desire to represent different individuals and the problems posed by large amounts of incomplete data. I have noted the shortcomings of the archive already: where records have not been taken or kept, a history based purely upon archival research cannot provide a representation of individuals. In this way, the power structures of the past, or present, continue to influence the work of historians and can dictate just which histories can be told and how we view the present. I wanted to think about a way of providing different representations of the past. This is not because I believe including fiction can help me as a historian create histories that are more accurate, more 'like' the past, or which pass what Demos describes as the 'ring-true test', but rather that help us to think about the past in different ways, to remember that individuals in the past took part in daily life and were more than the sum of the data collected about them.[9] If the limited traces of the past constrict and influence how we can think about it then are there ways we can attempt to combat such constraints?

This story starts in the archive. As part of my research into early Dutch football culture, I came across a magnificent source of information based in the archives of the *Koninklijke Nederlandse Voetbalbond* (Royal Dutch Football Association, *KNVB*) housed in the *NA* in The Hague. Within this collection of records were a number of large books, each containing lists of members of football clubs which had affiliated with the *NVB*. The earliest records in the collection were from 1893 when only a few clubs had joined, but they ran from this point up until the 1923/24 season. Initially, all the registers of the club members could be bound in one volume, but by the 1913/14 season, the sheer number of names, clubs and sheets from across the Netherlands meant that two volumes were needed; by the 1917/18 season, a third was added.

I remember my joy at having located these lists and setting off for The Hague from Utrecht. Traversing the eternally windy passage between The Hague *Centraal Station* and the building that houses both the *Nationaal Archief* and *Koninklijke Bibliotheek* (National Library of the Netherlands, *KB*) my pace quickened as I headed towards the books. Having passed through security, and after the confiscation of a rubber tipped pencil, I waited for the works I had ordered in the reading room – a nervous wait ensued during which I briefly contemplated how I could highlight the futility of the somewhat officious guard's work. Fortunately, the arrival of the documents calmed me somewhat. Flicking through the pages carefully, seeing the names of teams I recognised but which had since vanished, I felt content that my research had paid off. But, as page after page of almost illegible names mounted up, I encountered another emotion, not joy at having found a source but concern at what I was going to do with it. As I read the lists of names, searching for someone I recognised from my research, I was aware that there were hundreds that I did not. And this was just from 1910. How could I deal with a further twenty volumes of names within the limited research time I had left?

I thought about how I could use the names. I could find out which clubs were the most popular and from where they derived most of their members. With more research I may even be able to confirm addresses, to find family members and find out how people were employed. As the possibilities for further research grew, the time available to look at all the membership lists began to diminish. I had already limited my research to Rotterdam, for reasons I cannot quite remember, but even here I was faced with a confusingly large amount of data. Perhaps, I thought, I could select a few years here and there and look at the data from this period.

But just what form would this history take? Would it be a collection of statistics attempting to draw wider conclusions about the state of Rotterdam football? Would it be a piece of geographical research analysing where people lived and their propensity for playing in certain clubs? As I thought about how I could construct this history, I noted that the membership lists were collected on the 1 August each year. This date conjured up a vague memory of something I had seen while researching the building of the Sparta Rotterdam stadium. While searching for information on the Rotterdam *Gemeenteraad* debate over the proposals for the stadium in 1914, I had come across this date before. In the *Rotterdamsch Jaarboek* (Rotterdam Yearbook) of 1915, opposite page xxiii, there was an image of a telegram sent on 31 July destined for the mayor of Rotterdam. It read: 'All militarists and first-reservists come with all haste.'[10] Below this printed statement, was the handwritten date of when this action was required to be taken: 1 August 1914. This was not only the date when football clubs from across the Netherlands registered their members, but it was the first day of mobilisation in response to growing international tensions and fears of war.

Further research from newspapers in Rotterdam gave me some important background information about events in the first week of August in this year, and I decided that Rotterdam members in 1914/15 would be my focus for research. Data piled up: names, addresses, birth dates, death dates, locations, jobs, occupations, families. In all, 916 people had been registered with Rotterdam-based football clubs for the 1914/15 *NVB* season on 1 August; more would be added throughout the season. For each, I had more than just a name. But I had little else to help construct their daily life. Of course, for the famous members of the football teams, I could find a little more in newspapers or football histories. But, for others, there were no diaries, no journal entries, few reports in the newspaper and, for some, names remained obscure or confusing. I kept thinking about how I could represent this data and kept returning to the idea of a map to show where people lived. Following my initial research, I created nine maps, which I have included in the Appendix despite their imperfections. But what did this really tell us? That some people lived here and others there? That many Sparta members came from the north of the river? But what did this actually mean? I thought about working out who did which job and which club they played for. But something was not right. This would reduce all these individuals, all the many different people into statistics, to be accumulated and compared. Would this not go directly against my attempt to name and represent the forgotten in history, to show the contingency of writing history and the gaps it has within it?

After weeks of researching and thinking about how I could construct my history, I thought about incorporating fictional elements to link the individuals together within the wider Rotterdam context. Nervously, I considered what this meant. It would be breaking what I had been taught was the golden rule of history – separating fact from fiction. I realised that I had a choice. I could remain faithful to traditional procedures of producing history based solely upon historical traces found in the archive, but obscure the individuality of the members of Rotterdam football clubs by reducing them to statistical figures. Alternatively, I could ignore established historical practice and to try to represent, to name, as many of the individuals as possible in a narrative as people with lives and fears, but to alter their individuality by placing a non-attributed, personal, present-day voice to them. This chapter is the result of choosing the second of these options.

Before embarking on this imagined journey through different parts of Rotterdam in August 1914, I should be clear on what was researched and what was imagined – this history is not simply the work of a historian fed up of the archive. In researching this history, I followed similar procedures to my other histories, and to many other researchers, which would sit with those of more traditional conventional histories – and it should be said the research practice of most postmodern historians too. The names of members of Rotterdam football clubs, which included playing members and administrative members, were collected from the membership lists in the *NA*. They were verified for spelling and their addresses were checked in Rotterdam's *Algemeen Adresboek* (General Address Book) of 1914, 1915 or later if needed.[11] The locations and dates of birth for as many members as I could find, as well as any other familial relations, were referenced using the online genealogical records of the *SAR*. Events in Rotterdam and descriptive elements about the city and period were found in the *NRC* and other historical sources. Guidebooks and newspapers provided details about travel and other amenities. Contemporary maps of Rotterdam provided the ability to place the data and to think of a journey, which was geographically informed, even if it was temporally shifting and entirely imagined.

The membership lists of fourteen Rotterdam registered clubs were researched. These clubs were Sparta Rotterdam, VOC, CVV, RFC, De Concordiaan, Transvalia, Het Noorden, Feyenoord, UDI, USC, Neptunus, Leonidas, Lycurgus and DVS. My 'corrected' lists can be downloaded online for you and others to use and improve the data; they remain a work in progress which can be refined, added to and corrected. More information about each of the clubs concerned is set out in Table 3.1.

Some things were missing from the start. Rotterdam clubs – Excelsior, Groen-Wit and Xerxes – who appeared in the 1913/14 season did not appear in the archival record books for 1914/15 and, therefore, their members could not be included. This is also true of the many smaller clubs affiliated only to the local *RVB*.[12] In some cases it was impossible for me (and others) to recognise names or locations in the original text; these individuals will, sadly, be ignored by my history. Information which may have permitted a wider representation of the concept of *verzuiling*, the idea that separate groups based upon religious or political beliefs established their own clubs, was lacking. The lists I used were from only one organisation, the *NVB*, often considered to be a liberal organisation. As noted in my spatial history (Chapter 2), clubs were formed by those belonging to socialist, Protestant and Catholic groups especially after the First World War, and some other clubs may have included members from across the perceived divide. But I simply did not have the information to represent this. If I had, this would have been a different, and perhaps more significant history. The lists also do not provide representation of those who attended matches without being members, either regularly or sporadically. Like so many records, these lists represented a certain form of power, a collection of data, which excluded more than it included. The many thousands of supporters who attended matches in Rotterdam, who

Table 3.1 Rotterdam football clubs in the 1914/15 *NVB* member lists*

Name	*Year established*	*Home ground (Rotterdam unless indicated)*	*NVB League in 1913/14 (finishing position)*
Sparta Rotterdam	1888	Prinsenlaan	Western 1st Div (2nd)
VOC	1895	Schieweg	Western 1st Div (7th)
Neptunus	1900	De Heuvel	Western 2nd Div B (8th, last)
DVS	1903	Kethelweg	Western 2nd Div A (4th)
RFC	1904	De Heuvel	Western 2nd Div B (4th)
Transvalia	1905	Afrikaanderplein	Newly affiliated to *NVB* in 1914
USC	1906	Schuttersveld	Western 3rd Division B (4th)
UDI	1907	Woudestein	Western 3rd Division B (2nd)
CVV	1908	Waalhaven	Western 3rd Division B (6th, last)
Feyenoord	1908	Afrikaanderplein	Western 3rd Division A (3rd)
Leonidas	1909	Woudestein	Western 3rd Division A (5th)
De Concordiaan	1910	Schiebroek	Western 3rd Division A (7th, last)
Lycurgus	1910	not found	Newly affiliated to the *NVB* in 1914
Het Noorden	1911	Woudestein	Western 3rd Division B (5th)

* Table compiled from *Nationaal Archief* (*NA*), The Hague, *Koninklijke Nederlandse Voetbalbond* (*KNVB*), nummer toegang 2.19.123, inventarisnummer 246; *ING*, 'Databank Sport', http://resources.huygens.knaw.nl/sportbondenclubsperiodieken/gids/search; defunct Transvalia website, '*Beknopte Geschiedenis Transvalia*'; and Zevenbergen, *Rotterdamse Voetbalglorie*, p. 48.

may have considered themselves as integral parts footballing life in the city, are also absent and silenced.

As part of my construction, I divided Rotterdam into a number of geographical areas, which would help my narrative retain a sense of geographical coherence. For those that wish to use the data behind my story, I have provided references to books, newspaper articles, photos and other utilised documents. The maps show the locations of registered addresses for members in 1914 and there is a description of how I divided Rotterdam into different sections. I cannot be certain in all cases whether addresses were domestic residences, business addresses or another forms of contact address and we should always bear in mind official documents do not always tally with individual lives. But this story is comprised of many 'truthful statements', of what could be called 'facts'. The imagined, or rather, fictional aspect is how the narrative combines them together – the journey never happened and the words and thoughts of the individuals, where they appear, are from my own imagination.

In providing this imagined journey, my aim is to show that the lives of individuals matter in history, that too often gaps in the archive mean we can only represent individuals in certain ways, or often not at all. I wanted to construct a representation of life in Rotterdam during this week and to suggest how the individuals of the football field may have lived within it, not as abstracted statistics but integrated individuals. I believe that the existing traces of the past would not allow me to do this in the way I wanted and would have lead to many individuals being ignored. Secondly, I wanted to question whether history and fiction could mix effectively. Does knowing that elements of this story are acknowledged as 'fictional' change how you read it? Most importantly, I wanted to think, and invite you to consider, whether such experimental histories may be useful and, to echo Southgate's question, does the distinction between history and fiction really matter?[13]

To be clear, I believe that experimental history can help historians combat inherent power structures which lie within the archive, in the technology of collecting data and in how it is represented. Experimental history can highlight the importance of the narrative process in history and make readers question just where the borders between history and fiction are, and think about how many other histories and historians have been quietly playing in them without letting anyone know. What follows is my somewhat nervous experiment within the borderlands.[14]

An imagined journey in Rotterdam somewhere between 1 August 1914 and 7 August 1914

The telegraph office, 31 July 1914

At just before half past two, on the afternoon of 31 July 1914, a telegram intended for Mayor Zimmerman, requesting that Rotterdam be mobilised the following day, arrived in the head office of the Rijkstelegraafkantoor in Zuidblaak. The tensions in international politics outside of the Netherlands had occupied the office for the past few weeks and the noise of the telegram brought confirmation of what many had feared. Who would be required to fight? Would there be a wider war? Would the Netherlands be invaded? Just what would happen next? A. W. Gelderen, who had heard the telegram arrive, worked for the Rijkstelegraafkantoor. Within hours, work had been abandoned, bells began ringing across the city, masses of people gathered around notices in shops to find out what the news contained and announcements were made that the Netherlands was to mobilise.[15] The following day Gelderen was registered as a member of RVV Lycurgus, with his contact address listed as the Rotterdam Rijkstelegraafkantoor.

The southern Stadsdriehoek

A few hundred metres north-east of the Rijkstelegraafkantoor, in the heart of old Rotterdam, was the chemist shop of Sparta Rotterdam member J. Snoep, at Groote Markt 17. From here he and his son oversaw one of Rotterdam's busiest areas, and could see the steam railway viaduct, which linked the centre of the city to its northern and southern suburbs. In the centre of the square stood De Keijser's bronze statue of Erasmus, a reminder of the city's sometimes overlooked glories.[16] To the other side of the railway viaduct was the Middensteiger and the Hoofdsteeg, where fellow Sparta member F. Tillemans coordinated his perfume business.

To the south of the Groote Markt was the busy market site of the Blaak, with access to the Rotterdam's northern harbours. To the east was the Beurs, which was the location of the main Exchange, a fine sandstone building surrounding a courtyard flanked by colonnades and with a beautiful glass roof.[17] Above the Beursplein, the viaduct brought trains into Beurs station from north and south. As people flooded in and out of the square below, many had fallen in their haste. At the start of the week, both Tillemans and Snoep saw that the centre of Rotterdam was unusually busy. Mobilisation on Saturday 1 August had seen a large number of Rotterdammers rush to buy food and other goods, fearing that any war would lead to shortages. On 3 August, the rush for food had calmed somewhat, but the clamour for news had replaced it. On the Blaak, people headed into cafés and shops where the *NRC* posted regular bulletins of the latest news.[18] From the Groote Markt ran the narrow, fashionable streets of the Hang, where there were a number of shops including fashion boutiques and, rather usefully, the Doodewaarde mirror shop.[19] As the owners peered out onto the busy street, they wondered if any of the people had come to the Hang to shop, or if everyone was hurrying by to other parts of the city.

Some on the Hang were ignoring the rush and dreaming of the new football season. At Hang 49, lived Neptunus member J. Nacken. Along from him were another two members of Sparta Rotterdam: B. Spaapen, whose family were involved in painting and decorating, and J. H. Bouwman, a director at the Hammes company, specialising in roasting coffee and trading goods from the colonies in their shop on the Hang. Spaapen often talked to club-mate A. van Aken, who ran a game shop from his location on the Visschersdijk, around the corner from the Hang. As he walked past the shop, surrounded by a crowd of people, Spaapen noticed that Van Aken was swamped with people looking to stock up on food. He turned around and decided to come back later. Perhaps his friend might even put a little food aside for him.

Herman Alexander de Bij Jr was an auctioneer at the fish market and lived with his father at 35 Baan, just a short walk from work across the Leuvehaven Bridge. He had just registered with Sparta for the new season. He had been a fan of the game since his youth, and even though his father was reluctant at first, he often came with him to Prinsenlaan ground. North of Baan, the Van Hogendorpsplein was splashed with colour by the daily flower market. Around the square was the police station, the library and one of Rotterdam's most popular attractions, the Boijmans museum. Here one could while away time looking at drawings and paintings by the Dutch masters or some more modern artists. For those who found themselves in Rotterdam, it may have provided a useful distraction. As De Bij made his regular walk from home to work, he unknowingly passed the house of Th. Schreuder, who had registered for the smaller DVS team and was waiting for his coffee to be served.

On the busy banks of the Leuvehaven lived chemist and Sparta member Dr Adriaan Robertson. In the years before 1914, Robertson and his family had had a tumultuous time. With his wife, Henriette, Robertson had fathered five children, of whom three had died in infancy.

The youngest child, also called Adriaan, was born in May 1900 and his father hoped he would soon take up the sport. From their house on the east side of the Leuvehaven, it was a short walk to the ship-lined inlets of the Scheepmakershaven and the Wijnhaven, where the impressive spire of the Roman Catholic Zuiderkerk could clearly be seen.[20] The harbours on the north of the river were busy unloading apples and other fruit to be taken further into the city. Scheepmakershaven 29 was the home of Sparta member J. H. Wigleven Jr. Born in Prussia and married in Rotterdam in 1896, he had fathered a son in 1900 bearing his name. Wigleven was a manufacturer and trader, and his position on the Scheepmakershaven gave him close access to the Maas and the trading routes into Germany and beyond. Close to the Wigleven family at number 24 was the house of fellow Sparta member Louis Snoek, who was also involved in trade. While watching football, the two would often talk about business, new opportunities and the difficulties they faced with harbour workers. Not far from Snoek lived J. Boon at Scheepmakershaven 48a, who had just completed the membership forms for the much smaller RFC club. Still, at least it this would give him something to talk about with Wigleven instead of the dire news from the latter's homeland.

Between the Scheepmakershaven and the Wijnhaven ran the Gedempte Glashaven. On this street, line 3 of the Rotterdamsche Electrische Tramweg Maatschappij (Rotterdam Electric Tram Company) continued its journey between the Boompjes along the riverside and the Bergweg in the north. On the Glashaven, lived the Senn family, who ran a shirt-making factory. W. J. Senn had paid the membership for himself and his son, J. A. Senn, and like so many in the area was looking forward to being involved with the other men at Sparta. Parallel to the Glashaven ran the Bierhaven. B. Benenga's family had taken advantage of the massive expansion in the city and were involved as agents in Rotterdam's vast shipping industry; they had, of course, decided to remain living to the north of the river. Both Benenga and W. J. Blonk, who lived nearby, had joined Sparta. One street further along, the Klene family were involved in the lucrative chocolate and sugar industry which had grown in and around the harbours of Rotterdam in the years before 1914, largely on the back of imports from Dutch colonies overseas. Sparta member, F. J. Klene lived at Bierstraat 18b, and was preparing for the difficulties of bringing supplies from abroad if shipping was hampered. As Klene gazed across the busy Wijnhaven, its waters frothing with commotion, he noted that VOC member Ph. Rübsamen, was taking his daily stroll back from work.

Across the bridge, which carried trams to the centre of Rotterdam, was the address of Bouter & Zoon, a firm dedicated to trading securities and stocks. The financial situation in Rotterdam was becoming more perilous. On the Boompjes, not far south of the address of Sparta members A. E. and E. F. M. de Bouter, the impact of mobilisation caused public tensions. On 1 August, hundreds of people flocked to the doors of the Nederlandsche Bank looking to withdraw funds, causing a run.[21] Elsewhere in Rotterdam, the Spaarbank (Savings Bank) was stormed; paper money was no longer considered an accepted form of payment and a vast queue formed outside the Nederlandsche Bank, which would continue for much of the week.[22] The police did their best to contain the number of people, but things seemed to be different. Would the De Bouters suffer amidst the troubles or would their investments pay off as the trading map of the city was altered? More than this, would those people ever stop their incessant noise?

From their house at Groote Draaisteeg 20, the Van Dun family could hear the commotion at the bank, less than a hundred metres to the west. Situated between the Synagogue – north of which lived shipping agent H. Geerlofs with G. Geerlofs, both members of Sparta – the Nederlandsche Bank and the NHM buildings, the Van Dun family lived near one of Rotterdam's most important destinations, not only for trade, commerce and business but also for passenger shipping. Joannes Baptista Carolus Martinus van Dun had been born in Breda and moved to Rotterdam before marrying Maria Snijders in 1879, at the age of twenty-six. He had wisely studied to become an accountant, a profession for which there was great demand in Rotterdam. Van Dun's wife had given birth to ten children, one of whom died after thirteen days in 1880. Their three boys Joannes, Henricus and Andreas had all joined local football clubs although, strangely, they had not all opted for the same one. Joannes and Henricus, along with relative K. van Dun, had opted for Neptunus, where Joannes senior was president, while the impetuous Andreas had joined rival team UDI, inviting more than a few good-natured jokes.

Next door to the Van Dun family, lived seventeen-year-old Neptunus member Alfred Eduard Dehnert with his lawyer father Ernst and family. Capitalising on the passengers coming and going from the numerous ships was the nearby Hotel Batavia, owned by the Burggräfers, of whom C. Burggräfer had joined USC. If war broke out, would people still travel to Rotterdam? Would they be able to? Already there had been a warning that war would mean fewer ships docking in the harbours. But, for now, the panic had been good for business as stranded tourists and travellers desperately looked for somewhere to stay. 'Ah well,' thought Burggräfer, 'best make hay while the sun shines.'

And the sun was indeed shining, with the many waterways of Rotterdam acting like a mirror for the sun's rays upon the city around them. Across a small bridge from the Hotel Batavia was the Zalmhaven, which had flourished with the growth of salmon imports. Club membership flourished here too. Here, on the Eenhoornstraat, the Dirks family provided four members to the UDI club. On Houtlaan, were two members of USC: J. M. Borstlap Jr and C. J. Tettelaar. On the Zalmhaven itself lived two members of the Klip family who were members of Sparta. The bustling area to the east was home to passenger ships and further along the promenade, past the office of VOC member W. Bekker Jr, was a swimming school, popular with local children. Under the railway viaduct, in the shadows of the impressive Witte Huis office block, was the Gelderschekade, which was home to the café of F. A. G. Kortman. His teenage son, a Leonidas member, loved climbing to the top of the ten-storey office block to look over the whole of the city.[23] Sometimes, from the top of the building, he had tried to call down to his neighbour D. Visser, who was a Sparta member, but he never quite managed it.

A new bridge had been built across the Oudehaven from the Gelderschekade, which could carry the numerous horse-drawn carriages and transport vehicles to the Haringvliet. There, the English Episcopal Church had recently shut down and there was another hotel, the Continental, belonging to K. de Grooth. Three of his children were members of Sparta; one, G. B. de Grooth, hoped to play in the first team and had proved to be quite a talent already. W. Lammers, also registered at Haringvliet 24, was likewise a Sparta member and had been trying to find out if any old boots were going spare.

Nearby was the Maas train station, dispatching trains to Amsterdam, Utrecht, Arnhem and Germany. On 3 August, this usually bustling station reported that no trains had departed.[24] In the newspapers, various railway companies took out advertisements indicating that service was to be limited and altered. Beneath these adverts, in German and French, were official declarations in the name of the Kaiser's envoy in The Hague and his French counterpart; both French and German governments had decided to mobilise their own armies and requested conscripts to rejoin their units.[25] To those who lived on the Haringvliet, including two members of Sparta Rotterdam, the merchant C. H. W. Heusdens and traveller F. S. Ouwehand, the unusual quiet which greeted the streets around the Maas station seemed an ominous sign of what was to come.

The northern Stadsdriehoek

To the north of the Groote Markt was Rotterdam's main thoroughfare, the Hoogstraat, which separated the old harbours on the northern bank of the Maas from the congested inner district towards the station. On the Hoogstraat were numerous businesses and shops, both small and large, and set back from the street was the covered Passage arcade. The Peek & Cloppenburg store sold all manner of household wares from their spot on the Hoogstraat, and so too did Vroom & Dreesmann, near the America cinema. Cafés, fashion stores, wheel shops and private houses were dotted along the length of the busy street. Three sons of C. Lap, who ran a clothing company vying for business with the larger stores, were members of Leonidas, all lived at 36 Hoogstraat. Along from them, at 220, lived the Elze family. Simon Isaac Elze was a director at the male Jewish cemetery in the city. Simon's father had been involved in trade but had died in January 1912. Although his son Mozes Bernard Elze was only thirteen, Simon had always encouraged him to take part in sport and had eagerly renewed his membership of Sparta, even if the secretary there had neglected to note down his age. At Hoogstraat 325, J. A. R. Muhs owned the restaurant Zum Löwenbrau. K. E. W Muhs would often invite some of his Sparta club-mates back to the restaurant after a match to enjoy some hearty German food. As Muhs's restaurant showed, there was a large German influence in Rotterdam and, of all the Dutch cities, it was most at risk from a war between the Germans, French and British. It had excellent trade links to all, as well as a great number of inhabitants with friends, families and business contacts in each of these countries. The Muhs family wondered if war would see tensions in the city increase between those from different parts of Europe? But for one evening at least, they decided to forget football and talk of war and attend the local Thalia Theatre where the actors were preparing for a performance of 'Een Vorstenkind'.[26]

North of the Thalia Theatre was the Groote Kerkplein upon which was the Groote Kerk with its fifteenth-century Gothic architecture. In good weather, one could climb to the top of the church spire and see the impressive churches in the nearby cities of Brielle, Delft, The Hague, Gouda, Leiden and Dordrecht.[27] Nearby, at Groote Kerkplein 56, was Katan's Zon shop that offered repayment services. Israel Marcus Katan had started the business but, at eighty-seven years old, he was finding life increasingly difficult. Beset by a serious illness, Katan had little time for daily business operations and had passed these on long ago to his son, also named Israel. His grandson, M. Katan, devoted his

Sunday to playing football for Sparta, something the elder Katan had never understood. At Groote Kerkplein 50a was the Vaterland Passage Bureau. Those who worked there were keenly aware that the United States had noted its concern at the situation in Europe with a brief message in the 3 August's *NRC*. All US and Canadian citizens were requested to leave Rotterdam on English ships using this agency to help them do so. Reinforcing the confused and worried nature of many Rotterdammers, the message indicated that, after the 5 August, no tickets would be issued to those on the Continent. There was, the message read, 'no absolute certainty what would happen tomorrow or after'.[28]

North-west of the Groote Kerkplein was Oppert. At Oppert 61, those inside the building of the Vereeniging tot verbetering van Armenzorg (Association for the Improvement of Poor Relief) were already considering how to respond to the present crisis and how best to distribute their money.[29] Despite the numerous adverts from various food associations indicating that food was still plentiful in shops, any conflict was sure to have an impact on its availability and many seemed to doubt the reassurances.[30] The members of the association debated on the best way to deal with the influx of people into the port, but they all agreed that if war broke out it would be the city's poor who would be hardest hit. On the opposite side of the street was a billiard factory, which had been in operation since 1852 and had supplied many of Rotterdam's drinking establishments. Just a few doors down was the shop of Wolff & Zoonen. Josephus Johannes Wolff had fathered eight children with his wife Maria. When Maria died in 1889, Josephus was left to care for them, although he had help from time to time. With his two sons, he undertook work in many houses of Rotterdam as a plasterer. His first son, Jacobus Wolff had decided to fill his Sundays with football for Sparta and Josephus intended to watch as many games as he could. At Oppert 138 lived A. Keehnen who also worked in the decorating business. His main trade was as a wallpaper-hanger and upholsterer and he would often be recommended by Josephus Wolff. Theodorus Keehnen was yet another teenager looking for excitement on Sunday, although he had decided to join the smaller UDI club. However, compared to Het Noorden which only had twenty members, UDI seemed like a giant of the game. J. Koomans, who was involved in managing an office, had joined this small north Rotterdam team along with J. van IJperen. They often spoke about getting more members; after all, not all of them were available to play every week and they only just had enough for a team as it was.

Parallel to the Oppert, the Delftschevaart ran alongside a canal from the Hofplein to the Spuiwater. The canal itself was only just wide enough for two barges to pass side-by-side and the houses were tightly packed along both its banks.[31] At Delftschevaart 40, Theodorus A. A. Kreijns was a painter. His son, Theodorus, born in 1898, was one of those to register with the young north Rotterdam team of De Concordiaan which had been established in 1910 along Roman Catholic lines. Three doors down, at 43 Delftschevaart, W. T. Lammers ran a dealership concerned with hairdressing equipment which he sold throughout the city. Two of his relatives had registered at different clubs. J. Lammers had pledged his allegiance to the Catholic-aligned Leonidas while Th. Lammers had joined Neptunus, a club less bothered by any religious attachment. Together they would often look jealously towards their neighbours A. van Zijl and the architect Th. J. Aalbers as they returned from celebrating another victory for Sparta or VOC respectively.

Within shouting distance from the Delftschevaart was the Haagscheveer where three Sparta members lived. At Haagscheveer 30, R. van den Heuvel Jr had registered at the company address of R. van den Heuvel & Gebroeders van Buuren that operated car services between Rotterdam and Delft. The owner of the company was worried that all motorised transport would be required by the military should war break out, which would place their transport service in a difficult position; but for now, the increased number of lost travellers was particularly welcome. R. van den Heuvel lived a few doors down with fellow Sparta member P. M. van den Heuvel. At the end of the road was the shop of A. G. Bol. His son Jan Bol had just turned eighteen and all summer long he had dreamed of breaking into the Sparta first team, of playing with 'Bok' de Korver and 'Cas' Ruffelse, and perhaps of even catching the eyes of some young women on the sidelines. But now, with the prospect of war on the horizon, these dreams took on a slightly more painful and uncertain form.

To the north of the Haagscheveer was the Delftsche Poort, a giant gate on the border of the heart of old Rotterdam with the station beyond.[32] On the Delftschepoortplein lived L. Scheepsma, a member of Neptunus, near the tobacco warehouse of K. Schaedtler & Co. From the square itself, Scheepsma could see the dark blue and cream electric trams rattling into the Hofplein.[33] The Hofplein was home to cafés, shops and the distinctive façade of the terminus of the Zuid-Hollandsche Electrische Spoorweg-Maatschappij (South Holland Electric Railway Company), which sat at the end of a viaduct adorned with sculptures and reliefs of animals fashioned from concrete. The bright white façade on the Hofplein housed the Loos restaurant and passengers had to find their way to the glass-ceilinged station via a side entrance.[34] From here, the new railway took passengers through The

Hague to the beautiful seaside resort of Scheveningen just 28 kilometres away. In the *NRC*, the resort had placed an advert to calm those who could no longer holiday abroad because of the political situation, promising a suitable alternative nearer to home.[35] Although just thirty minutes away, the concerns of war that had occurred in Rotterdam made the picturesque late summer evenings on the beach seem further away than ever.

Noordereiland

In the middle of the river, to the south of the centre of Rotterdam, was Noordereiland, which had been established after the development of the harbours on the southern side of the Maas in the late nineteenth century. It was home to many dockworkers.[36] Shipbuilding and metalwork had become the dominant forms of work in Rotterdam's harbours, although in recent years tobacco and margarine manufacture had also proved to be important parts of the city's trade.[37]

On 1 August 1914, a number of individuals from the island had registered as members of Rotterdam football clubs. Across the bridge from the centre, which offered wonderful views of the city on both banks, ran the wide Van der Takstraat. The street cut through the centre of Noordereiland and took people to the south of Rotterdam, as well as providing trams for those who needed to turn back. Named after the former city architect responsible for linking the Noordereiland to the mainland, the street also housed the Spaarbank, which saw queues outside it on 3 August. Next door, H. J. M. A. F. van der Eerden had fought his way through the queues to arrive at work and had noticed that he had left his VOC membership papers in his desk. On the northern side of the island was the Maaskade, a wide tree-lined road that ran alongside a small quay where local passenger boats departed and arrived. The busy road had seen extra excitement in 1911 when a passing boat, the SS Gutenberg, had exploded leaving debris and what was left of its boiler on the road to the bemusement of locals.[38] Running the entire length of the island, the Maaskade was home to a variety of individuals and businesses. Near the bridge, the Fritschy café-restaurant offered superb views of north Rotterdam, as well as the many trams, cars and horses crossing the waterway.[39]

The Maaskade was also home to a number of football club members. At Maaskade 78, next to the Fritschy, was the Van Driel family. Willem van Driel was involved in trade, but had died in 1911 at the age of sixty-six. His three sons remembered how enthusiastically Willem had followed their stories of playing football when growing up, and even the rivalry between them. In their early twenties Henri and Gijsbertus were members of VOC, hoping to become not only the best team in Rotterdam but also in the Netherlands, while W. van Driel, like so many other Rotterdammers, was a member of Sparta. Gijsbertus was already thought of as one of the best goalkeepers in the Netherlands, but he found it difficult to stay with the same team for long; he used to play for both DFC and Sparta, but this year he would be wearing the distinctive hooped jersey of VOC.[40] This was not the only case of split loyalties on the Maaskade. Further along, at Maaskade 92, father and son A. Emmerie and A. Emmerie Jr had also joined two old rival clubs, VOC and Sparta respectively.

At the western end of the Maaskade was the Prinsenhoofd, an area that offered a launching place for small boats and had been the stage for the centenary celebrations of Dutch independence in November 1913.[41] On 4 August 1914, VOC member B. C. Boogaert 't Hooft, wondered whether he would witness another celebration as he read the news of Germany announcing war on England and France in the evening edition of the *NRC*.[42] Although Mayor Zimmerman had promised to introduce legislation to keep the cost of food affordable, he was unconvinced.[43] He put down his paper, grabbed his coat and set out to the centre of Rotterdam, not quite sure why, but hoping he would find some stores left open willing to sell him something.

'Father, have you read the news?' asked Sparta member Q. van Beijnen. A trader by profession, Van Beijnen knew that his father, Johannes, had predicted things getting worse. He trusted his father and realised that as director of Scheepvaartmaatschappij Holland-Friesland (the Holland-Friesland Shipping Company) his father would need to act straight away. 'Yes, son. We had meetings today about what to do. It does not look good,' replied Johannes. Other companies had already taken the decision to suspend sailings; with Germany at war with France, the North Sea would become a contested area. Van Beijnen was sure to be asked what information he had when he saw other footballers on the Prins Hendrikkade. J. J. van den Akker, G. A. Burger and W. E. Knip had all registered for VOC and would no doubt be eager to hear the news.

In the centre of Noordereiland was the Burgemeester Hoffmanplein, an attractive tree-covered square with a monument to the engineer Stieltjes who had planned the harbour development on the southern side of the Maas.[44] It was also home to M. Bol who had joined Neptunus. To the east of the bridge, beyond the railway line, and parallel to Van der Takstraat, was Feijenoordstraat. At the southern end of the Feijenoordstraat were the warehouses and work sites of the

Nederlandsche Stoomboot-Reederij (the Netherlands Steamboat Company). Four buildings up the street from the company, at Feijenoordstraat 40b, lived the sailor and Neptunus member D. Zevenbergen, along with a civil servant from Ghent, P. F. Leenknegt, and J. Leenknegt, who was registered with Lycurgus. At number 26, M. J. Viergever was attached to one of Rotterdam's smallest clubs, Transvalia. Every week during the season Viergever would travel over the Koninginnebrug past the Stieltjes monument, past the lines of the Rotterdamsche Tramweg Maatschappij (Rotterdam Tramway Company, RTM), past the docks and harbours of the great passenger steamers, and to the home of the club on the grassy fields of Feijenoord's Afrikaanderplein.

The south

South of the river, across the railway viaduct, were the great new harbours designed to bring passengers, oil, ores, grain and other goods to and from the city. The area south of the Maas had been developed considerably in the latter part of the nineteenth century and was home to both the Rijnhaven and the Maashaven, which could berth the largest of ships carrying a vast range of goods from around the world.[45] These goods flooded in and out of the factories and warehouses of the new production industries, but the industries had been hit hard by the first day of mobilisation. On 3 August, the *Rotterdamsch Nieuwsblad* reported that in offices up to a quarter of workers were unavailable for work, on the tram network several hundred conductors had been taken off duty and industry was also struck by a diminution of labour.[46]

On Rosestraat was the Rotterdam terminus of the RTM, which since 1905 had ferried passengers from West Brabant and the islands of Zuid-Holland to the harbours of Rotterdam. Outside the station, cabs often waited to whisk passengers further into the city.[47] The street was full of small shops, dealers in cigarettes, carpets, hairdressers, cafés and bars, as well as the numerous dockworkers who lived close to the harbours. At Rosestraat 46, A. J. Weber had registered for Feyenoord; so too, at 330b, had Th. J. Paul whose father was a dockworker. Parallel, to the east, ran the lengthy Oranjeboomstraat with the Wilhelminakerk flanked by trees at one end. On his way from Noordereiland to the Afrikaanderplein pitches of Transvalia, Mr Viergever would often stop in one of the popular cafés on the Oranjeboomstraat. Usually he would find a fellow Transvalia member to talk to. In fact, he was somewhat spoilt for choice, as many of the small club's members would come in to the café before a match.

B. Smits was related to P. L. Smits, a local wheelwright; L. de Rijke lived at the same address as Q. de Rijke who operated a crane in the harbour, loading and unloading goods from the berthed ships. Many of those members who lived in the south had connections to the docks. In nearby Stampioenstraat, A. Vogel was the son of a dockworker, and liked to join the discussions before a game. And it wasn't just Transvalia members who congregated at the cafes on the Oranjeboomstraat. J. H. Akveld, a twenty-year-old teacher's son, was south Rotterdam's sole representative of Leonidas, and would sometimes stop by on his way to the Woudestein pitches in east Rotterdam.

On the other side of the railway, next to the Spoorweghaven, was the Afrikaanderplein, the home of south Rotterdam football. On this large, open, grassy square, the teams of Feyenoord and Transvalia played. Two Feyenoord members also lived on the square, A. van Dokcum and G. P. de Graaf. In the south, the initial war panic which surrounded the busy squares of the Blaak, Beurs and the banks of the Boompjes was seemingly not present; there were some benefits to living here. On the Paul Krugerstraat, experienced ship's captain Pieter Willem Levasier could see the pitches from his front door and was a short walk from the team changing room, based in the café of F. W. J. Waltmann at Joubertstraat 61a–65a. The usual talk of business and football had subsided in the off-season and now it was talk of war that took the lead. As ships to the city became fewer, there would certainly be less need for a ship's captain and it was perhaps best, thought Levasier, to stay at home anyway.

Feyenoord members A. Koonings, P. and J. Meulendijk and J. van Rikxoort had registered at Joubertstraat 63 and always looked forward to their time in the café. One street to the west, C. van de Velde was another Feyenoord member with relatives working on the docks. Waltmann's café was not the only one around the Afrikaanderplein to be involved in football. On the north side of Bloemfonteinstraat, where it joined with the Hillelaan, Petrus Josephus Mulders ran a café. He hoped that he could capitalise on the football played on the square on Sundays and wanted his eighteen-year-old son, Frederik Petrus Mulders, to persuade some of his Transvalia team-mates to come back to the café for a drink after matches.

Around two kilometres to the west of the Afrikaanderplein, beyond the Maashaven, was Charlois, which had only been incorporated into Rotterdam in 1894. For part of the way between the Afrikaanderplein and Charlois ran the Brielschelaan, home to Dr Huijsman; it was also home to Rotterdam's two southernmost members of VOC. The doctor's two young sons, J. C. Huijsman and J. C. F. Huijsman, were both fourteen years old – born ten months apart – and had quite a way to travel to the pitches in northern Rotterdam. Charlois was some distance from the centre of the crowds in the Stadsdriehoek and was easiest to reach via a ferry from the park in the north. Charlois was a small community of streets centred around a church and was growing as the wharfs and harbours to the north expanded; it was home to CVV, a young club with its changing facilities at the Charloissche Kerksingel 86, in the Hof van Bourgondië café.[48] The owner of the café was J. L. W. Holkers, who had divorced his first wife in 1906 and remarried in 1908. As a café owner, Holkers got to know most of his team-mates well and the café was the centre of club life for a small team like CVV. Nearby, A. Huizer and B. van Ooijen had also signed up for the new season and were hopeful that their post-match drink in the café would be able to continue.

The Kaatsbaan ran from the church and was where A. van der Steen and his two sons lived. Van der Steen ran a sales shop and had just registered both himself and H. van der Steen to join CVV, although J. van der Steen was pestering his father to sign him up too. To the south was the long Katendrechtsche Lagedijk. At 294 lived H. Pors, a workman, with his father W. Pors, both part of the local team. Next to them, H. van de Ent had also joined. Closest to the church was J. van Eijk. On Tuesday evening, Van Eijk returned home from the factory where he worked to talk with his family about the day's events. He had been born in Charlois when it was still an independent town and was pleased to be attached to his local team, although the commotion of Rotterdam was sometimes a frustration. The problems on the trams in the centre were not a great concern to him, as he worked close to Charlois, but Charlois had changed a lot in a short time. Petroleum tanks and docks now punctured the landscape of the southern banks and nearby the giant mouth of the ever-growing Waalhaven was another reminder of the rapid change that had happened in Rotterdam.[49]

Stationswijk

The scene around the Delftsche Poort Station, in the north of Rotterdam, on the morning of Saturday 1 August, demonstrated that times had changed. Although it was the first day of the school holidays, the station was not full of children and families heading to the beach. Instead, a long stream of young men dressed in uniform arrived in response to the mobilisation orders. Although most reservists were locally based, some first-reservists, who had previously served, had to travel by train to their destinations, either locally or further afield.[50] On the pavements, vestibules, streets and waiting rooms, the men said goodbye to the neighbourhood and their loved ones. Many were brought to the station by their girlfriends, wives and parents who accompanied them to the entrance of the stations where empty trains rolled into the platforms to be stormed by eager young soldiers; their family and friends looked on and waved a sombre farewell.[51]

In the streets around the Delftsche Poort station, the site for this unusual and uncomfortable busyness, there were many who had registered for local football clubs, mostly Sparta or VOC. At Stationsplein 1, Jacq van As was a businessman, uncomfortable both with the political situation and the sudden number of people outside his house. Van As had registered for Sparta. Further along the Stationsweg, was the house of the Ruffelse family. The activity around the station was especially painful for those who lived here. W. H. Ruffelse Sr had been an inspector on the Hollandsche IJzeren Spoorweg-Maatschappij (the Holland Iron Railway Company), which operated from the Delftsche Poort station. Sadly, W. H. Ruffelse had died three weeks previously, at the age of sixty-one. As his sons read the morning newspapers, which announced that the trains had been commandeered for military use and that the public would only be welcome on most trains after midday,[52] they thought of their father and how he would have loved making the new timetables and directing confused passengers. Ruffelse's two sons, Wilhelmus Hendrikus Ruffelse Jr and Caspar Ruffelse, were both members of the Sparta club. Caspar, or 'Cas' as he was known, was part of the Sparta first team, one of the Netherlands' best players and had represented the national team three years earlier against England. At Stationsweg 30, his club team-mate Henri de Groot, sometimes called Henk, sometimes Hugo, but better known as 'Huug', had qualified as an architect. De Groot's cheeky smile could often be seen at the Sparta ground in Crooswijk and he had also broken into the national team, scoring both goals in a marvellous 2–1 victory over England the year before in The Hague.

To the south of the Stationsweg was the Diergaardelaan, which led to the Rotterdam zoo. The magnificent architecture of the Stationsweg continued along this road.[53] J. Zwartendijk (a trader in colonial goods), P. A. Zwartendijk and thirteen-year-old F. C. Drescher had all registered for VOC. Businessmen P. Ribourdouille was registered for Sparta and lived in the street next to the zoo with many other businessmen. Despite the troubling times, the streets of the city were still busy with a number of families who were looking for a distraction from the upheaval and heading towards the zoo; a number of children and those without anything better to do also seemed to be loitering around the centre of town looking for some form of excitement.[54]

On the northern side of the station, the situation appeared calmer. On the Stationssingel, two VOC members from the Van de Schoor de Boer family noted that the sound of trains coming and going drowned out the sounds of the soldiers on the Stationsplein. The nearby Spoorsingel was home to insurance underwriter C. van der Plas who was already concerned about his business; luckily he had made sure that he was not responsible for damage caused by war. Van de Plas often went around to the Leeman family, at Spoorsingel 23, and sometimes he would go to matches together with the three VOC members of the Leeman family and his son.

Next to the still, blue waters of the Proveniersingel was the Proveniersplein, where VOC member J. A. Rietdijk lived.[55] On the adjoining Proveniersstraat was the shoe shop of Johannes de Beer whose sons were members of De Concordiaan. Northwards on the Walenburgerweg was the house of sixteen-year-old VOC member Jan Lodewijk Marie Bloemen. His father was the head commissar at the telegraph office, which had seen so much activity since the call to mobilisation; it was not only the streets around the station that seemed unusually busy.[56]

West Coolsingel

VOC member Mr Van Cleeff lived near the popular Tivoli theatre, which on the evening of 1 August was preparing for an eight o'clock performance.[57] Close to the Remonstrant Church, on the banks of the Westersingel, was the school of Mr Schreuder. On Tuesday 4 August, he had allowed his school, which was empty for the vacation, to be used as a registration point for a female volunteer society. The newspaper advert from the previous day had urged women with any free time to come and sign up to help the mobilisation effort. The society would be affiliated to the Dutch Red Cross who were already busy elsewhere in Rotterdam.[58] Opposite the Westersingel to the south was the Eendrachtsweg, a long fashionable street famed for being home to many artists, lawyers, teachers and manufacturers. On its western side, a long stretch of water bordered by shrubs and grass formed a beautiful space to promenade for well-heeled Rotterdam residents.[59]

One street to the east was the narrow Eendrachtsstraat, which, thanks to the tall towers of the Eendrachtskerk, was often in shadow. On this road was the house of P. W. de Jong and further up the road lived fellow UDI member P. de Jong, who worked as a carpenter's apprentice. For both men it was a long trip from here to the east of the city where UDI played their home games on the Woudestein; fortunately, the tram stopped near to the pitches. Opposite P. de Jong was the trading firm of P. W. van Dalsum. Van Dalsum was the son of another businessman who held a position at Van Berkel's patent office. Originally from Amsterdam, he had achieved success relatively young and lived alongside his younger brother Jacques Philippe van Dalsum who was a Rotterdam native; both men had registered for Sparta.

The often-bustling street of the Oude Binnenweg was home to shops of all types and sizes, from the large Vroom & Dreesmann to the watch seller and goldsmiths of G. Brunott. At Binnenweg 73, next to the family grocery shop was K. van der Burg, a member of Neptunus. Nearby lived Sparta member A. H. Douw who was the son of a private teacher. On the Aert van Nesstraat, two roads north, was the Groote Schouwburg, with its impressive façade. The Groote Schouwburg was once home to plays and opera and for many was the centre of Rotterdam's cultural life, even though it often lost money.[60] Kindly Mr Douw told some confused and disappointed travellers that the Schouwburg did not have shows on in July and August: 'I recommend the Thalia Theatre in the centre, I hear they have a new play on.'[61]

The road was also home to other members of football clubs. J. H. Kooiman, who was a director of a stable-keepers' association, had been told that the export of horses had been banned shortly after mobilisation, along with other products.[62] On 31 July, Kooiman had been warned that his horses may be requisitioned for use by the army. He would receive compensation if this did happen,[63] but felt compelled to remark sarcastically: 'Great, but what exactly am I supposed to buy to replace them?' He put down the paper and mumbled to himself as he looked out of the window to the streets below. On Saturday morning, the streets of Rotterdam saw a stream of horses make their way to the grassy fields of the Heuvelterrein and Woudestein, where pitches used for football had been transformed into temporary stables.[64] J. Kooiman registered as a member of Sparta.

To the south of the Aert van Nesstraat was the Van Oldenbarneveltstraat, which began near the Calandmonument in the east. Here was the distinctive building of the Coolvest Hospital. Capitalising on the proximity of the hospital was Firma Linden Jr, which traded in medical instruments and furniture. If one thing was certain it was that a war would mean that surgical instruments would be in great demand. A. Linden was registered for Sparta. Further along the street was the Koopman Dance Academy where it was possible to gain instruction from C. and M. C. Koopman. Sparta player J. W. Koopman also lived here. Fellow Sparta member K. Vuijk operated as a decorator in a family-run business and, further along the road, the Coenen family ran a business trading religious articles. C. and J. Coenen had registered to play for east Rotterdam's Leonidas Club.

South of the Binnenweg, the Zwarte Paardenstraat was home to many boat workers and clothes makers. J. W. Smit had registered for the small RFC club, although the club secretary had forgotten to note dowen his house number, which would make communication a little more difficult. Nearby, the house at Witte de Withstraat 55 was a busy place. The building was home to railway agents, post agents and a gymnastics teacher, as well as a Cooperative Pension Society. It was also the postal address for J. O. Bender of DVS and F. Hoekzema, A. Koops and W. Scharenberg of Sparta. Along from the bustling doors of Witte de Withstraat 55, was the address of Louis Weinthal, who was involved in his father's cigar business and manufactured the products from his base in Rotterdam. In the late nineteenth century, he had been a prominent athlete and footballer. Next door, H. H. W. Rutteman was a member of the VOC club and they would often talk about the glory days gone by, with the younger Rutteman always looking for tips. Weinthal was also the consul for Guatemala and had spent much of Monday 3 August hastily making business enquiries. Both he and Arthur, his son, were members of the Sparta club. But it was not just business that was worrying Weinthal on this August evening. His wife, Clara, was from Iserlohn in Germany. If war broke out between the Netherlands and Germany, would she still be safe here? Would she want to stay? The days ahead promised to be difficult.

The west and the park

In the newer parts of Rotterdam, to the west of the Westersingel, it seemed that one could not kick a ball without hitting a football club member. In the southern part of the area was the park, where concerts were often held in the summer and a café afforded pleasant views over the Maas.[65] On 5 August, the bad news from abroad had led to more panic in the centre of the city. The border with Germany had been difficult to cross since 1 August, but by 5 August the Scheldt waterway near Antwerp became heavily restricted as well.[66] On the evening of Tuesday 4 August, England had declared war on Germany; warring parties now surrounded the Netherlands. In the park, the evening's concert by the corps of the Koninklijke Scherpschutters (Royal Sharpshooters) had been cancelled; many of them may have been needed for more serious business. Next to the park, the Heuvelterrein, which saw the gathering of horses on Saturday 1 April, was home to RFC and Neptunus.[67] To the west of the park, three new harbours were criss-crossed with railway lines and occupied by cargo warehouses. On the banks of the Maas, between the Sint Jobshaven and Schiehaven was the site of the Rotterdam Lloyd Steamship Company with its vast steamers, now so much in demand.[68]

Around the park, a number of new, long, well-populated streets had emerged in the recent past and most were residential in nature. On the Westzeedijk, H. Geensma joined RFC, partly because it was so easy to get to games, but others had made different choices. The Ebeling family had cause for sibling rivalry; Karel A. Ebeling Jr had opted for Neptunus while his brother, J. Ebeling, had registered for their rivals RFC. Not far away, on the Veerhaven, the large Van 't Hoff ship-brokerage family had a similar experience with brothers Johan Jr and Johann Philipp M. splitting their allegiances between Rotterdam's two most popular clubs, Sparta and VOC.

If Rotterdam could be said to have had a football street, it was here, on the Mathenesserlaan. Despite its position on the edge of the city, it had excellent transport links and one could catch tram number ten nearby towards the Delftsche Poort station. VOC was well represented here and two families had done their best to swell the numbers. At Mathenesserlaan 348 lived the Neuerburg family. They had four children of whom only Reinhard, just twelve, had been born in the city. But as with his brothers, E. Neuerburg and the two H. Neuerburgs, he had also registered for VOC. A few steps along the road were the Stenger family. Geert Stenger had been born in Farmsum, Friesland, in 1858 and had become a commander in the Holland-Amerika Lijn. In the *NRC* of 3 August, the company had placed an advert indicating that the SS Gorredijk would still be travelling to Cuba, Mexico and New Orleans on 18 August.[69] That felt like a long time away and things were changing quickly on the docks. Stenger had married a local woman, Pieternella Oelssen, in Rotterdam in 1883 and together they had eleven children. Eight of these were male, all but one of whom had joined VOC. The eldest, J. G. Stenger, had moved to New York but still remained a member. Another six of their children had continued their membership at the club. Though her children and husband did not know it, Pieternella loved to go and watch matches at VOC. She left home after them and arrived back before them on Sundays to ensure that she would not have to face too many questions. At the ground, she blended into the crowd like anyone else, shouting and screaming, especially when one of her children was on the wrong end of a foul.

Around the Mathenesserlaan many other club members lived, including L. van Zandvliet, the president of the south Rotterdam-based Feyenoord team. H. A. den Held was involved in the large sporting-goods firm Den Held Sporthandel and had registered as a VOC member. A keen sportsman and familiar face of the Rotterdam sport scene, he also hoped that he could persuade some of his club-mates to buy their goods from the family store. His elder brother, Cornelis Johannes, was an official contact for the *NVB* in Rotterdam and a vice-president at VOC, living on the Westzeedijk. A new football season would not only mean more time with his friends at the club but the opportunity to find new places to sell his goods. The Hörburger family, on the Burgemeester Meineszlaan, had three members playing for VOC. Arnold Hörburger was one of the Netherlands' best players and had made his debut in the 7–0 defeat of Belgium in 1910. His brother Anton had been close to the Dutch national team and this year he hoped he would finally get his chance. Together the three brothers formed part of an impressive VOC team.

On the Nieuwe Binnenweg, two men had been affected by the rush to buy food among many Rotterdam citizens. Both Lycurgus's H. J. G. Bolk and Sparta's M. A. Hoogerbrugge were involved in the trading and regulation of food: Bolk was connected to the control of grain and Hoogerbrugge was involved in the trade of potato-meal. Both these staples were much in demand during the weekend and local authorities were considering regulations to limit the cost of such products. In the newspapers, adverts had been taken out to indicate that bread and butter were still freely available, but if Rotterdam's trade links were cut then where would new supplies come from? The newspapers had urged citizens to understand that producers and vendors were in difficult positions, but everywhere people were in a difficult position. Elsewhere on the road, Sparta members J. C. F. van de Roer and L. P. Hoogendijk discussed their connection to the building trade and how war might affect this. As the changes in the previous few years had shown, Rotterdam was a fast-changing, fast-growing city and always needed architects and building technicians; but it also needed money, and neither of the men were sure where this would come from.

On the Claes de Vrieselaan, football was never far from the discussion in the local café. At Claes de Vrieselaan 145, Leonidas member

H. Kleijn ran an office and, next door, Sparta member J. M. Kerkhoff operated his own electrical technician's business. The Vellenga family had three members attached to VOC: S. L. Vellenga was an engineer and C. H. Vellenga was a ship's assistant, while a third, S. R. Vellenga, also lived at Claes de Vrieselaan 50. Perhaps the inhabitant of this street most famous to Rotterdam football fans was Johannes Marius de Korver. 'Bok', as he was affectionately known to friends and fans, lived at Claes de Vrieselaan 12 and during the day was a civil servant for the Municipality. He was much better known for his inspirational performances in Sparta and Netherlands jerseys. From his position in the midfield, he was at the centre of the action and was famed for his hard running and good passing. He had played in the first official Netherlands international and during his thirty-one games for his country had often been captain. Bok had led the team in a famous victory against England Amateurs in March 1913, when his good friend Huug had scored twice; he preferred to think about this match rather than the return defeat in Hull. Now De Korver had other worries. He had planned to marry his girlfriend, Henriette, but more concerning was that he was to be mobilised.[70] As he packed his equipment and headed to the station with Henriette, he wondered when he would see her, Huug or the fields of the Prinsenlaan again.

Crooswijk

At the Hollandia café, on the Crooswijkschesingel, bulletins from the *NRC* were posted on the wall. The *NRC* morning edition of Saturday 1 August was lacking the usual previews of sporting matches for the weekend ahead. In their place, it sombrely noted that the times were too serious to discuss sport, which was, after all, entertainment.[71] The main sport weekly, *De Revue der Sporten*, announced a halt to publication because of the war.[72] That morning thousands of men had travelled to the Schuttersveld just to the north of the café. In the past years, the rectangular expanse of grass had been frequent host to gymnastic competitions and was the home of the USC team.[73] On that morning, at 6 o'clock, it was a meeting place for those responding to the call to mobilise.[74] To the north of the Schuttersveld, bordered by the Algemeene Begraafplaats (General Cemetery), was the Prinsenlaan stadium of Sparta Rotterdam. Sparta had been formed in 1888 and had become the most successful team in Rotterdam. For members and supporters, there was hope that they could reclaim the title, which HVV had won in spring 1914.

Sparta member, A. van der Pluijm, lived at Hugo de Grootstraat 145, which was adjacent to the Veemarkt, where cattle and milk were sold every Tuesday.[75] He noticed on Tuesday 4 August that there were fewer people in the street and at the market. There seemed to be fewer cattle too. That evening, the *NRC* indicated that there were only around half the usual number of animals for sale.[76] On the other side of the Veemarkt was the Boezemsingel. At Boezemsingel 136b lived the Van der Sluis family. Jan van der Sluis Sr was a trader in fruit and vegetables and had already noticed a problem in obtaining them. His wife, Elisabeth, came from a Dutch town just metres from the German border in Gelderland. Their two sons Jan Jr and Chrisitaan Frederik had joined the VOC club. Downstairs, at Boezemsingel 136a, E. J. Eilers ran a car-trading business. Military requisitioning of vehicles was bound to hit him hard and he was not sure when he could import any more. His son, Cornelis, had joined Sparta as a member. Along the road, H. J. Brandes had also registered as a member of Sparta, but he was concerned that his job as a trader of meal would be hampered by problems obtaining different foodstuffs.[77]

North of the Boezemsingel was the Goudscherijweg, where Neptunus's H. J. J. van Seventer ran an office. West, past the shops and residential houses of the Goudscherijweg, the Crooswijkscheweg ran towards the Schuttersveld. On the street lived J. van Gelderen, a member of Het Noorden, and J. J. Oostbaan, of the UDI club. Not far from the Hollandia café, was the house of J. Buskop, a Sparta member and director of the Vereeniging van Grondeignaren (Society of Landowners). J. Buskop's brother, also J. Buskop, was a legendary figure at the Sparta club and within the Dutch sporting scene in general. He had helped to establish the Nederlandsche Athletiekbond (Netherlands Athletics Association) in 1897 and had been both a board member of the NVB and a secretary of Sparta. He had played as a goalkeeper in Breda and also worked as a journalist for the *Athleet* and *De Sport* publications.[78]

Although USC played their games on the Schuttersveld, they had few members who lived in the vicinity, having moved from the Heuvelterrein at the start of the 1912/13 season. One member who did live nearby was J. A. Spruit at Pootstraat 47a. To the north, past the Schuttersveld and the cemetery, two of the Rietveld family were members of UDI. The elder Rietveld was a gravedigger; his son Nicolaas Laurens Rietveld was also a member of the club. Thoughts of graves were, mercifully, a long way away from the celebration that the Welschen family had planned on 5 August. Despite the bad news from outside the Netherlands, the Welschen family were celebrating the marriage of Sparta member Johannes Welschen to Maria van Beek, who was born in nearby Dordrecht. The family ran a timber company on the Crooswijk that specialised in making barrels and, of course, coffins, and Johannes's two brothers, Henricus and Nicolaas, had joined the Leonidas club. Cheers rang out around the house as family and friends tried their best to ignore the throng of people in the streets and the continuous, depressing news reports posted across the city.

The north

W. A. Hensen lived next door to Mr Gillesen's café where *NRC* bulletins were posted. On 7 August, he came back from the Roman Catholic Cemetery, where he was a director, to his house on the Noordsingel to find out the latest news. The news reports did not seem to get any better. In the centre of the town, there was a large number of German immigrants who had fled England and were desperate for accommodation. On the Boompjes, named after the scraggy elm trees dotted along its length, the banks were mobbed by people looking to withdraw their money;[79] the mayor's declaration of the day before seemed not to have calmed the rush.[80] There were still very few cargo vessels to be seen. On the river, Thursday 6 August had seemed more like a peaceful Sunday, rather than a busy trading day.[81]

At the same address as W. A. Hensen – Noordsingel 48 – lived H. Hensen who was a member of one of Rotterdam's smaller clubs, De Concordiaan. Membership of De Concordiaan and Het Noorden was strong in the north of Rotterdam and the majority of both clubs' members lived here. For De Concordiaan, this was no surprise, as they played their home games to the north of Rotterdam in Schiebroek.

At Jacob Catsstraat 43, in sight of the Calvinist Noorderkerk, Het Noorden members Pieter and Paulus Beijen Arkenbout waited for their father to come back home from his job in the butter and cheese industry.[82] Despite more adverts noting that there was no reason for abnormally high prices in dairy products, there seemed a greater clamour for them.[83] In the week after the mobilisation, other associations, businesses and organisations tried to reassure the Rotterdam public that normal prices and service would continue, some even promised price reductions.[84] However, by Thursday 6 August, the Association for the Netherlands Paper Trade had made it clear that the political and economic situation meant that the cost of paper would rise by 10 per cent from Friday onwards.[85] Knowing which goods were cheaper or more expensive was becoming increasingly challenging. At Jacob Catsstraat 71, lived Het Noorden member H. P. Lorier, the only son of Joost and Adriana.

To the south, the long Noordsingel ran both sides of a narrow waterway.[86] Here, between different members of Rotterdam's football clubs, M. G. Buskop, another brother of J. Buskop, ran a stable and, like his brothers, was attached to Sparta. Nearby, the Prussian-born F. W. Pflitsch was a cooper and was naturally concerned about developments in his homeland. Both his sons were members of VOC. On the Noordsingel, Johannes Peters was preparing another batch of bread for the oven – customers had been reassured that bread was still available and even after a small rise in the previous days it was still cheaper than other places had been before the war.[87] His children, Jan and August, were affiliated to DVS.

At Noordsingel 30, J. A. P. de Bel worked as a clerk, while next door W. C. Hartman ran an accountancy firm and was also a bookseller to teachers. The two neighbours often discussed how their respective teams, VOC and Sparta, had fared during the season, something which in recent years Mr Hartman had enjoyed more than Mr Bel. Opposite Mr Hartman was another divided house, that of the Rogmans. W. J. Rogman and Koenraad Rogman had joined Sparta and H. Rogman had joined VOC. Koenraad was a noted traveller and despite the club rivalries the family was relieved, given the international situation, that he had no trips scheduled in the next few weeks. On the Eerste Pijnackerstraat, frequent absences from home brought similar anxiety to the family of Eduard Korsten, who also travelled for a living. Both he and three of his children had joined De Concordiaan. The youngest, Antonius Korsten, was just fourteen but had already got used to the rhythm of football on Sunday.

The ground of Rotterdam's great VOC club was north-east of the centre on the Schieweg. VOC could lay claim to being one of Rotterdam's oldest clubs. While it had been born out the merger of two local clubs in 1904, these clubs, Volharding and Olympia, were established in 1895 and 1896. P. van Muijden lived at Schieweg 6 and had the misfortune of being a Sparta member near to the VOC ground. He would often have to fight his way in the other direction as thousands of spectators came to watch VOC. When not involved with Sparta he worked in a bank in Rotterdam. On the Bergweg, W. J. Beukers was the son of the director of the Beukers & Rijneke Company and F. M. van der Meulen was a manufacturer of cables and steel; both were attached to Sparta. Also on the Bergweg, at the Municipal Hospital, the Red Cross had requested eight nurses to help with ambulance service on 3 August.[88] In the days since then, the Red Cross had increased its operations not only in Rotterdam but the rest of the Netherlands. Across the city, support services and committees had sprung up as people volunteered to help with the problems of health, work and housing which had arisen since the declaration of war between Germany and England. The growing influx of people to the streets of Rotterdam made it clear that the Red Cross would need every one of the extra 1,860 sleeping places it had found.[89]

The east

In the eastern suburbs of Rotterdam were the popular fields of the Woudestein, home to Leonidas, UDI and Het Noorden. The spacious fields had been used for a variety of sporting events, including horse racing and, most spectacularly, the flights of pilot Jan Olieslagers, the 'Antwerp Devil', in 1910.[90] In August 1914, the fields were used for a less exhilarating purpose, as horses gathered to help with the war effort. On 5 August, the Vredehof, a field north of the Avenue Concordia, was the site of a gathering of motor cars. The day before, the mayor had let it be known that under article 33 of the Inkwartieringswet (Billet Law) the military commander of land and sea forces could request cars to be at the disposal of the army. Those with vehicles, both private and otherwise, were requested to bring their vehicles and accompanying trailers to the field for the army to make a decision on their utility.[91]

For VOC member E. W. Kup, who lived on the Avenue Concordia, the increased number of cars instructed to go down this road was causing a headache. His neighbours, the Liesveld family, and their two DVS members, were also concerned at the prospect. The mayor had given instructions to those coming from the west of the city to use the Plantageweg, which for Sparta's C. Naujoks, was an unpleasant surprise. As he discussed what his family were going to do with their summer break, he found himself shouting at the noise caused by the stream of motor cars rattling down the road. In the same building, Neptunus's H. Friederich also cursed the extra busyness around his home; he could not hear Naujoks's shouting above the din.

To the east of the Plantageweg were the gasworks, which loomed over this part of Rotterdam, somewhat dwarfing everything in the vicinity.[92] They cast shadows on the Oostzeedijk in the south. Here, A. Brussaard, the butcher, and B. Brussaard had registered for Lycurgus. The grain-broker G. van Geffen lived at Oostzeedijk 192; while at Oostzeedijk 64, C. van der Graaf was the secretary for the Nederlandsche Tuinbouw Vereeniging (the Netherlands Horticulture Association); both men were members of Sparta.

At his house on the Esschenlaan, Sparta Rotterdam president M. J. Overeijnder sat down to read Friday 7 August's evening newspaper. A merchant by trade he had become familiar with the problems that the conflict was causing within Rotterdam. The news remained worrying.

On the Boompjes, crowds were still trying to exchange paper money for more solid forms of currency. At the dock of the Batavia Line, usually one of the busiest places in the city, it was eerily quiet. On Saturday 8 August, two boats were due to set sail from Tilbury docks to Rotterdam; these were the last scheduled to arrive in the port. Letters to and from Germany could only be exchanged if they were in German. The Red Cross and other organisations still sought volunteers to help in their operations and at the docks a vast number of Americans were desperate to leave Rotterdam on one of the final boats leaving the city.[93] Overeijnder was busy trying to secure a new ground for the Sparta team. The expansion of the Crooswijk cemetery meant his team had to move from the Prinsenlaan, but in what sort of Rotterdam would a new ground be built? Leading Sparta, with the expectations of players, fans and the city, was not always an easy task. As he looked at the final tally of members for the year, his eye was drawn to familiar names in places overseas. How he wished they were here to help him.

Further afield

Many members had been spared the confusion and panic in Rotterdam during the first week of August, although they had their own concerns. Some had concerns close to Rotterdam, in neighbouring Vlaardingen, where many DVS members lived. Some members could still follow their club from relatively close at hand. 'Don't worry,' urged Leonidas's J. J. van Woensel, from his house in The Hague, 'once the commotion is over, we will be able to get to Rotterdam.' Like Van Woensel, other members of Rotterdam clubs lived in the province of Zuid-Holland, in Delft, The Hague or Schiedam. The president and former captain of VOC, D. van Prooye, lived in Leiden. But some others lived further afield. In Berlin, E. Liffmann had joined VOC; in Dusseldorf, N. Schultz had registered with Sparta. In London and Paris, A. J. van 't Hoff and C. J. A. Musly hoped that they would still be able to hear news of DVS. In Medan, Indonesia, G. Stok was an honorary member of Sparta, while elsewhere in Indonesia H. Grimmen was one of a number of VOC members. In North America, VOC member J. van der Leck was based in Montreal and G. van der Zee was in New York.

During the first week of August 1914, Rotterdam saw a great clamour for food, for ships and for information. Some of those desperately searching for news were members of Rotterdam football clubs who, every now and then, passed a familiar face on the street and asked about the new season, a way to distract themselves from the chaos around them.

Outside Rotterdam, as news of the international situation grew worse, others, even with no hope of attending a match during the season, felt themselves also a part of the sporting life of the city. Perhaps this was a way to stay in touch with a city which they were not sure when they would be able to visit again.

London, December 2015

What is it that a history with 'imagined' elements can do which other histories cannot? I have to say that they certainly do not bring a sense of ease within the historian. The sense of nervousness with which I began the story never faded throughout. Even though I had acknowledged that elements of this story would be imagined, I found that this did not free me in the way I had thought. For some reason, it was harder to write 'imagined' elements than those I had researched. With each name I included, I wanted to make sure I had not made an error, that I did not create people who did not exist, that I had not confused people who had the same name, or that I did not create fantastical events in Rotterdam which I had no evidence for and that I did not resort to cliché or stereotype. I struggled with every name I excluded from the narrative, and there were many. Just why was I excluding this individual instead of others? Could I not concoct some reason for their inclusion? Adding thoughts or speech to individuals was especially difficult. Each time I gave voice to the individuals of the past, I became more aware that the words were mine and not theirs, that I had no 'official' records to fall back on to corroborate my story. Even if the archive cannot provide the historian with access to the past, it does provide an enormous amount of comfort for their contructions.

This history also did not provide answers to many interesting questions, such as differences between the lives of players and administrators, the role of religion or politics in club life, why individuals may have chosen certain teams over others – particularly within one family – or even how close members of different teams were to each other. While there are hints throughout the history of the involvement of those from different religious backgrounds, which may suggest that for football clubs pillarisation may not have been a priority, these remain hints rather than conclusions. Perhaps an important element of 'imagined' histories is that they can leave us asking such questions, leave us wanting to find out more and to question the historian and their work. I certainly hope this is the case.

In many ways, this history is no different from others. I had to choose what to ignore and what to include, which things supported the story and which did not. This history has gaps which sometimes I tried to bridge with imagination, by placing certain people somewhere to help drive the narrative. But this is no different from other histories, where the imagination of the historian is used to bridge the gap between pieces of information. Indeed, a great deal of history is concerned with imagining why certain individuals did certain things; while the historian may use numerous forms of data to form an opinion, this act remains a creative process in the mind of the historian based upon their own concept of logic and reason. In this respect, the differences between history and fiction may be ones of scale rather than nature.

I believe that histories, which acknowledge their imagined nature, can do three things. The first is that they allow the historian to create new and different histories. Without the use of 'imagined' elements, I would have been restricted to a statistical representation of individuals based upon what remained in the archive. Imagination allowed me to attempt to represent the life of football club members within the everyday life of the city, and to represent Rotterdam life in an often-ignored period. I believe that history needs to find ways to represent the often mundane acts of daily life, and that imagined histories can help do this. Secondly, imagined histories can remind us that history is only ever a proposal, a construct, and that it is there to be challenged and questioned. They can allow both historian and reader to be more open about what is happening in the production of history and to think about which stories are being told and which are not.

Finally, I believe that imagined histories can encourage a greater number of people to take part in thinking about the past from their own perspective; should not this be the job of history today after all? History requires multiple voices and the freedom to create; it requires dissent and new ideas – especially those with which we disagree. And, if we do disagree, we can take solace in the fact that there is always another history to tell.

4

Discourses about Football: Role of Daily Newspapers

The link today between the media and sport is very close. The growth of television and the internet, in addition to print media, coupled with a range of financial incentives, business opportunities and markets, has made the dissemination of sport an enormous international business. In the Netherlands, a dedicated sport channel provides access to the two professional Dutch leagues, as well as many from across Europe. Outside the Netherlands, the *Eredivisie* is broadcast across the world. Sport and, in particular, football, has never been so easily accessible around the globe or as intrusive into daily life; advertisements, endorsements and sponsorship place sporting stars into our homes and city spaces on a regular basis.

For those involved in early Dutch football, things were somewhat different. With the exception of physically attending matches, or discussing them with others who had attended them, the printed word was the only method of gaining information about what was happening in the world of football – both inside the Netherlands and outside of it. The position of the print media – daily newspapers and weekly magazines – as primary disseminators of information gave them a privileged position in shaping how people perceived football and its relationship to wider society. Bourdieu notes that 'the very fact of reporting, of *putting on record* as a reporter, always implies a social construction of reality that can mobilize (or demobilize) individuals or groups' and, while he refers primarily to television news, such reporting can create its own reality effect.[1] Bourdieu also suggests that the pressures of competition in journalism mean that over time newspapers become more homogeneous and similar in what they report.[2] In relation to football, how the media represent matches, actions, individuals and values is important to the constructed 'reality' of the game and the discourses which are spread about it.

In this history, I will use daily newspapers to represent how discourses about football were constructed in the early twentieth century. What football was for, which values it privileged and how it was seen to link to wider society form a central part of this history. How newspapers reproduced discourses, which were disseminated to their readers, is an important aspect of representing how football positioned itself in Dutch society and how its growth was linked to wider discourses of values. The role of the sportsman, the fans, the administrators, referees and the representations of different identities in the press will all form part of this history.

But this history has an agenda. While thinking about the role of football in Dutch society in the early twentieth century, I read Foucault's *Discipline and Punish* and this provided me with a series of sceptical questions about the link between sport and society; it is the inspiration for this history. The idea of 'discipline' and the construction of docile bodies through forms of training was one which has remained with me and which had lead me to question how sport operates in society today. While Foucault used the prison, the school and forms of punishment as the basis for his work, I could not escape the idea that sport was another way to extend concepts of discipline, docility and efficiency into wider society; that it was not just the world of work or education which constructed docile and useful bodies, but also our leisure and free time.[3] I want to experiment with these thoughts; perhaps something useful may emerge.[4]

This history of early Dutch football will suggest that football was part of a wider disciplinary mechanism. Similarities between the discourses of football and others in society allowed football to align with other organisations in Dutch society and spread disciplinary techniques more widely within it. Following its formal organisation, football demonstrated many of the tactics and techniques which reproduced discipline in society, including an increasing segmentation of time; increased training of movements; examinations, ranking and measurements; the construction of norms; a system of internal regulations and penalties; and the observation of participants. These techniques spread to all areas of the game, including administrators, referees and spectators. The media had an important role in reproducing discipline in society, even if they did not do this in a uniform way. This history also suggests that footballing discourses could provide a framework for the expression of identity, which was both malleable and able to reinforce segregation and stratification.

This history is about how football came to reinforce certain discourses in society and the authority linked to them. I cannot deny that I have a sceptical view of how authority is exercised in society, and this has influenced this history. Since reading Foucault, my scepticism about the role of sport in society has grown; the almost daily reports of organisational scandals in sport, which occurred while I was writing this history, certainly did not radically alter my view.[5] At the heart of this history are two questions I keep asking myself: 'Is the thing I love to do really part of wider discourses which I do not agree with? Can something I enjoy so much really be bad for us?' One of the discourses often related to sport, sometimes by those in positions of power, is that sport and politics should not mix. Central to this idea is the idea that political interests are not a part of sport, that ideologies, opinions and 'causes' should not infiltrate sport; there are too many examples of where this has happened in the past for this idea to really be taken seriously anymore.[6] In this history, I will demonstrate that politics and sport are not separate things which can be mixed but, rather, that certain ideas associated with 'discipline' are deeply entrenched within sport, just as Foucault suggested they were entrenched within society; politics is an integral aspect of sport and has been from the beginning. Sport is not a separate entity from society, culture or politics, but is a powerful method of reproducing certain ideas and discourses. My hope is that by outlining how sport does this, we can change the discourses it spreads today.

The press and sport

In 1882, the first sporting weekly magazine appeared in the Netherlands under the title *Nederlandsche Sport*. In the later part of the century and the early twentieth century, more sporting magazines began to appear: *Het Sportblad*, *De Sportkroniek* and *De Revue der Sporten* all focused on a number of different sports. However, such publications were often aimed at 'insiders', those who were already aware of the clubs, matches and activities of various sports. In newspapers before the turn of the century, sport reports often came under the oversight of the Home Affairs editor and were sporadic in their appearance, with sailing, rowing and skating being the primary focus of the small number of articles which appeared.[7] Around the turn of the century, newspapers began to report on aspects of football, particularly where there was involvement with teams from abroad. Matches between Dutch players and those from Belgium or England, including sailors' teams in Rotterdam, occurred before the turn of the century and the interest which they attracted prompted the press to become more actively engaged in football. Before 1900, efforts to spread the popularity of football, along with the growth of the game in urban centres, saw an increase in press reporting. In 1895 footballer and cricketer J. C. Schröder became the sport reporter for *De Telegraaf* and in 1896 Jan Feith became the reporter for the *Algemeen Handelsblad*. However, before 1900, football remained only the third most reported sport in Dutch newspapers.[8]

After 1900 interest in football grew and it was not uncommon for members of the public to be charged to watch important matches. The press also played an important role in popularising and spreading the game and articles often advertised lectures, meetings or new regulations. It devoted space to promoting the social good of football and this propagandising role is perhaps not surprising given that those involved in sports journalism were often involved in playing sport themselves. In 1902, *De Telegraaf* appointed John Coucke, a football enthusiast and later secretary of the Amsterdam *Sportpark*, as its sport editor.[9] In 1909 H. A. Meerum Terwogt, the noted Rotterdam football referee, football administrator and former RAP member, became a sporting editor at the *NRC*; he had previously been a journalist in *De Revue der Sporten*.[10] As football became more normalised in everyday life, the press devoted more space to it.

This history focuses on the representation of football across five newspapers from both Amsterdam and Rotterdam in the period between 1910 and 1920. These newspapers are, from Rotterdam, the *NRC* and the *Maasbode* and, from Amsterdam, *De Courant*, *Algemeen Handelsblad* and *Het Volk*. They were selected for a variety of reasons, both historical and practical. On the practical side, the newspapers had all been archived and were easy to access at the *KB*, either in person or online; this was not the case for many of the weekly sporting publications.[11] Historically, I considered that each of them might have the possibility of creating its own 'reality effect' and discourses, either by virtue of their location, political affiliation or intended audience. As well as providing news for a different city, the newspapers were considered to represent different constituencies. The *Algemeen Handelsblad*, *NRC* and *De Courant* were all broadly attached to liberal political perspectives on the world. The *Maasbode* was noted as a fiercely anti-liberal and anti-Protestant paper, which developed into the most widely read Catholic daily, and *Het Volk* was the daily newspaper of the *SDAP*, linked both to a political party and the aim of spreading socialism.

Each of the different newspapers had a different audience in mind. In 1893, Henry Tindal established both *De Telegraaf* and *De Courant*; the latter was intended to be a populist newspaper, though certainly not socialist. Under the stewardship of Hendrik Holdert, *De Courant* developed into the most widely read daily newspaper in the Netherlands with circulation figures in 1910 of over 100,000, more than four times as many as *De Telegraaf*. For comparison, Amsterdam's other major liberally orientated newspaper, the *Algemeen Handelsblad*, could only boast 17,191 subscribers in 1914.[12] The different papers also had different approaches to sport. In the same year as the *NRC* appointed Meerum Terwogt – who would remain its sports editor for forty-four years – the *Algemeen Handelsblad* appointed G. J. Nijland as its sports editor.[13] In both *De Courant* and the *Maasbode*, sport formed an important part of the paper, especially on a Monday, though in each newspaper the focus on various sports and stories often differed; one point of similarity, however, was that the First Division of the Western *NVB* League was the most reported form of football.

By contrast, *Het Volk* only began reporting on sport in around 1912; perhaps due to the scepticism of many orthodox socialists towards sport. Even after starting to report on sport, space devoted to it in *Het Volk* was much less than in other newspapers. Yet, while the newspaper was relatively late to reporting about football, it demonstrated a certain flair for it. The first line of Monday 29 January 1912's football report read: 'We live in the time of the impossible, or rather, in the time where things which were once thought impossible now appear possible.'[14] The report went on to say that many would have laughed if you had suggested that men would fly like birds in the sky, sit on trains far from home and talk to their wives on a telephone, finishing the opening paragraph indicating that if you had suggested the Sparta–Ajax game of the previous day would end in a goalless draw, people would have laughed just as hard.[15]

Discipline, efficiency and time

The role of the body, of how it was controlled, understood and shaped, is of fundamental importance within Foucault's concept of discipline. He noted that in the classical age, the body was located as an object and target of power. It was both useful and intelligible, and docility was an important factor in the relations between power and the body; the docile body was an economically productive body and it could be trained and made more useful. By the eighteenth century, the way that the body was being transformed and improved had changed. Rather than aiming to control the body as a whole, it was the efficiency of the body that became a primary concern for those in positions of authority. Control of the body became connected to the regulation of gestures and movements and operated in increasingly small ways. This change in how the body was linked to mechanisms of power meant that there was a constant coercion over the body, over its actions and its movements. Individuals internalised rules, regulations and operations and in doing so became more docile and more useful within a capitalist economy. It is this regulation of the body which Foucault calls 'discipline'; it is different to slavery as it does not require the physical appropriation of the body, but its effects can be just as great.[16]

The emergence of discipline was not sudden, but slowly started to operate in many areas of life. Foucault notes how schools, military centres and hospitals all became sites where different techniques were implemented which furthered the aims of bodily discipline. These techniques represented a new 'micro-physics' of the body; they were about detail, about a meticulous fussiness and were connected to regulation in all areas of daily life.[17] I would suggest that organised sport was a further site where the techniques of discipline were in operation, techniques that not only aimed at shaping the behaviour of individuals but also how they moved, how they acted and how they saw the world around them. Organised sport is entwined with discourses which limit and permit, which train the body to act in certain ways at certain times and newspapers played an important role in constructing and spreading these discourses throughout early Dutch football.

The history of football stadia in the Netherlands demonstrated how space was linked to a discourse of values, how certain spaces became coded with messages, how certain spaces were enclosed and given new purposes in the city. Individuals became delineated in the stadium by virtue of their position, but were still part of the wider whole; they could be ordered, mapped and instructed how to utilise the space most efficiently. The control over spatial distribution was one aspect of enforcing discipline over the body, using the space of the city to locate certain values of order, regulation and measurement within the body.[18] But spatial constraints were not the only link to discipline that football demonstrated. Foucault noted that ranking and measuring was one of the key aspects of discipline. It enables knowledge to be created about a series of individuals and to map their progress against each other and a perceived norm.[19] And rankings and measurements were an integral part of organised sport: match results, goal-scorers and league tables all helped provide a way to assess the multiple number of individuals involved in football, to rank them and, as a consequence, master them. Newspapers distributed such rankings to their readers, giving league tables and match scores throughout the season, establishing football as a location for continuous ranking and measurement.

However, rankings were only one aspect of sport's disciplinary nature. Coupled with ranking tables came timetables and the regulation of time itself. Foucault noted that the control of activity is a key technique for spreading discipline throughout society and the regulation of time is an important element in the control of activity.[20] Regulation of time allows certain actions to occur at specific times and not others. And time and timetables were important within the discourses of Dutch football. There was a certain temporal pattern which developed through the imposition of league football in the Netherlands. Playing games in the *NVB* leagues meant adherence to a certain set of temporal constraints; matches occurred on Sunday afternoons, they would be of ninety minutes in duration, with a break of fifteen minutes in-between. Thus football provided a new temporal construction to the week and specifically to Sunday. This disruption and reconstruction of the temporal formation of Sundays is perhaps one reason why orthodox religious groups so disliked the practice of football. But through football, time was coded with certain possibilities of action and for those individuals who took part in sport, such temporal coding became a natural occurrence.

Temporal demarcation was also important for newspapers as football began to play a more prominent role in the press. A specific time and place for football reports emerged; in the daily newspapers, this was Monday, the day after league matches. Throughout the period, the press began to exhibit a remarkable uniformity in how it reported football matches. The exuberant style of *Het Volk*, noted above, was uncommon in match reports during the early part of the twentieth century. Most match reports, which were brief in nature, followed a rather formulaic pattern. For the Sunday league matches, reports would appear in the following day's edition of the newspapers giving information on scores, scorers, the passage of play and often the weather. These reports gave readers the basic information about the match and how the teams performed. Reports, especially earlier in the period, would often start by indicating the time of day, where the match was played and the players' positions, before continuing with a description of the course of the game, often in two parts: 'A fine rain, misty weather and a good field [...] At 2 o'clock HVV came onto the pitch and ten minutes later Sparta [...] Sparta won the toss and chose to defend the goal on the town side. HVV kicked off at

2:20 [...]'[21] On some occasions the report demonstrated that it followed a similar fashion to the match: 'The referee, Mr Willings, divided the game, as often happens, into two periods of 45 minutes, and to come to a fair and accurate reproduction of the course of the game, we can safely follow his example. This is because there was a great contrast between the two teams.'[22]

Football time was measured and repeatable, there was a pattern to what was to be done and when it was to be done. Matches had two halves of forty-five minutes, the season opened and closed, annual meetings occurred at a similar time, significant international matches occurred around Easter and special tournaments, like those for the *Zilverenbal* in Rotterdam, ran at the start of the year.[23] Throughout this period of time there was consistent ranking. Leagues pitted teams of similar qualities against each other and those who finished in certain positions were deemed worthy of progression to a higher league in the next season – the next period of time. Time was measured and supervised by the referee, the club and the organisation. Referees were responsible for calling teams to the pitch at the appointed hour and ending the game and the *NVB* was in charge of when teams played each other or if this was to be permitted; the *NVB* sanctioned matches against international clubs and was responsible for creating the fixture list. The regulation of time was an important part of sporting practice. Each week was separate, measurable and repeatable. Just as the world of work and school had a timetable, grades and exams, so too did the world of organised sport. Each match, or part of the season, was part of a wider temporal series of steps.[24] Football was not an escape from work, but merely a way of reproducing and embodying its temporal structures.

Training and schools

In the disciplinary system, certain periods of time are associated with certain acts. If Sunday was for matches then the week was when training would occur. Foucault highlighted the importance of training and exercise as a method of instilling discipline in the body. Through training one learns to perform set movements in space and time, to perfect them, to become efficient. One also learns to respond to small gestures and to bells, rather than physical force.[25] One comes to learn what is expected of the body and through repetition and practice, disciplinary power becomes embodied; each minor correction leaves its trace on the body: 'to punish is to exercise'.[26] While Foucault focused on schools and the military, one cannot ignore the similarities between military or scholastic education and the process of sports training. Through training, the footballer learns how to move, when to move and also to be subject to the authority of a whistle. Training places the individual under supervision and locates him or her within the concept of the group – it distinguishes, regulates, ranks and observes – it shows how the individual can fit within the concept of the team and creates a number of other individuals who can fit into this place.[27]

Despite this, many in the Dutch educative system had serious misgivings about the role of football in Dutch society, particularly for the young. In 1910, the *Algemeen Handelsblad* outlined that a committee had been established in light of complaints about the value of football in schools.[28] Concerns were particularly high amongst teachers in Gymnasia, which were considered the highest level of secondary education in the Netherlands and had seen an increasing number of students form their own clubs. In August 1910, a report was presented to the annual meeting of the *Genootschap van Leeraren aan Nederlandsch Gymnasiën* (the Society for Teachers in Gymnasia of the Netherlands) in The Hague which highlighted that the most common complaints against football in school were: '1st: It requires too much exertion; 2nd: it is rough and causes injuries; 3rd: the matches and the travel linked to them; 4th: the young men are so taken by it that they are no longer interested in schoolwork.'[29] The report outlined a series of suggestions to overcome such problems, which again illustrated certain temporal and corporal considerations. Those younger than fourteen should not be permitted to play in schools and there should be a medical exam before students were allowed to participate in matches.[30] Thus, from an early age, sport could be used as a way of placing the idea of the medical exam into society and act as a method for gathering information about the body and its functions.

The most contentious area for the educators was competitive matches. At the meeting, members were warned of the problems attached to students who were cheered each Sunday at games and celebrated in the newspapers; competitive matches had become too much about winning and getting one's name in the paper. To combat this, it was suggested that competitive matches should be limited in size and needed to take place in local areas, although some journeys would be of pedagogical worth for slightly older students. Those at the gathering heard that football was of immense use if it was practised under the guidance of 'a wise leader', either a teacher or a player with experience.[31] Thus, for the young, training and exercise were seen as the essential aspects of football in schools. The *NVB* had been keen to ensure that football gained acceptance among Dutch educators. In February 1910, a communiqué from the *NVB*, published in the *Maasbode*, highlighted that competitive matches needed to be halted or scaled back:

> We can only demonstrate the worth of this, our game, with participating pupils, who have been instructed, for a long period of time, under expert guidance and that the competitions between school teams must not be permitted to be a surrogate for this, as it will promote a confusion of ideas, which will block the distribution of real school-football, and this 'competitive character' will turn away many whom we desire to win over [to our game].[32]

In 1913 the *Algemeen Handelsblad* ran a report about school football in The Hague, indicating that certain rules had been suggested which would restrict the participation of young students against older students as it was suggested that this was a cause of over-exertion, a lack of enthusiasm and led to poor play. The new regulations recommended a maximum of ninety minutes of activity per week for students and that school matches needed the leadership of a teacher to ensure that pedagogical value was maintained.[33] Football, as with other aspects of school life, was being measured, regulated and supervised.

By becoming part of the educative process for young men, football became further normalised, accepted and championed as a way to construct the 'correct' set of values. As Graafland noted in his communiqué:

> The committee considers that football training for school pupils, under the expert leadership of a teacher, a leader or a chosen captain, is of immense worth in the physical formation and the character building of the male youth, and the committee is of the view that this game is a benefit, more than any other form of physical education, and it should be spread.[34]

Emphasising the educative aspect of football gave the discourses of football access to a wider audience and fulfilled part of the *NVB*'s propagandising mission. Football became more widely accepted by pedagogues in the Netherlands because the *NVB* had demonstrated that they and educators both had similar discourses of values; both wanted 'correctly' to educate the younger generation and used similar techniques to do so. The techniques were those of discipline and of constructing useful, docile bodies, which could be trained to perform the 'correct' movement at the 'correct' time, without the use of physical force.

The match as exam: constructing the sportsman

Despite the desire to limit school football and organised matches for the young, newspaper reports demonstrate they still occurred on a regular basis in Rotterdam and Amsterdam.[35] For adults, competitive matches were much less contentious and regular league matches formed a central part of the *NVB* organised football structure. They also formed an important part of the process of discipline. Within the match, the player could put their training into effect. The match could function as a form of exam, a way to demonstrate that the player had learnt the rules, perfected the techniques and understood the values required of them. The player could be placed under an observing gaze, could be ranked, measured and evaluated against an ideal, or normalised, figure, all while retaining the air of individuality.[36] By disseminating match reports, newspapers played an important role in constructing and reproducing discourses of values in football and they subtly reinforced an idea of the footballing 'sportsman', one in which the body was used 'correctly' and to maximum utility.

Throughout the different newspapers in the period, match reports exhibited a similarity in the language used to indicate positive or negative attributes of players or teams. The following examples from across the period give an indication of how certain terms were linked to a positive image of the player or team:

> It was not only because all cohesion was missing, that the Spartans made glaring technical errors, but because there was also no spirit or fire within the Red-White Rotterdammers.[37]
>
> The Ajax attack was a good unit; in general, they played a better game and were dangerous, in particular, through their enormous speed.[38]
>
> In the last moments, the Spartans tried everything to eliminate the ugly lack of goals. De Groot tried beyond measure, but he was checked time and again in his attack by the solid, hardworking defence of Ajax.[39]

Players should work hard, play together, be spirited and be quick. In a similar manner some terms were given more negative connotations:

> The Amsterdammers, spurred on through this unexpected luck, continued to work with enthusiasm, in contrast to which the Spartan defence gave a lax display.[40]

> Teamwork was absent in the attack of the visitors, which the players tried to compensate for with rough play.[41]

> A drawn game (3–3) was the result of a pretty poor game, in which VOC worked hard and Ajax held the idea that the championship is theirs and that there was no need for more effort. Poor sportsmanship apart from anything![42]

In these cases, physical excess, laxity and lack of effort were seen as attributes which should be curbed. Crucially, the last of these excerpts links a lack of effort to the concept of 'sportsmanship', and in such a way, press reports played an important part in constructing the concept of the 'sportsman'.

The concept of the sportsman and its attached discourse of values was part of reproducing the discourses of discipline. In combination with the established sporting regulations, discourses surrounding the sportsman formed part of a micro-system of punishment within football. Foucault outlines that, within a micro-system of punishment, certain actions, which are not against the general law, become punishable; deviations of time, use of the body, gesture, behaviour, speech and other acts can all be punished and this further places the individual within a framework of punishment.[43]

Formal regulations are an important part of this micro-system, as the *NRC* reminded readers in 1918:

> One of the Haarlem defenders gave away a penalty with a deliberate handball and the consequence was inevitable: Ajax led 2–0. It is remarkable that so many people, outsiders as well as insiders, are still of the opinion that a penalty-kick should only be given if there is a chance to score. Yet, this is an entirely false view. The regulations state that a penalty-kick must be given if the referee establishes a deliberate touch of the ball with the hand. If a chance to score exists or not makes no difference to this point at all.[44]

In football, as with other sports, regulations provide an aspect of this micro-system. Within the game, infringements carry their own penalty, and newspapers played a role in distributing the regulations to a wider audience.

However, newspapers also played a part in reproducing other aspects of this micro-system of penalties which were not connected to formal regulations. Teams or players that challenged the discourses of values or sportsmanship would receive their punishment through widespread public criticism. This was the case with a report on the Sparta versus Ajax game of 1918 where the play of the Amsterdammers was called into question by the *Maasbode*.

> Referee Willings was in charge and this was fortunate, because without his firm hand the play of the Amsterdammers would have been less pleasant. People know what we think of the Amsterdammers' system. The 'hacking', the pushing and the throwing which these 'amateurs' make use of, is so condemnable that even the most neutral spectator said to us yesterday 'I am happy that Sparta have won, because of the unpleasant play of the Amsterdammers.'
>
> Ajax began immediately with a dishonest trick.
>
> [...] Van der Wolk led several nice attacks; once, he created a beautiful chance for the inside-trio, but the Sparta centre-forward was not energetic enough; moreover he was guarded by the Ajax defence in the so-called 'forceful' manner.[45]

It seems that this reporter felt that Ajax had, on occasion, contravened the rules of the game, but more than this, their play had fallen short of the standard expected from a sportsman. The report also highlighted scandalous fouls and dishonest tricks used by the team. Poor sportsmanship did not only involve contravening the written rules, but those which were more subtle, as indicated after a match in Amsterdam: 'VVA beat DVS 7–1. The Rotterdammers [DVS] played the match with a great number of replacements. People whispered that they had done this intentionally. But surely this can not be true; this would be very unsportsmanlike.'[46] The reports served to highlight the limits of what was considered acceptable in the discourse and acted as a broader reminder of what not to do. Likewise, the individual who deviated from his role in the team, such as the Haarlem player Houtkooper, was singled out for criticism: 'Houtkooper, with his ball-hogging, on many occasions gave the Ajax defence a helping hand.'[47]

Non-compliance with the norm of the sportsman resulted in public criticism, but also served to differentiate between the acceptable and the unacceptable; it put the actions of the individual or team under further observation. Through the discourse of the sportsman, football was able to provide a norm against which everyone could be measured; to paraphrase Foucault, it enabled a measurement that gradated all the aspects of a supposedly equal society and shaded individual differentiation. In this sense, while the sportsman can be seen as an ideal, to be striven towards, it is also a concept that permanently divides, distinguishes and shows the failings of the individual.[48]

But there was a problem. While the language and terminology used to demonstrate positive or negative attributes was similar across the period and in different newspapers – for example, reports never praised a deliberate handball or players who were too rough – how this linked to action was subjective and fluid. This is demonstrated by two further reports into the Sparta versus Ajax game of 1918. Where the *Maasbode* had highlighted Ajax's 'hacking' and 'pushing', the *NRC*, also from Rotterdam, provided a somewhat different tone to its report:

> While some complained about play that was too forceful, we would like to impart our opinion that we cannot generally go along with this view. There happened, here and there, and more from Ajax's side, some isolated incidents that would have been better not taking place, but the game as a whole was certainly not too wild or too rough.[49]

The *Algemeen Handelsblad* summed up the game in even less critical terms, suggesting Ajax were unlucky to have lost and that a draw would have been a fairer result.[50] *De Courant* felt Ajax fully deserved to win; the Sparta defence was certainly under pressure, not because of rough play from the Amsterdammers but because the Sparta attack had been listless.[51] This difference suggests that while the discourse of values, and the concept of the sportsman may have appeared to be similar throughout the period, it was actually capable of being used to mean different things.

The link between action, language and meaning was not fixed, but capable of shifting. While the discourse of values gave the appearance of similarity, of unanimous understanding, it was perceived subjectively; similar actions could be positioned differently within the discourse. This space between action, language and meaning, this fluidity, permits those without authority to use their own power to move within the confusion of the discourse, to push the boundaries of just what is acceptable. But it also allows those with authority, such as the media and sporting organisations, to reframe discourses able to cope with such changes. Where language can be used dexterously to refer to action and meaning, then discourses, narratives and other concepts may sometimes subtly shift while appearing to remain stable. Thus, the sportsman as a concept, as with many other concepts, is at once both loaded with meaning and meaningless. To fail the test of sportsmanship is to be decried, to be marked out as abnormal, but what exactly this means is fluid, subjective and anything but fixed.

The sportsman as amateur

Another such term, and one intimately linked to the sportsman in early Dutch football, is the 'amateur'. Ajax had fallen foul of this term in their style of play.[52] As Richard Holt suggests, amateurism was not just purely about playing without pay. The tenets of amateurism in Victorian Britain appeared to be linked to a set of values concerning the correct way of playing the game; sport should be played correctly, for joy, with style and above all without taking unfair advantages. Money played some part in the concept of the amateur. The 'Gentleman Amateur' was a man who played the game correctly, without concern for the negative influences of money; if money were to be introduced, it was thought, then the importance of winning would challenge existing values and make success more important than the 'correct' playing of the game. Practically, this also meant the exclusion of many from poorer backgrounds within high-class British sport, as well as protecting existing power structures.[53] While football in England had seen the development of footballers paid to play, in the Netherlands this was still forbidden.

In 1910, a report in the *NRC* demonstrated the position of the *NVB* towards professionalism:

> The board of the *NVB* pronounces as its opinion that the discussion concerning professional football in the press is very excessive, it declared itself to be against professional football, in any form in the Netherlands, [and] considered it harmful for this sport and the [Dutch] people, and shall therefore fight against it as much as possible.[54]

The use of the terms 'professional' and 'amateur' were part of a wider discourse of values in football and, by extension, society. To accuse an individual or team of professionalism or to question their amateurism was a loaded term, and it was one which would be understood by the reader. The following excerpt about the creation of a new team in Dordrecht demonstrates that the use of the term could be provocative:

> The five attacking-players of DFC, who, after the general meeting of last Tuesday, have departed from the Dordtsche 1st Class team, have, with some other DFC players, formed a new club and this – somewhat naively – with the name of: 'Amateurs'! As if to say that Lotsy and associates are not this.[55]

At an *NVB* board meeting in 1914, discussions became heated when Haarlem-based Eendracht Doet Overwinnen were accused of professional tactics, in this case overly rough play.[56] However, the meeting demonstrated that what constituted amateurism was not clearly defined. While there were a fixed set of rules that defined the amateur, connected to expenses and the receipt of money, there was also another, unwritten set of regulations which were linked to the subjective discourse of values that allowed a degree of movement.

To be accused of taking part in 'disguised professionalism', as was Gé Fortgens of Ajax in 1912, was to have one's sportsmanship and character questioned. In different newspapers, Fortgens was accused of benefiting from dinners, lunches and travel, all paid for by his club – it perhaps did not help that he was not from one of the older, elite clubs. Fears that professionalism was finding its way into the game saw the *NVB* establish a committee to investigate 'shamateurism'. However, while it was noted that there was sometimes creativity around the amateur regulations, no players could be considered professional.[57] The debate, however, indicates both the power that terms such as 'amateur' and 'sportsman' can carry and also how fluidly they can be applied. Debates about amateurism in Dutch football would continue until the 1950s, when professionalism was formally accepted as part of the discourse.[58]

While one could be subject to criticism, playing football also brought gratification and this was an essential part of the disciplinary system; it not only gave participants some benefits for continued participation but it also provided a delineator between the 'good' and the 'bad'.[59] Newspapers could highlight individuals who were worthy of being singled out. One man who seemed to embody all the 'good' attributes of the sportsman and amateur was FC Dordrecht's Dirk Lotsy, who received a great deal of praise for his performance in the Netherlands game against Germany in 1914. In Amsterdam, November 1910 saw the last home match of AFC midfielder Togneri, who was moving to the Dutch East Indies. *De Courant* reported that following this performance supporters of AFC lifted him onto their shoulders and carried him aloft to the clubhouse.[60] The following week, the newspaper ran a full story on his final game for AFC, accompanied by a photo, a rare occurrence in newspaper match reports.[61]

In Rotterdam, the Sparta player De Korver gained a great degree of fame, earning the nickname 'Bok' or 'Billy-goat'. He was the first to be featured in a new series in 1919 within *De Revue der Sporten* under the title 'Stars of the Football Pitch' and was said to be 'Holland's most popular footballer'.[62] Other footballers also received more attention. This happened when extra efforts were made to get to matches, such as Karel Heyting's eighteen-hour journey from Paris to play for HVV,[63] or when they suffered misfortune, such as Versluys of Willem II who missed a train and, as a consequence, an important national championship game.[64] By providing such reports, the newspapers could demonstrate that through football one could receive gratification and that individual achievement would be noticed. At the same time, the media were reproducing the discourses of the sportsman, who was gifted on the pitch, loved off it and went to extraordinary efforts not to let their team-mates down; by the start of the 1920s, the media were starting to turn sportsmen into sport stars.

Administering order and regulation

Players were not the only subjects of newspaper reports. Administrators, organisers and authorities were often represented in newspapers and the reporting of committee procedures formed an important part of the sporting press in the early twentieth century. This had two functions. One was to inform those who had an interest in the proceedings of committees what had been discussed and decided – to disseminate rules and regulations to participants in the game. The other was to demonstrate that football was a game of order, regulations and of properly exercised authority. Throughout the period, newspapers reported on administrative developments in various organisations, such as the *Fédération Internationale de Football Association* (International Federation of Association Football, FIFA) – which the Dutch *NVB* had been instrumental in establishing in 1904 – the *NVB* and local and regional organisations. On many occasions, different newspapers provided details about meetings, including official procedures, votes and discussion points.[65] Reports note that the meetings are conducted correctly; where there is dissent, it is discussed and concluded following the rules of the organisation. If there was a discourse that demonstrated how a sportsman should behave on the pitch, there was also one attached to those who conducted the affairs off it.

Newspapers used their sports pages to highlight the achievements of committees, presidents and administrators. In 1910, *De Courant* highlighted organisational success and good order: 'Finally a word of praise should be expressed in relation to Mr M. C. Blöte, the diligent secretary-manager of the Zwaluwen, who organised this game in an exceptional manner.'[66] They followed this in November: 'The board of Forward, who discharged their duties as hosts in such an outstanding manner, deserve, for this, to be specially commended.'[67] In the *Algemeen Handelsblad,* the secretary of the *Sportpark,* and fellow sport journalist, John Coucke was praised for his tireless work in making sure the 1914 international against Germany took place.[68] In November 1910, praise was heaped upon club boards that ensured their pitches were kept in good order meaning that, despite inclement weather across the western Netherlands and the cancellation of many league matches, two games could go ahead in the Watergraafsmeer. While the Amsterdam teams of 1910 may not have been particularly good, the city could take pride in its horticultural achievements. The *Maasbode* also praised the pitch conditions at a small Roman Catholic tournament in Arnhem, which was visited (and won) by the Rotterdam club Swift. Indeed, the report focuses more on the procedures and formalities of the day than the football. Only two lines refer to the matches while we hear about the welcome and refreshments, the engraved trophy, the prize giving and some 'appreciative words' from the president.[69]

The year 1910 also saw an attempt by members of Rotterdam and Antwerp football circles to organise a match after the usual international match between Belgium and the Netherlands, held in Rotterdam each year, had been moved by the *NVB*. While the *NVB* came in for criticism, the report is keen to outline how the new game would be organised, when it would occur, how the money would be distributed, and crucially how the organisation committee of the game was to be formed in both cities.[70] Likewise, clubs or individuals that caused problems for good order and organisation, especially in terms of late arrival, were condemned: 'That [the game] could only start almost half-an-hour too late, which threatened to disturb the precisely scheduled programme, must ultimately be ascribed to the non-appearance of some of the Ajax players, an event which was not sufficiently condemned.'[71] Football was presented as a game of order, structure and regulation and the correct administration of the sport was just as important as the playing of matches.

Reports on football also emphasised the charitable nature of the game – both the sportsman and the administrator were involved in a charitable act for the benefit of society. Players in a poor match between

VOC and Vitesse were spared criticism 'given the charitable goal' of the match.[72] A charitable game occurred for the families of the *Vlaardingsche Lugger*, a boat that had sunk after colliding with a mine in the first months of the First World War.[73] In 1914, the president of the *NVB*, Mr Warner, spoke, in forceful tones, about comments that had come from outside the game, comments that were 'more negative than positive' and that had ignored the fact that the organisation took part in its share of charitable work.[74] By reporting events off the pitch, the media constructed and reinforced the importance of time, order and charity within the discourses of football and demonstrated that football was of value for Dutch society as a whole.

Committees, infringements and punishment

When regulations were challenged or order broke down, newspapers were keen to demonstrate that there were efficient procedures in place. Early Dutch football was not without conflict; there were disagreements over how clubs conducted themselves on the pitch, over the concept of professionalism, and about why certain clubs had not been in the appointed place at the correct time, as was the case in 1918 during an *RVB* discussion over the non-appearance of a CVV team.[75] Yet, with disagreement came a procedure, a vote to resolve the issue or a new committee established to investigate complaints. Where rules and regulations were broken, there were committees to consider and impose punishments. The *NRC* reported one such committee meeting of 21 November 1910, which was established to deal with complaints arising from matches. On this occasion, a referee had lodged a complaint into problems in the Haarlem versus Quick match. While a committee considered further action, Haarlem were prevented from playing games on their own ground. A further committee was established to consider complaints regarding a game in Groningen.[76] Who sat on committees was established at regular intervals and announced by the *NVB*. From military football committees to school football committees, and from protest committees to statistical committees, the *NVB* established a range of panels to oversee and measure the efficiency of every area of the game;[77] a range of individuals were involved in collecting this knowledge and using it to regulate the game.

Corruption, bribery or trying to gain a sporting advantage outside the permitted rules naturally resulted in punishment. In May 1914, during the *Begeerkrans* tournament for Regional Football Associations, the captain of the Brabant Association was condemned for submitting a false team sheet in their match against the Amsterdam association; once discovered, the team were prohibited from further participation.[78] Worse came in 1918, when reports surfaced of attempts to bribe a referee by the president of Watergraafsmeer-based De Spartaan. A letter from a concerned Amsterdammer suggested that not only was the president of the club guilty but so too was the referee, who should not have received the dubious visitor, and even the *NVB* board member who discovered the collusion through questionable means.[79] With a suspected infringement in regulations came further investigations and the imposition of punishments aimed at deterring future repetitions. By reporting the administrative procedures connected to football, newspapers reinforced the concepts of discipline within football. They not only demonstrated infringements would be punished by those in authority, but reproduced the idea that football belonged to an ordered, regulated and correctly administered system of authority. Football helped to reproduce and cement these ideas within the social body and within the body of the player and administrator.

Organisational issues also caused tension in early Dutch football, including the mobilisation of many Dutch men at the outbreak of wider conflicts in Europe in 1914.[80] With many players moving to different parts of the Netherlands, the existing league structure was suspended and changed. As a result, between the 1914/15 season and the 1917/18 season, a number of changes occurred. The 1914/15 season was designated as a *noodcompetitie* (emergency competition), which had no formal classifications or relegation and promotions. While the First Division of the Western League remained largely intact, the Second Divisions were fragmented into different departments. By the 1917/18 season, the Western First Division was split into two parallel divisions, Western 1A and Western 1B. The new structure brought tensions with it. While both leading divisions were theoretically equal in the league structure, the clubs in the A division considered those in the B division to be of lesser quality and were keen to ensure that if a restructuring occurred, they would not be incorporated into a new division alongside these 'lesser' teams.[81]

By the summer of 1918, the twelve clubs in the A division had threatened to resign from the *NVB* if their concerns were not addressed. The clubs suggested that they would not enact this threat if a general meeting of the *NVB* proposed acceptable terms. However, a letter from the *NVB* published in *De Courant* noted a problem. The letter pointed out that as the clubs would have formally resigned before the meeting, they would have to be readmitted to the *NVB*, where they would have the same status as newly registered clubs and would have to follow the same regulations and stipulations as these clubs in joining. Furthermore, by resigning, they would not be in attendance at the meeting; thus any chance to come to an agreement would be diminished.[82] The tensions between these clubs and the *NVB* in early Dutch football highlights that certain clubs, often older, elite clubs, were becoming dissatisfied with how the game was being organised and that they wanted to force a change in the running of the game. But it also indicates that the administration of the game, in common with the game itself, had penalties for those who did not use accepted procedures. To resign, rather than use the established protocol, was not to fit in within the constructed framework.

Criticism of the *NVB* could also extend to its own regulations. In 1918, *Het Volk* published an article, which first appeared in *De Telegraaf*, accusing the governing body of imposing regulations which hampered the spread of the game. The article stated that many clubs in Nijmegen were finding access to pitches in the area difficult to obtain and their survival was threatened. Worse still, the Roman Catholic organisation in the area was planning to build eight new pitches available to hire for a low price; those clubs aligned to the Roman Catholic organisation would find it easier to use such pitches. The *NVB* regulations were, warned the report, causing 'anaemia' in the Nijmegen Association and pushing some clubs to the rival Roman Catholic organisation.[83] On this occasion, the regulations of the *NVB* were criticised because they risked pushing football clubs towards a rival organisation and thus diminishing the possibility of spreading the *NVB* discourse of football and its ability to shape Dutch society.

Surveillance: the referee, the fans and the media

The role of the referee was also important in the newspapers of the period. It was sometimes limited to purely functional aspects; he would ensure that the players were in the right place at the right time, blow the whistle to start each half and do the same to end it.[84] In some reports, the referee is almost a silent presence, not mentioned during the game, except for the important administrative aspect of beginning and ending the match. But the referee could also be subject to surveillance, supervision and measurement. Subtly, the referee's performance, particularly towards the end of the period, began to be measured and recorded. Such was the case with the compliments of Referee Willings's handling of the Sparta–Ajax match in 1918, as well as his role in the international between Germany and Belgium in 1910.[85] But other less positive reports also appeared in the press. In 1918, *De Courant* noted the following: 'Yet, on one occasion, [Racing Club Haarlem] were still unfortunate. Towards the end, the ball was clearly played by one of the Blauw-Wit defenders with his hand inside the [penalty-box]. Evidently, the referee was one of the few, if not the only one, who did not consider this an infringement.'[86] In the same year, the *NRC* presented another account of a refereeing mishap:

> Mr Veldhoven [the Referee] could not establish, possibly bothered by the sun, that HBS had scored a goal. Van Hemert, who was under the impression that [the goal] was scored from an offside position, took a free kick, upon which HBS protested and demanded a goal. [DFC player] Lotsy, gallant as ever, had seen that the goal was scored and immediately supported the protests of HBS. The referee recognised that a goal had probably been scored, but was not able to award the goal as he had not seen it being scored. He therefore acted, in our opinion, perfectly correctly by not allowing [the goal] to stand, but advised HBS to formally protest, which has now happened.[87]

With increased public and press interest, the referee – responsible for observing and regulating the players on the pitch – became observed himself and subject to critical scrutiny. Thus, particularly by the early 1920s, the idea of the match as a form of exam was extended to include the referee and also the administrator. The match was the culmination of good administration and organisation; it was a location where one could measure the performance of players and referees against the written and unwritten regulations of the discourses of football; and it was a site which could be part of the enforcement of discipline, authority, procedure and order. The match was not only a location where players came under an observational gaze but one where referees and administrators did too. While Bale notes that the installation of closed-circuit cameras and electronic ticketing towards the end of the twentieth century demonstrated how stadia were transforming into modern-day panopticans, where spectators and their behaviour were observed and data collected, we can see from the start of the game that the element of surveillance was crucial.[88]

Spectators and their behaviour were also the focus of reports in early Dutch football. Reports that previously focused on what was happening on the pitch began to mention how spectators behaved, bringing them within the normalising discourse of football. In the stadium, spectators were the subject of order and regulation, and this was reinforced in the press by reports which represented spectator behaviour. Reports demonstrated how football enabled individuals to change their behaviour:

> There were people in the stands, men and women, who we otherwise only knew as calm, formal members [of society], who would make every effort under all circumstances to preserve a conventional calmness, who now erupted, who joined in the celebration in the great triumph of the Dutch public; who waved hats and handkerchiefs like maniacs and were red from excitement; who had themselves – in short – become immersed in the game, who had become full-blooded football supporters.[89]

Het Volk added: 'Everything was thrown in the air, hats, umbrellas, caps, and bags, people seemed to have gone mad. Son-in-laws embraced their mother-in-laws, a completely unknown woman next to me threw her arms around my neck and screamed in my ear: "Göbel, Göbel" [the Dutch goalkeeper].'[90] These reports suggested a positive transformation of the citizen; here in the space of the stadium they were allowed to act in ways that were unthinkable in other parts of their lives; the space coded how they could behave. These two reports also give a brief and rare glimpse of women in football. The discourses of football of this time were presented as an almost entirely male domain, though muted female voices do sometimes come through. From the end of the nineteenth century, formal regulations prohibited women from participating in organised football and unwritten regulations provided little space for female sporting activity.[91] Football was, after all, something that was said to educate the male youth of the country. This was one more discourse of early twentieth-century society from which women were largely absent.

While sporting space could promote a change in how people acted, spectators were still expected to behave 'correctly'. Match reports sometimes noted poor sportsmanship from the crowd, as was the case at a game in the *Sportpark* between AFC and Willem II: 'The "Reds" [AFC] are a club that play attractively; they were not followed by many supporters; as a result, the enthusiasm in [the Sportpark] had a particular Ajax flavour, and, thus, qualifies as an example of poor sportsmanship.'[92] In this case, the attendance of Ajax fans supporting their fellow Amsterdammers was construed as unsporting.

Elsewhere in Amsterdam, *Het Volk* noted that fans sometimes got carried away and that on one occasion during the *Scheepvaartbeker* 'feelings outside the lines ran so high that in one place there was spirited fighting'.[93] Where spectators were observed to have transgressed their regulations, they would also be punished. In Almelo, in the east of the Netherlands, the *NRC* reported on the prohibition of football matches as a direct result of members of the 'younger generation' carrying on in an 'unseemly' manner, which had seen the police deployed. It was stated that if similar instances occurred then further bans would be imposed and that 'it is now up to the public, and especially the younger generation in Almelo, to give some thought as to whether they value seeing football matches or not'.[94] Spectators were expected to know the boundaries between exuberance and unseemliness, and if they did not then punishment would follow. With more spectators attending matches, more people fell subject to surveillance, to the micro-system of punishment and to the normalising concept of sportsmanship. Football increasingly became a location were everyone was being observed, ranked and measured against the discourses of the game and society.

Those who broke or challenged the established discourse of football too strongly could be punished formally through disciplinary structures or informally in the press. Football was an instrument of discipline. It constructed a normalised figure against which one could be measured through observation and examination. It allowed individual satisfaction and success through conforming to the norm and playing well. It contained its own system of rules and penalties through which the individual could be disciplined and punished. Football was an activity where training and punishment focused upon modifying the acts of the individual and in cementing the disciplinary techniques within a docile body.

Constructing identities through football

Newspapers played an important role in linking local identity to football and in demonstrating that football was something which could play some role in promoting a civic identity. In the history on sporting space (Chapter 2), I demonstrated stadia were linked to the desire to improve the prestige of a city or country. While the newspapers had a circulation beyond their city of publication and each covered matches from outside their locale, match reports had a local focus. In both Amsterdam and Rotterdam, coverage was tailored to a local audience and to the success of local teams. Local success was an affair of note, while a rival city's success received a more cautious treatment, as was illustrated in a report in the *NRC* about the eighteenth annual *Zilverenbal* tournament held in Rotterdam: 'People know that if Willem II win this tournament again, they will permanently get to keep the trophy in Tilburg. A real spectre for all right-minded Rotterdammers!'[95]

The concept of the local summer trophy being taken from the banks of the Maas to the southern city of Tilburg is seen as a negative event, not just for the local teams involved, but also for the city. In Amsterdam, similar reports occurred in *Het Volk* as Ajax Amsterdam struggled in the 1913/14 season: 'it would not surprise us if, in a short time, we see the Ajaxied [Ajax] at the bottom of the table again. Think about this, Men of Amsterdam!'[96]

Although there was a wide coverage of football in the Netherlands, it was only with local teams that the newspapers in Rotterdam or Amsterdam displayed this degree of emotion. It was at its highest in times of success or trouble. As Ajax came closer to the 1917/18 national championship, the sense of tension and importance increased in *Algemeen Handelsblad*. In February, the newspaper reported that, should Ajax's success continue, Amsterdam would be able to celebrate a championship 'after many long years'.[97] In April, when Ajax claimed the championship, the paper exclaimed that '[f]or the first time since 1899 (RAP), Amsterdam has the champion of the Western First Division within her walls'.[98] Amsterdam newspaper reports were keen to remind their readers that these metaphorical walls were part of the capital city of the Netherlands and that there were certain expectations attached to this. With such reports, newspapers were reinforcing the idea that football was an important aspect in the life of the city and that it was an activity which had an impact beyond simple match results.

And it was not just at times of success or failure that match reports reinforced elements of civic identity. Teams, and individuals, were referred to as '*onze stadgenoten*' – our fellow citizens – on a regular basis. Teams from other cities were given the moniker of Hagenaars, Utrechtenaars or Haarlemers, depending on their origin and those from Rotterdam and Amsterdam were also Rotterdammers and Amsterdammers. The use of such demarcations reinforced the idea of football as an activity linked to identity and as an event of importance beyond the individual or club.

But the reports did more than this, they constructed a framework for identity demarcation which could be changed and transformed depending on who was being talked about or who was being played. When Dutch teams travelled abroad, they were no longer Utrechtenaars, Rotterdammers or '*onze stadgenoten*', but were instead '*onze landgenoten*' – our fellow countrymen. This was the case in 1910, when HVV undertook a tour of Germany and played against Duisburg: 'In general, the opposition played very roughly against our fellow countrymen. Again and again, when the Dutch play in Germany, there are complaints about unfair play and faulty refereeing.'[99]

The focus of identity in this case changed, but the language of its application was similar; these were 'our' people, they belonged to the reader, and on this occasion were the victims of unsporting behaviour and poor refereeing. In 1914, the Netherlands versus Germany match saw many newspapers refer to the Dutch team as '*de onzen*' – our boys – again demonstrating a link with the reader and a wider concept of perceived identity which football could help construct, reinforce and define. Some reports made the link between football and national identity clearer. In the *Algemeen Handelsblad,* the reporter commented on the crowd:

> The sight of that sea of people, those thousands of people who waved everything they could hold or grab in rapture, was truly great, was enchanting. It seemed that Hollanders could also become enthusiastic, wildly enthusiastic, like no other people. And forgive me, it is especially good that it is this beautiful open-air sport which gives rise to such a noble outpouring of enthusiasm.[100]

While seemingly focusing on identity, these reports were also constructing and reinforcing the discourse of football as a positive activity for society. For those in the sports press, who were often intimately connected to the running of the game, match reports gave the opportunity to demonstrate that football was important to the city and to the nation. The use of these identity markers may have had a role in constructing different identities, either civic or national. My own work has not focused upon the reception of reports or how different individuals interpreted their identity through them; however, I believe the reports played a part in promoting the discourse of football within wider society by placing it as an activity which was important to the reader. It constructed a framework for talking about identity, one which could be transformed depending on the circumstances, but one which always demonstrated a link between the reader, football and wider society. Such a framework also reinforced the idea of differentiation in society. The reports contributed to an idea that there were clear, fixed, distinctions between things which could be identified with, such as people, teams, cities and nations. It provided a language to frame this allegiance and allowed for identities to be ranked and subsumed where necessary. This discourse was another way in which the concepts of regulation, order and measurement could be reproduced in football and society.

It was not only the sporting press which entered into the discourse of football and identity. A self-described, and rather excitable, 'layman' at the Netherlands versus Germany match did not hold back:

> At half-past two, the men, who would soon contend for victory, appeared; eleven white [shirted] and eleven orange [shirted] lads. The music played; first the [German national anthem] and then the Wilhelmus [Dutch national anthem]. And suddenly your heart really pulsated, as now you were on the cusp of it; no longer just two teams, but two nations stood opposite each other. In our time of increasing internationalism it still means something. No train, bicycle or car, no international congresses and world organisations of any kind, no 'alle Menschen werden Brueder', and no socialism can erase this – the sense that our young boys go into the field, flesh from our flesh, blood from our blood. The game of football, the most popular game of our time, opens new perspectives, panoramic views of our innermost feelings, of what sleeps deep within us, of our love for our own land, our own language, our own traditions, and above all our own race.[101]

The layman continued:

> It is the absolute sacrifice of our own [self] and the suppression of our [own] spontaneity. The French do not stand out because of the team-play, so I hear, of their side. It doesn't surprise me! From the battle of the Golden Spur something has always been lacking ... in the team-play of the French. And nor is it surprising that the Germans, in such a short period of time, have made such an impact within the game of football as they appeared to demonstrate – to competent judges – yesterday. Discipline is in their blood.[102]

Football could be linked to national, even racial, qualities, to historical failures, to individual constraint and explicitly to discipline. It was an activity which was part of an older form of national identity untroubled by new-fangled technological inventions or political persuasions and it was something that provided the opportunity to criticise the French, even in their absence.[103] Reports of this nature were rare in the sporting section, but this one suggests that as football became more popular, the interplay between different discourses of football, society and culture became ever more closely related.

Similarities and differences

So far, I have focused on how the different newspapers displayed similarities throughout the period. On many occasions, newspapers simply reprinted communiqués, letters or other newspaper reports relating to football, contributing to a similar representation of the game across the various media. The nature of football reporting, focusing on results, teams and locations, meant that there had to be a degree of similarity. Scores did not change depending on the newspaper. The different newspapers also used the nicknames of teams in reports. Often these were linked to the kit colours worn by the teams. Thus, in Rotterdam, Sparta were 'our red-white fellow citizens',[104] while in Amsterdam it was Ajax who could be referred to as 'the red-white team'.[105] The Dutch were 'oranje', Blauw-Wit of Amsterdam could be the 'Zebras' on account of their vertical stripes, AFC could be the 'Reds',[106] while HVV could be the 'Black and Yellows'.[107] Elsewhere other nicknames emerged as Velocitas Breda were the 'Cadets', 't Zesde were the 'Militarists' and GVC of Wageningen were the 'Farmers'.[108] Such names spread a specific language of the game across a wider area, providing the readers with a knowledge of team kits and perceived identities; for those who did not know, the shorthand could perhaps also act as a form of exclusion as official names did not always appear in football reports.

But there were also small differences in content, which provided the readers of the different newspapers with a different perception of football and its activities. In the *Maasbode*, Roman Catholic competitions, such as the one held in Arnhem, received more coverage than in the other newspapers. There were reports on the establishment of a Roman Catholic Association in 1910 and about the expansion of the local Catholic association in Nijmegen in 1918.[109] More reports appeared which focused on Roman Catholic clubs, such as Roomsch Katholieke Voetbal Vereeniging (Roman Catholic Football Club, RKVV) Graaf Willem II, RKVV Leonidas and RKVV Bredania.[110] These clubs were not among the best or most popular in the Netherlands, and they often did not come from Rotterdam, but reports about their activities indicate that the *Maasbode* saw Catholic football as something of importance, perhaps something which needed to be promoted; its readers would have received a subtly different presentation of the football world – a different 'reality effect'.

However, the appearance of results for Catholic teams was not always a regular feature and coverage in the *Maasbode* was overwhelmingly dominated by match reports from the *NVB* Western League. In *Het Volk* there were sometimes results from the *AVVB*, but this also occurred in other Amsterdam newspapers and their coverage was dominated by the *NVB* Western League. In this sense, football reporting was not greatly pillarised into separate political or religious world-views; indeed, before 1920, it had become increasingly similar in terms of its coverage. In the *NRC*, *De Courant* and *Algemeen Handelsblad* there were reports on international developments in FIFA and reports on Belgian, German and, in particular, English football. There were sometimes reports on office football and, depending upon which city the newspaper was published in, reports on local tournaments. These reports were, with the exception of those relating to English league football, usually sporadic in nature and often focused upon different matches in different newspapers.

By the end of the second decade of the twentieth century, football had become the main focus of sport reporting and one particular form of football became the dominant discourse: football organised by the *NVB*. The *NVB* league and in particular the western divisions were the prime focus of all the newspapers examined. This extended to the Catholic-oriented *Maasbode* and the socialist-oriented *Het Volk*, even though they included other forms of football. That *Het Volk* began covering sport at all in 1912 demonstrates that there was an increasing demand for its representation and newspapers responded to this – or indeed created it. As Bourdieu suggested, the media representation of the football world began to replicate itself and it spread this dominant discourse. Whether this similarity continued when new footballing organisations aligned with Protestant, socialist or Catholic world-views emerged in the 1920s is something in need of further examination.

Sport today

This history was intimately connected to the present, to concerns that organised sport, and particularly football, is connected to discourses which promote a certain kind of power, one which reinforces existing authority structures; a concern that sport, something so important in my life, encourages a docile, disciplined body. No history inspired by Foucault's work can escape this present-minded aspect, or his link between discipline and the development of capitalism. I am concerned that in its initial development, football demonstrated many of the aspects of discipline, which Foucault links to socio-cultural developments from the nineteenth century onwards. My Foucauldian experiment has provided a history which questions the role football played in early twentieth-century Dutch society and particularly its role in reproducing discourses which promote order, regulation and increased observation of others and of the self.

In the development of Dutch football after 1900, one can see that those in charge of the *NVB* made efforts to demonstrate that the game had a social worth and that it had a similar discourse of values as education. To be an active part of the Dutch education system gave football the opportunity to play a part in the lives of many young Dutch children. But it also demonstrated that the discourses promoted by school and sport were similar; that they were both attempting to construct individuals who were respectful of authority and who could perform specific tasks appropriately and efficiently. In both school and sport, training is at the centre of a disciplinary nature. Students and players learn when to do certain things and when not to; the year is divided into different periods of months, weeks, days, hours and minutes and each of these is coded with their own function and possibilities. Individuals are expected to learn where to be and what to do, and to do so without external coercion – a fixture list or a whistle is all that is needed. To be part of the game is to accept the imposition of discipline on one's own body.

Both training and matches allowed participants to be measured and evaluated against both the written regulations and the unwritten norm of the sportsman. The sportsman was a vague yet powerful figure, which encapsulated the perfection of the player. And the match was a place where each individual could be tested against this construct. Each player in the team was not only playing the opposition but was playing a mythical sportsman. The match acted like an exam at the end of a specific period of instruction, where individuals could demonstrate they had learnt the correct skills, techniques and attitudes, but it also gave the opportunity for visible punishment; not physical punishment like in previous centuries, but punishment for seemingly minor infractions, for using the wrong part of the body to perform a certain act, for doing so in the wrong place or at the wrong time. To play was to be punished.

But the concept of the sportsman was also fluid and this was demonstrated in the media. Different actions were (and are) perceived subjectively, and the vagueness of the discourses which made up the sportsman allowed space for different interpretations. The discourses promoted in the media meant that one had to work hard, play fairly and be a team player, but these were also concepts that had subjective interpretations. As demonstrated by the difference in perception of team and individual attributes in the media, the sportsman was a construct of different terms which were themselves constructs; they combined to make a term which was both powerful and vague: a term which, like 'amateur', could be fluidly taken advantage of, or ruthlessly enforced.

Administration was a central part of the sporting world. Football was demonstrated to be a game of order, regulation and procedure. Here, too, deviations from the norm were punished by withdrawing the possibility of matches and imposing bans or a reduction in status. In this sense, administration was as important a part of sport as playing; I believe it still is. To play sport requires organisation and, in a period where sporting organisations are increasingly placed under an observational gaze, perhaps we need to question more rigorously both the way we play on the pitch and the organisations that regulate sport. If we do not, attempts to use sport to promote equality within society will fail as the same discourses which operated to exclude women, and to rank, measure and segregate each individual will continue to be reproduced.

Observation was a key aspect in the development of football in the Netherlands. With the increasing popularity of the game, not just represented by more teams, players and spectators, but by more media attention, it brought more individuals under an observational gaze. Players, administrators, referees and spectators all became watched, and watched each other. Physical expressions of power and authority were not needed to ensure that individuals behaved well, performed properly or acted correctly, because everyone was being watched by everybody else and this was being monitored by an increasing number of societies which could do so on an increasingly minute level. Football and in particular the *NVB* were part of this increased observational gaze which helped reproduce discipline within society.

And this was reproduced in the media. While newspapers did not replicate each other completely, they all began to devote more space to football and specifically to the *NVB* form of the game. In this way, the *NVB* form could become the dominant form of the game in the Netherlands. The media also constructed a specific framework for attaching identity to football which could be used to demonstrate the importance of sport to the reader in different circumstances; reports gave the reader a chance to feel attached, whether it was to a player, a club, a city, a nation or even a race. Such reports both used and reproduced the discourses at play in wider society to further spread those of football and reinforce existing discourse of discipline.

This history places the development of sport firmly within wider cultural and social development. Sport is not just something which reflects or responds to the outside world, but is an intrinsic part of reproducing and constructing the world around us. In the case of early Dutch football, sport gave the opportunity for the techniques of discipline to come out of the school, prison or military and to enter the free time of an increasing number of people. In this sense, leisure became no different from work, education or politics; it became part of the same discourses of order, measurement and punishment. Sport, as football did in the early twentieth century, plays an active role in promoting discourses which encourage differentiation, ranking and sublimation of the individual to the whole.

As I end this history, I am left with more questions than answers. Am I being overly cynical? Have I been too influenced by Foucault's narrative drive without looking for other explanations? Should I have taken more account of individuals? I feel the answer to all of these is perhaps 'yes'. I feel a sense of unease when reading this history; a sense that it is an experiment that does not quite work, which is not quite as solid as I want it to be, which is fuelled by urgent concerns about the role sport plays today, but where the urgency has hidden some greater insights from my view. I have a sense that, as the deadline for publication of this work looms, and as with no other history in this work, there exists scholarship of which I am not aware. While this is always the case with any research, sometimes it leaves a greater feeling of unease, a desire for just a little more time.

But I believe the risk of not presenting an entirely convincing argument is one of the risks of experimental history. Such histories are there to be challenged and they can perhaps capture something which other histories cannot – a sense of urgency is sometimes important. If history is to be an experimental kitchen, we cannot be afraid to cook up something which is not to everybody's taste or which may need something added to it.

I want this history to be challenged, not because I believe that it is wrong or misleading, but because I still do not have answers to the questions that concern me most and it is only through continued debate and proposal that we can think about any tentative answers. Is sport really just a way to extend power over a wide group of people? Does it really promote segregation, conformity and the embodiment of authority within the body? Is the freedom I feel when I play football really just a myth? Is sport really good for me? And most concerning, with all of these questions and many others swirling around my head, just why is it that I still love it so much?

5

Van Aalst and Sport: Diaries and Historical Research

This history is about the link between form and content, about how constraints and influences external to the past, in sources, intentions and ambitions, shape and construct how the past is represented. It is a history about how the act of writing, of constructing and of remembering is an essential part of the production of history and how this changes what is produced.

I remember that this history was born not from considerations about the *content* but from what *form* I wanted the history to take. Before embarking on the research for this history, which was the last one I researched, I had considered a few things. I had completed my research for the history on Rotterdam during the first week of the First World War and, with the need for a perceived balance, I wanted to construct a history about Amsterdam in the same period (partly with the idea that this period has received less attention in histories of the city, especially in English). I wanted to construct a history which put an individual – not necessarily a 'famous' individual – at its centre and which focused on the idea that history is about different individuals and their stories. In addition, I wanted to take an individual involved in football and examine how the sport was part of their everyday life, what role it played and how it was reported or viewed.

During my research into the construction of a football stadium in Amsterdam, I became aware of the diary of C. J. K. van Aalst, the president of *MENS*, who oversaw the project from start to finish.[1] Copies of this diary had been digitised and made available online, taking away much of the hard work of archive research. The source seemed to fit the form of my history and it had another advantage. An email from March 2010 between myself and the *Huygens Instituut voor Nederlandse Geschiedenis* (Huygens Institute for History of the Netherlands, *ING*) demonstrated that the nature of the resource was important for my research.[2] I introduced myself via email, outlining that I was researching the history of a member of the Amsterdam football circle and that I had noticed the diary of Van Aalst in their collection. Rather than going to the enormous effort of clicking through the pages of the diary online, or having to physically move to an archive, I asked if they had a simpler form of the diary for me to navigate; I wanted a much easier solution. Not only this, I was concerned that the original diary files would be handwritten, which, after looking at numerous minutes from football clubs, I discovered not only took me much longer to read but were often indecipherable to me, even given my own awful scrawl. I slipped in the somewhat plaintive question, 'Is [the diary] typed? – I can't read old Dutch', by which I believe I meant handwritten Dutch.[3] Looking back at this question, I was struck by the sense of trepidation and nervousness that so often accompanied my research. Cringing somewhat at my poorly phrased admission of struggling with handwritten documents, I realised that I had overtly constructed how this history could represent the past before having done any research into the subject matter itself; I had chosen what was to be studied, partly to complement my other research, to fill 'gaps' in what I had already done, and I had chosen material which was easy to access and, crucially, easier for me to read from my laptop, rather than spending more time in archives. After all, time is an is not an endless commodity, even for historians.

As I tried to forget how many sources I had either overlooked, skipped over or deliberately ignored for this history, I looked at the copy of the diary that the *ING* had kindly sent to my address in Utrecht and eagerly anticipated writing a history of how Van Aalst had attended great matches, how he had discussed sport and business, how he had responded to contentious issues and to the value of sport in Amsterdam, about how he made great links between sport and social tensions and about his family and the war. As this history will demonstrate, I did not find this. Throughout the diary, Van Aalst barely mentioned sport, and certainly did not provide any great insight into its practice or operation. The lack of attention Van Aalst gave towards sport suggested two things to me. First, Van Aalst, as director of the *Sportpark* and a board member of the *Amsterdamsche IJsclub* (Amsterdam Ice-skating Club, *AIJC*), while central to the practice of sport, did not actually seem to care too much about it. There is no evidence that he participated in sport and little that he attended sporting events in anything other than a purely administrative capacity. Secondly, I needed to change what this history was going to be about.

This history underwent many changes between its conception and this representation. Many of these were never written down or thought about for too long. This history is not about how football worked within the everyday life of someone within Amsterdam sporting circles. Instead, this is a history based upon a few entries in Van Aalst's diary. These entries, which were sometimes short, hinted at other aspects of life in Amsterdam between 1914 and 1918, of which I had previously not been aware. They hinted at social tensions, problems of neutrality, attempts to deal with refugees, humour; some of them even had tangential links to sport. They were vignettes, often small and not necessarily highlighted by Van Aalst himself, but ones that resonated with me.

How one can use diaries in historical research is not a new debate. As Paperno suggests, one thing that should not be done with them is to treat them as if they provided unmediated access to either experience or fact. Yet, they are often privileged in historical research; perhaps it is the sense of immediacy or presence which gives them a form of authenticity.[4] But diaries, like other forms of writing and representation, are not magical texts giving us access to the past. A variety of different researchers have used diaries in their work in different ways: they have been used as a way of researching subjectivity and the construction of identities; as ways of reflecting on the construction of time in different periods; as a reflection on the self; as something that links private and wider social contexts; and as documents to be studied by literary scholars examining their form and structure. However, this history is about my approach to history and about why I chose certain vignettes and ignored others – it is about constructing something from the numerous possible different stories. In this case, the diary is 'an empty vessel, or an adaptable tool, at the disposal of its users for the purposes at hand'.[5]

One of my purposes in this chapter is to represent some unfamiliar stories about the past, but just as important is my desire to demonstrate how the emotions and attitudes of the historian can shape history and how the process of construction can shape the historian. The use of a diary, a text so attached to a fixed concept of time, allows me to experiment with 'non-linear' representations of time and with representations tinged by my own memory. This is a history where 'affect and memory become essential elements' in constructing the story.[6] Braidotti notes that these elements are an important part of a new 'posthuman' methodology for the humanities that incorporates increasing creativity, trans-disciplinarity and scholastic diversity.[7] Far from posing a threat to the practice of history, they are elements which permit new avenues of thought and creativity and new ways for us to consider our relationship with the past, with how it is constructed and with our own memory.

Van Aalst and sport

The copy of Van Aalst's diaries sent to me by the *ING* consisted of typed versions of the original entries, beginning on 26 August 1914 and running until 13 May 1918. I decided to find out more about the man who wrote it. Cornelis Johannes Karel van Aalst was born in the North Holland city of Hoorn, on the banks of the IJsselmeer, on 7 May 1866. His father, Dirk, was a reformed preacher and his mother, Jacoba Maria de Ruyter, was descended from the Dutch admiral Michael de Ruyter. Cornelis was earmarked for business from a young age. After attending the *Hogereburgerschool* (a higher tier of Dutch secondary school) in Hoorn, he was educated at the *Openbare Handelsschool* (Public Business School) in Amsterdam. Upon completion of his final exams in 1885, the young Van Aalst went to work trading tropical goods in the firm of Gustav Briegleb in Amsterdam, a company known for providing a good education to young men with an interest in pursuing a career in business. Three years later, at the end of 1888, Cornelis took the entrance exams to join the *NHM* and on 1 January 1889 was accepted into the corporation. Immediately, he was posted to the rapidly growing department in Batavia (modern-day Jakarta); by May 1891, he had become the head of the department.[8] During this early period of his career, he married Tjalda Anna Petronella Hoorweg.[9]

His business success continued and by 1895 he had moved to Surabaya, in East Java. The following year he became the leading businessman there and his involvement in the development of the Klampok sugar enterprise gained particular praise. In 1898 Van Aalst became a director of the *NHM* in Singapore, which at this time was the fastest growing market in Asia. With the cooperation of the governor of Aceh, new agencies were opened for the *NHM* in Palembang, Rangoon, Bandjermasin and Kotaradja. In Sebang, Van Aalst worked on the development of the harbour, to take full advantage off the opening of the Suez Canal, which was intended to be a twice-weekly destination for Dutch shipping companies. In 1902, he returned to the Netherlands and was invited to become a member of the Amsterdam delegation of the *NHM* with responsibilities for banking and trade.[10]

By 1910, Van Aalst was one of the most recognisable and influential people in the Amsterdam and Dutch business world and was raising a family.

He was also involved in the development of the *Sportpark* in Amsterdam. From 1912 onwards, he was first the president of the *MENS* and then, after 1914, the president of the board of the stadium. He was on the board of the *AIJC*, which used space behind the *Rijksmuseum* for skating; during summer, cricket and equestrian events were held here and occasionally football matches. This involvement in sport seems to have been a new development for him. Van Aalst was not one of those who donated to the first aborted attempt to build a multi-sport stadium in Amsterdam in 1908. Despite this, I thought that it was reasonable to expect that Van Aalst would have provided some information about his involvement in the sporting world; after all, I thought, if I were involved in the Amsterdam sporting scene, I would fill my diary with a plethora of details about matches, players and events. That I did not find this indicates that sometimes the historian's reason and logic is different from those whom they research; if a historian may be permitted to be disappointed in the past then I certainly was.

As head of the board of the *Sportpark*, Van Aalst was involved with meetings and key decisions. However, during the period of the war, his daily connection to the new stadium and its finances was severely diminished by the more pressing needs of international trade. Entries connected to the *Sportpark* appear briefly in the diaries, with few, if any, entries connected to sport for the whole of 1917 or 1918. Some entries in the diary are simple records of the fact that Van Aalst had attended a meeting, no further details are added:

> **5 October 1914**
> 1 – visit to Vliegen about the Sportpark.[11]

A few days later Van Aalst suggests what the meeting may have been about:

> **7 October 1914**
> 1.15 – with Vliegen about the Sportpark. He now promised me a 75-year lease and will quickly ready the documents.[12]

The change in circumstances in Amsterdam had brought the financial success of the stadium into question only months after its grand opening. The process of renegotiating the lease demonstrated that the financial future of the ground was in jeopardy, as too was the reputation of those who had invested in it. During the latter part of 1914, Van Aalst's dealings with the stadium were almost entirely concerned with extending the lease on the ground, obtaining a mortgage and persuading the Municipality to accept the proposal.

The daily operation of the *Sportpark* saw other unexpected issues arise. In September 1914, Van Aalst notes:

> **30 September 1914**
> 12.30: Coucke let me know about a military festival that was scheduled for 13 October without our knowledge ([at the] Stadium), by Captain Van der Meijden. General Ophorst said that we should publish a communiqué [indicating] that the Board knows nothing of such an event. Believed that the money from earlier military festivals for the Support Committee was handled strangely.[13]

Here, Van Aalst hints that charitable events staged to help victims of the war saw corruption or, at least, something a little odd. But, as with many of his entries, such interesting elements are not elaborated upon. There is no record of a military event occurring in the *Sportpark* on the date suggested and no mention is made again of Van Aalst's concerns; the repeated highlighting of the distance between my interests and those of the author were starting to pose a problem for this history.

In 1916, Van Aalst provides an entry in his diary about a proposed staging of the Dutch Olympic Games in the stadium, but he seems a little uninterested with the potential sporting events.[14] I discovered that a Dutch Olympics took place in September 1916 when the various facilities of the stadium were put to good use for a range of sporting events. To coincide, *De Revue der Sporten* published articles about the origins of the ancient Olympics, the modern variant and how, owing to the war, the proposed 1916 Olympics would not take place. The Dutch Olympic Games was its replacement and according to the magazine, a celebration and 'a blessing for our people' who had been spared the monstrosity of war and who could celebrate the influence of psychical education on a healthy life.[15] If it was supposed to be a celebration, it seems many people had not got the invite. Photos showed Sparta Rotterdam in action against Willem II of Tilburg in front of, at best, a quarter-full stadium; Sparta would win the final match of the tournament 4–0.[16] A hockey match between Amsterdam and Togo – from The Hague – also took place in front of 'next to no public', while a korfball match between two mixed teams did not receive much more attention.[17] Van Aalst's name is not mentioned in the magazine and, likewise, Van Aalst does not mention the staging of the Dutch Olympics in his diaries.

In July 1916, Van Aalst wrote about a military festival to be held in the grounds of the stadium, but again his entries demonstrate that he was more concerned with following the correct protocol and administration than with the playing side of sport:[18]

> **13 July 1916**
> 11.30 Sportpark. General Meeting.
> I said, in connection with the forthcoming visit of Her Majesty the Queen to the military sport-festival on Saturday, that I could only welcome Her Majesty, as President of the Stadium, if I was invited to do so, as the stadium had been hired to the Olympic Committee and they were in actual fact the hosts.[19]

His diary entry about the event itself, while giving an insight into his conversation with the Dutch Queen, was not replete with sporting information:

> **15 July 1916**
> Upon the arrival and the greeting of Her Majesty, Her Majesty came to me and said 'I am so happy to be able to see your Stadium again['] and asked me to accompany her above [to the reception].[20]

Following the reception, Van Aalst accompanied the Queen on a tour of the festival during which time he records her discussions about her husband, who was in Switzerland; her desire to move palaces on account of the damp in the *Huis-ten-Bosch* in The Hague; the problems regarding British and German trade regulations; and a need to be kept informed of pressing issues. He concludes:

> After we visited the games, Her Majesty and I walked inside the stadium, attended a running match at close distance and when we were close by the entrance to the stand, an army of photographers stood, who took photos. I said 'Majesty, I apologise that the photographers were there', to which she laughingly replied 'I am sorry that I didn't have my parasol, which I would usually put up on such occasions.'
>
> In the Boardroom a cup of tea was brought, for which we had made our silver service available.

> After that, Her Majesty spent some time in the stands watching the matches and after this she departed, with the reassurance that she had found everything delightful.[21]

The visit of Queen Wilhelmina to the stadium was clearly an event of note for Van Aalst, yet his own interest in sport is limited; it seems the Queen may have taken more interest in the games than he did. Van Aalst's involvement with the *AIJC* is also mentioned, but again it is a matter of protocol and organisation; he attended regular meetings but little is mentioned, although he describes a celebration for the porter and the desire to create a commemorative book for the club.[22]

While reading an entry from February 1916, I felt a sudden sense of excitement. In this entry, Van Aalst describes how the secretary of the *Sportpark* had approached him for his help in setting up a new sporting newspaper. The first mention was on 10 February and this was followed two weeks later:

> **26 February 1916**
> Again at the office. Coucke asked for support to establish a sporting newspaper. The publisher Nunes and furthermore Kokosky and Elte want to help him. The first with 6,000 guilders, the 2nd with 1,000 guilders – but more following this, and Elte with 3,000 guilders.
>
> In total he needs 22,000 guilders. I said that I was prepared to lend him 5,000 guilders, which he could use to take shares, but did not myself want shares in the newspaper. I was well prepared, so as not to ruin him regarding this matter, for him to authorise me to bear financial responsibility for the shares for a limited time. This will happen if the affair goes badly.[23]

The entry suggested that sport was gaining more attention. Why else would Coucke want to begin a new newspaper? It demonstrates the sums needed to fund such a venture and how business networks were used to find the capital. But again, Van Aalst is more interested in the financial side of the enterprise rather than anything to do with its content. My initial excitement at this entry soon disappeared when only one brief further entry appeared relating to the idea; it is never made clear what sort of newspaper was planned, who was to write it or whether it actually succeeded. This particular entry could be seen as a metaphor for my interaction with Van Aalst's wider diary – an initial sense of excitement, snuffed out by dead-ends and Van Aalst's own lack of interest. I was starting to think that this source should be treated as a sort of hostile witness; discussions about the private life of the Queen were all very well, but were definitely not what I had been looking for.

I had put a lot of effort, and importantly time, into reading and noting Van Aalst's diaries – all for some brief mentions of a few meetings about sport. I considered whether I should ignore what I had found, whether it was one of those instances where research does not give us the material we need to provide anything of use or relevance. I vaguely recall anxiously looking at my notes and the diaries and wondering what to do; my response varied depending on the hour and my mood. Fortunately, I decided to re-examine what I had found; if there was not enough to provide a new representation of Van Aalst's role in sport or of how sport linked with wider daily life, were there any other stories I could tell? Although I had initially skimmed over many of Van Aalst's entries relating to discussions of trade and political affairs, I decided to reread them in the hope of finding new angles, new histories to think about. Under this new pressure, where sport was no longer a driving force, there were a number of stories which I had ignored at first – stories and entries which now interested me, which suggested that I could construct something about daily life in the Netherlands during the First World War.

Trade and business

During her visit to the *Sportpark*, Wilhelmina had asked Van Aalst about German and British trading issues. While this may or may not have been small talk designed to pass the time while walking between receptions and races, it was certainly a very well-chosen topic. When conflict between Germany and Great Britain broke out, it immediately threatened the position of the Netherlands, both physically and in terms of its economic interests. With the Dutch government following a policy of strict neutrality, Trade Minister Treub and Foreign Affairs Minister Loudon were keen to ensure that trade between Dutch and German businesses was not viewed by the Entente Cordiale as a method of avoiding the British blockade on contraband goods entering Central Europe. Equally, any Dutch attempt at preventing free trade along the Rhine, which would result from accepting the British blockade, may have been viewed by the German government as a provocative act in contravention of the 1868 Rhine Shipping Treaty.[24]

In response to this situation, Van Aalst was asked by Treub to head a committee of influential businessmen which would keep the British government informed of Dutch trading activity. This committee, which would be given the title of the *Nederlandsche Overzee Trustmaatschappij* (the Netherlands Overseas Trust, *NOT*) was, at least in theory, established as a private company independent of the Dutch government, designed to provide a plausible barrier between the operations of Dutch businessmen and the government, ensuring neutrality and avoiding the ire of the German government. Traders who wished to import goods to the Netherlands had to do so through the *NOT*, signing a contract promising that the goods would not be exported to Germany and providing a deposit against this occurrence. The British agreed that *NOT*-guaranteed goods would be permitted to pass to the Netherlands through the blockade.[25]

Van Aalst became the president of the *NOT* and as a consequence held a great degree of influence; the *NOT*'s size grew and during the war they would employ over a thousand people.[26] Many of Van Aalst's diary entries during the war, particularly during the early period, relate to issues of trade and meetings between various diplomats and trade attachés. The tensions caused by British actions featured in September 1914, when Van Aalst highlighted that, while the British detention of Dutch ships could be in contravention of international law, he feared that Britain could in practice 'do anything' and that if the Dutch 'were not careful, the whole sea could be shut off and our telegraph lines could be cut'.[27]

Van Aalst also expressed concern at the number of German businessmen in Rotterdam, which could give rise to Entente suspicion, and his diaries highlight divisions between businessmen in Rotterdam and those in Amsterdam. While Amsterdam's trade was focused on international and imperial deals, Rotterdam, by virtue of its links to the Ruhr, relied on Central European trade.[28] On 12 September 1914, Van Aalst had been made aware that *Wambersie & Zoon*, a Rotterdam firm, had offered help in the sale of thirty-six boats through a Dutch middleman working for Germany – a sale that did not occur due to government intervention. However, Van Aalst remained worried that the large number of German workers in Rotterdam firms could do a great deal of damage to the Dutch reputation and possibly their neutrality.[29]

In November 1914, Van Aalst was called to see the British trade attaché, Sir Francis Oppenheimer, to discuss suspicions about the Rotterdam-based businessman Anton Kröller, who was suspected of helping the German government agents in Rotterdam, and whether the Batavia Line shipping company had given the German government information about minefields.[30] While Van Aalst assured Oppenheimer that these suspicions were groundless, his diaries also indicate tensions between businessmen in both cities over the composition of committees and that Van Aalst was accused of being overly critical of the Rotterdam Bank.[31] The *NOT* under Van Aalst found itself negotiating between fears in Britain of German favouritism, fears in Germany (perhaps more grounded) of British favouritism and the differing interests of businessmen and politicians within the Netherlands. Van Aalst's own interests also seemed to profit from the period.[32]

Negotiations about trade deals and economic agreements were certainly not the primary focus of my research, but within the detailed accounts of these meetings I noticed sentences that intrigued me or made me smile. Such sentences often revolved around how individuals were said to have tried to get around the trading regulations in a number of ways. Traders from Germany were said to have labelled goods 'Made in Holland' in an attempt to breach the blockade and sell them on the international market.[33] In March 1915, Van Aalst reported that some Dutch traders had loaded a ship full of contraband tobacco while declaring that it contained rubber, ensuring that the *NOT* had to remain ever-vigilant againt those trying to make a surreptitious profit.[34] Van Aalst held meetings about alleged corruption in the tea trade and further communication about problems in the rubber trade.[35] My favourite story of illicit trading, and possibly the moment which gave me the greatest pleasure in producing this history, was one mentioned by Van Aalst on 30 May 1916. On this day, he notes how one exporter had been given special permission to export a number of milking cows and pedigree cattle, as payment for other services he had rendered. However, later it appeared that these cows were simply ordinary cows, which had been left unmilked for four days or had their udders inflated with bicycle pumps.[36] As I imagined how exactly one went about inflating a cow's udder, I imagined that my reaction to this particular entry may not have been the same as Van Aalst's, who was clearly coming up against new and increasingly ingenious attempts to avoid regulations.

Elements of humour were not abundant in the diaries, but some examples of dry humour occurred. The German trade attaché, Dr von Hartogensis, during trade negotiations on the sale of tin, requested that Germany should be given a greater amount of tin than Switzerland, as they 'have nothing except snow from Mont Blanc' to trade.[37] Van Aalst suggested that he should be given the Iron Cross for his help with the trade; von Hartogensis came back a month later:

> [Dr von Hartogensis] was very grateful and began again to talk about an honour, [but said] that the 'Iron Cross' was not possible!!

> The man appears not to have understood that [Van] Vollenhoven and myself were making a joke.[38]

Humour sometimes does not translate well.

Belgian refugees in Amsterdam, October 1914

Van Aalst had many dealings with von Hartogensis; in his diary, he reports his first meeting with him in November 1914:

> **14 November 1914**
> 12 – Dr Van Hartogensis [*sic*], the German trade attaché, came to visit. A very friendly, cool-headed man, who made a positive impression. He spoke very good Dutch, [he] had studied in Leiden for three years.[39]

However, a month later the tone had changed and a meeting between the two revealed that the Dutch government's fear of threats was not without reason:

> **21 December 1914**
> 2 – Dr Hartogensis [*sic*] came again to press the point about tin [...] He then started to become somewhat rude, ending with threats 'between ourselves', that Germany would ban all, or at least most, exports to the Netherlands, [he] ended with the question, what had we actually done for Germany? I advised him of the 200,000 Belgian refugees, who we fed daily; he didn't care, Germany would not have had to do this to Belgium if Belgium had let her pass through etc. etc. I told him not to talk politics, upon which he said, that people in Berlin could lose their patience, [that] he had done everything to attempt to get something 'sensible' from Holland, but if that did not work 'would it really make much difference for Berlin to get one more enemy?'[40]

The entry highlighted the political tensions involved in Van Aalst's work, but also hinted at something I was not familiar with, namely the issue of Belgian refugees in the Netherlands. I decided to go back to some of the entries I had at first only glanced at in search of sporting information. Van Aalst had first, and briefly, mentioned the invasion of Belgium on 8 October 1914 after a meeting at the Batavian Petroleum

Company with the company director, politician and former Dutch Minister for War, Hendrikus Colijn. The entry is only a sentence long and notes that Van Aalst had warned Colijn that his writing on the war entitled 'Military Necessity' had raised unfavourable sentiments.[41] Colijn responded that he was free to say what he wanted, in reply to which Van Aalst reminded him that as he was a former, and now current, politician that this was actually not the case. The entry, like so many of Van Aalst's diary entries, yields almost nothing about wider events, or his own opinion of them. Yet the German advance into Belgium in the first weeks of October saw major upheavals which, as Van Aalst's entry from December of that year hinted at, would have important consequences in the Netherlands.

In late September 1914, Antwerp was placed under siege by advancing troops. Held up by the ringed fortifications, the siege continued into October. By 6 October, the city's authorities had urged residents to leave and three days later, only around 10,000 of the city's 400,000 residents remained. Antwerp fell under German army control by 10 October.[42] Those who had left the city often did so in a state of panic; those with the means left by car while the poorer carried their possessions on foot, forming long lines of people streaming towards the nearby border town of Essen and the awaiting trains. For some, especially the elderly, the journey was difficult and those who had suddenly become refugees searched for food and shelter. For the majority of those that left during the first weeks of October, the Netherlands offered, at least temporarily, a place of refuge. Home Affairs Minister, and Minister-President, Cort van der Linden assured refugees that they would be fed and they were welcomed into the Netherlands.[43]

In the southern Dutch towns around the border with Belgium, cities swelled with those from Antwerp and its surrounding districts. The cities of Bergen op Zoom and Roosendaal grew from around 16,000 residents to around 50,000 in the space of a few days. In Putte, a small town of 1,298 residents, 4,000 refugees arrived. Many of them camped in parks, on the street or went in search of other shelter, as local family homes were already full. In Hulst, streets were filled with straw to provide those sleeping there some comfort and across Zeeuws Vlaanderen, classrooms were used to provide shelter. The vast numbers put a strain on local facilities but also on the military who were required to ensure that fleeing Belgian soldiers were not amongst those crossing into the neutral Netherlands; many soldiers did cross the border and when they were discovered they were sent to internment camps. To ease the situation, refugees and internees were moved to other parts of the Netherlands.[44]

The newspapers reported on the great numbers of refugees entering the Netherlands. On 7 October, the *Algemeen Handelsblad* carried a report from a journalist making a journey in the areas around Antwerp; the journey changed from a scene of peace and harmony to one filled with rows of people eager to leave, people not looking back, but heading north, 'where the still-unscathed Holland had to be, where people could sit in a house without the threat of their roof or cellar being blown out, where the villages and cities stand upright, and do not form black, ruined lumps'.[45] On the same day, the newspaper reported that a local support committee for Belgian refugees had been set up in Zwolle. The committee hoped to find lodgings with individuals who needed money and in that way 'both sides could be helped'.[46] As the number of refugees increased, other charitable organisations were established and spontaneous events were organised. Thursday 8 October saw the announcement of an evening of songs to be held in the small room of the Concertgebouw the following Tuesday, which, in part, would be for the benefit of Belgian refugees.[47] On 11 October, the football match in Dordrecht between DFC and Sparta Rotterdam saw a collection by soldiers for Belgian refugees at half-time.[48]

Fig 5.1 Concertgebouw, Amsterdam, 2016

Reports on Belgian refugees in the Netherlands increased in size. By 9 October, in addition to the reports on the passage of the war, half of the inside page of the *Algemeen Handelsblad* was devoted to stories from around the Netherlands about Belgian refugees. In Vlissingen, the situation was worse than before as thousands arrived by boat and train. In Utrecht, around 150 refugees had been given shelter under the roof of St Catharine's convent. In Breda, organisations went from door to door trying to find accommodation as hundreds of new refugees arrived on each train. Around 2,000 were housed in public buildings, while others slept in shops or factories and the army gave what food they could. The head of the Rotterdam Municipality had sent a telegram to the director general of the State Railway Company to request a temporary halt to trains for refugees as there was nowhere to house them. The Hague was a scene of full stations, trains and platforms, with some passengers receiving gifts from the public.[49]

Many refugees came from the border through Rotterdam to Amsterdam. In Amsterdam *Centraal Station*, 'on the chairs, sat old women, old men, whose angst and misery could be read on their faces [...] Next to their parents sat children with tired, pale faces, with rings under their eyes because they had not slept'.[50] Outside the station, a crowd of people awaited the refugees, some forming groups to hear the news; others, who had already fled Antwerp, tried to find out what had happened to their homes. Throughout the day and night, trains arrived bringing new people, some of whom were moved to the newly finished Stock Exchange, to be given food and hope of shelter.[51] In addition to the Stock Exchange, refugees were brought to the Artis Zoo, the Diamond Exchange and to the Bijenkorf store.[52] The *AIJC* saw many of the early refugees from Belgium housed in the club facilities and many different individuals provided help across the city.[53] The Municipality also played its part, giving 9.10 guilders to Belgian families of four refugees, substantially more than was allocated to the unemployed.[54] The *Algemeen Handelsblad* started a campaign to provide refugees with reading material as a form of relaxation, particularly for children.[55] Not wanting to be left out, some businesses advertised that they could provide products at 'extra low prices' for the refugees.[56] But still more was needed: 'never has the need to help so many, and immediately, felt more urgent than now, when the consequences of dire world events are also felt in the Netherlands'.[57]

By 11 October, the number of refugees in Amsterdam had grown to around 14,000. It was decided that the city was full and in a message to the station commander at Roosendaal, Amsterdam was closed to further refugees.[58] The front page of Sunday 11 October's *Algemeen Handelsblad* carried an advertisement from the *Centraal Comité voor Huisvesting* (Central Committee for Housing) calling upon other regional committees to offer shelter outside Amsterdam.[59] Inside, one of the refugees from Antwerp, Jef Deman, had taken out advertising space to inform his parents that he was well and staying in Holland.[60] By Monday 12 October, attempts were being made to encourage refugees to return home; a communiqué from the German commander in Antwerp assured those who had left the city that they would be safely welcomed back.[61]

Within the Dutch government, the scale of the refugee crisis had caused tensions between Minister of War Bosboom, who wanted to encourage refugees to return home, and Cort van der Linden, who was happy to continue to provide hospitality.[62] A policy of so-called 'soft pressure' was suggested as a means to encourage refugees to return: not exactly ushering people out of the city, but certainly not providing the most hospitable conditions either.[63] In Amsterdam, the need for space saw proposals for warehouses and hangers to be used to hold many of the refugees; this was both a practical step to deal with the lack of other spaces for housing the refugees and also fitted with the policy of soft pressure. The hangers used for the refugees, which became the central location for distribution of food, were poorly heated and had limited facilities for washing and sanitation. It was thought that only those who really needed help would stay here. However, the use of the hangers prompted a critical response from many in the city and by mid-November, those who remained in the hangers were moved to other camps established for refugees across the Netherlands.[64] The initial influx of refugees saw around 719,000 rehoused across 831 different municipalities; other figures suggest that nearly 1 million refugees were absorbed into a country of no more than 6.3 million people.[65] After October 1914, many refugees returned home and following this period the Dutch government gave the poorer refugees a choice between returning home or spending time in one of the refugee camps which had been established in Uden, Ede, Nunspeet, Gouda or Veenhuizen.[66] By December, the number of refugees in the Netherlands was estimated at around 124,000 and of those only around 2,500 refugees would remain in Amsterdam for the duration of the war.[67]

Returning to Van Aalst's diary I was surprised and then increasingly frustrated, even angry at his entries. On the day after reports about the elderly sitting shocked in the Amsterdam central train station appeared, Van Aalst recorded only one entry, connected to the receipt by Cort van der Linden of a telegram unconnected to the flow of refugees in the Netherlands. The same was true for the following day. Indeed, Van Aalst makes no mention of the refugees until 29 October, when a man called Stuart comes to ask about how he can set up a support committee in the Indies for the Belgian refugees.[68] With the exception of Van Aalst's meeting with the German trade attaché in late December, there are no entries that deal with the Belgian refugees in the Netherlands before 1915, when Van Aalst is asked to help establish businesses or committees to help Belgians in the Netherlands.[69] The absence of any comments or personal reflections connected to the personal upheavals in October 1914 struck me as odd. How could he not comment at all on the plight of refugees, on the situation in the Netherlands or even perhaps on how he was annoyed that he could not get somewhere because of the masses of people? Were these diaries really intended as his personal private recollections, or where they written with posterity in mind?

But the lack of emotion was in keeping with the rest of his diaries. I learnt that his wife's birthday in 1914, 9 October, was celebrated in The Hague at her mother's house, but nothing more;[70] that in January 1915 he travelled with Tjalda to Rotterdam to visit his brother Dick who was ill and who advised him not to consider taking the position of mayor of Amsterdam;[71] that in March 1915 Tjalda suddenly became very ill, with the doctor giving little hope and that her brother and sisters had been called,[72] but that by January 1916 'thanks to the good condition of Tjalda and the presence of many family members' they had all enjoyed a very pleasant silver wedding anniversary.[73] If this diary was not one where I would find great personal insights into football matches and sport, it was equally not one where I would find great personal insights into his private life, or his observations on daily life in Amsterdam; this was a diary about meetings, about the price of tin, about discussions with men of influence and import. It was tedious, it was frustrating – it was not doing what I wanted it to do. But the irritation I experienced while looking at page after page of meetings was sometimes punctured by a sentence or a word which hinted at something in his life which moved beyond the realm of trade and into the individual and the personal; be it his wife's illness, the Dutch dealing with Belgian refugees or, as happened in late 1915, the arrest of a newspaper editor, who also just happened to have been a successful Amsterdam footballer.

The arrest of Kick Schröder

4 December 1915

In the evening, at 8 o'clock, Mr Holdert from 'The Telegraaf' hassled me about where the shoes were, the ones given to me by Sir Francis,

> the ones which would sway the process against Schröder [...] then he said: 'You do know that Schröder has been arrested don't you?' I answered that I did not and he requested that I read the paper. Indeed, the whole story was inside. As I considered this imprisoning a 'political' error, which was very inconvenient to us in the NOT, where the relationship with England had been difficult because of the established smuggling, I telephoned Treub.[74]

When I first read this entry, I was interested in the story, but I was unaware of who exactly had been arrested, or what shoes had to do with it. Van Aalst's entry again focused on the political and economic consequences for the *NOT*, which, by this time, I had grown a little tired of. But later, having found few comments on sport, it was one of the entries I decided to return to. Quickly it emerged that Schröder was not only an important member of the Amsterdam media, whose arrest highlighted tensions between the policy of governmental neutrality and free speech, but that he was also a well-known footballer in the latter part of the nineteenth century.[75] The opportunity to look into new sporting exploits was too good to turn down.

For anyone who had seen Amsterdam football around 1900, J. C. Schröder, commonly known as 'Kick' Schröder, was a familiar figure.[76] He played football in the 1890s for RAP, based on the Schagerlaan on the outskirts of Amsterdam. His obituary notes that, for the older generation, Schröder's play was one of the great attractions for those who came to watch RAP. He demonstrated a 'natural, enthusiastic sort of play, which made a greater impression because it was without fear, and hard, really hard! Schröder was a feared footballer for more than one reason: the most prominent one was that he played so well.'[77] Obituaries sometimes seem to overestimate the importance of the individual concerned, but in Schröder's case, the claims that he was an impressive player seem at least partly born out. In 1894, Schröder captained a Dutch representative eleven against a touring Felixstowe team in Rotterdam; the match ended with a 1–0 loss for the *Bondselftal* in front of a small but enthusiastic crowd.[78] In April 1894, he was involved in a match with Maidstone FC who were short of players – naturally, the captain did the honourable thing and switched sides.[79]

As with many sports enthusiasts of the late nineteenth century, Schröder did not confine himself to football. He was interested in equestrianism and was also involved in the Dutch athletic organisations and cycling clubs. However, his other love was cricket, and it was in this sport that he gained particular attention in the Netherlands.[80] He played the game from his early youth and continued into the twentieth century. I found records of his contribution of thirty-seven runs for the Amstels Cricket Club against Rood en Wit from Haarlem in 1894 and others in 1913 for a Dutch team against an English representative team.[81] He would often captain his cricket teams, 'and what a captain' he was.[82] As a player he was an all-rounder, he excelled with the bat and was a good fielder and bowler. But most of all he was a very good wicket-keeper. If his obituary is to be believed, his game did not desert him in his later years, and 'it was not so many years ago, that we saw, that "Kick" had not forgotten it'.[83]

But, by late 1915, Schröder was involved in a contest far from the cricket field. He had become editor of Holdert's *De Telegraaf* newspaper and as such was responsible for ensuring that the articles published within it did not threaten the neutrality of the Dutch government. While the press could freely report the movements of foreign armies, they were censured from giving opinions on the merits of the war or on the conduct of the warring parties.[84] However, the concept of strict neutrality was difficult to enforce, partly because of the emergence of foreign press agencies that distributed various forms of propaganda within the Netherlands.[85] Newspaper editorials could also be the subject of foreign influence and were the focus of Dutch government attention. But there was a constitutional right to free speech in the Netherlands, meaning that enforcing rules about neutrality was difficult. In the parts of the Netherlands where a 'state of siege' existed, the military could take stronger action and prohibit the movement of certain individuals or the publishing of certain newspapers. This was implemented inconsistently and publications were not banned regularly or if they were, it was not for long periods of time.[86]

The arrest in December 1915 was not the first time Schröder had come into conflict with authority in his role as editor. Throughout 1915, *De Telegraaf* had repeatedly published allegations accusing Germany of colluding in smuggling across the Dutch border.[87] In February 1915, he was accused by Lieutenant J. Mallinckrodt of receiving money from the British government for writing his editorials. Following legal action, Mallinckrodt withdrew his accusation. In June 1915, Schröder wrote an article openly critical of the German government, stating: 'At the centre of Europe lies a troop of unscrupulous scoundrels who have caused the war.'[88] He was briefly arrested, but later acquitted of endangering Dutch neutrality.[89] If the arrest was intended to stop *De Telegraaf* publishing critical articles then it did not work. On Saturday 27 November, *De Telegraaf* took the rival *Nieuwe Courant*, or possibly the *NRC*, to task over their accusation of prompting mistrust amongst the allies with exposés about smuggling and the *NOT*. The piece ended with an assurance that *De Telegraaf* was not going to be silenced:

> We will not hesitate from challenging a government, and a collaborative press, which, under the mask of 'true neutrality', provides Germany with the most necessary of living needs through an irresponsible export policy, through which it enables the war to continue and not only commits treason against its own fatherland, but also to humanity, which would be better served by a stronger, more morally high-standing government.[90]

According to *Het Volk*, it was this piece that had prompted Schröder's arrest on 4 December and Holdert's call to Van Aalst. It is unlikely that Van Aalst learnt of the arrest in the socialist daily newspaper *Het Volk*; however, influenced by Van de Vooren's article, I had a copy of this to hand and they gave a full description of how Schröder had been detained upon returning to his home on the banks of the Amstel:

> On Saturday afternoon, Mr Schröder was in town with his partner buying things for the St. Nicholas festival. At around five o'clock he came home. Later, four policemen, who had waited for his arrival, arrived. There were two inspectors and two detectives, all in plain clothes.
>
> They informed Mr Schröder of the reason for their visit. [Schröder] sought permission to be placed in contact with the editorial staff of the newspaper to which he is connected and with his counsel, Mr J. Kappeyne van de Coppello, who advised him he should accompany [the police].
>
> Mr Schröder bade farewell to his dismayed family, who would have a most sad St. Nicholas celebration.[91]

Schröder was transported by tram to the *Leidscheplein* and then on to the Palace of Justice.

> The substitute Officer of Justice, Mr Jorissen, waited for the arrested man there and informed him that his taking into custody was made in the name of the magistrate's court, [...] in connection to a contravention of Article 100 of the regulations relating to criminal law (bringing the neutrality of the state into danger).
>
> After Mr Schröder was informed of the arrest warrant, he was taken through the busy part of the city, on foot, to the Huis van

> Bewaring [Custodial House]. Mr Schröder may receive food and drink from outside the prison and was given permission to send for a few books from his personal library.[92]

That Van Aalst considered this arrest as more of a 'political error' demonstrates that he was more concerned with the image it would present to his colleagues in Britain and France than the issue of press freedom. In a private meeting with Minister-President Cort van der Linden, on Sunday 5 December, Van Aalst expressed his dismay. While he felt the editorials of *De Telegraaf* had 'gone far too far, in connection with the so-called smuggling', he added:[93]

> I anticipate that in France and Britain this imprisonment will be treated as a pro-German act, under pressure from Germany, further, I am almost certain, that 'De Telegraaf' will fight more strongly, I think I know our People, there must be no muzzling of free speech and above all the awkwardness on St. Nicholas Eve will bring the oversensitive public to protest.[94]

Van Aalst's fears of a strong reaction from *De Telegraaf* were accurate. In the Sunday edition of the newspaper, Holdert took the opportunity to address his readers:

> If people think that they can change the position of De Telegraaf, then let me clarify that this will not be the case. I will continue to defend that which I believe to be good and just. I clarify here that I am pro-allies and will do everything to defend the allied cause.[95]

Van Aalst's concern at the public reaction also proved to be well-founded. In the week following Schröder's arrest, *De Telegraaf* ran large daily sections containing letters in support of its editor. The majority came from Amsterdammers enraged at the perceived loss of freedom on their streets, but letters also came in from other parts of the Netherlands.[96] M. de Visser indicated that whatever one's own political, religious or personal standpoint, the arrest must be seen as an attack on free speech.[97] J. F. Niermeijer, from the University of Utrecht, expressed sympathy for Schröder's wife, sending an open letter praising Schröder's service,[98] while J. R. Heuckeroth urged that a monument be built to Schröder, that his articles should be collected into a book and published under the title 'I accuse!'[99] Twenty-five lecturers of the University of Amsterdam urged the Minister of Justice to use his influence to free Schröder.[100] To quote

Van de Vooren, *Het Volk* 'was kind enough to give the names of the professors who had *not* signed the call'.[101] Other individuals took to somewhat more creative methods of protest. Dr J. van Epen composed 'Holland, for shame!!!' in which the Netherlands is portrayed as a land bent on making money, shrouded in mist, covered in dirt and silent about the injustice around it – with the notable exception of Schröder, of course.[102] Martin Liket composed 'In whose name ... ?' dedicated to Barbarossa – the pseudonym of Schröder – questioning whether the Netherlands was being governed in the name of the Queen or the Kaiser.[103] On some occasions, French and English poems appeared and an unnamed 'Irishwomen' dedicated a poem to the imprisoned editor.

Political cartoonist Louis Raemaekers, who often published his work in *De Telegraaf*, produced a series of illustrations which demonstrated a mix of contempt for German aggression, inept Dutch government responses and showed Schröder as the preserver of freedom, liberty, neutrality and justice. On 23 December, under the title 'Free' Raemaekers drew Schroder as a lion who had been let out of his cage.[104] Perhaps the most creative, or most bizarre, response was the publication of a song on 9 December 1915, with full sheet music and lyrics, entitled 'Schröder in the Slammer'.[105] My lack of musical talent prevented me from attempting a full rendition of the five verses praising all of Schröder's virtues.

As Van Aalst feared, there was condemnation from abroad. In the French press, *Le Figaro* intimated that the arrest was unwarranted and motivated by the German embassy.[106] According to *De Telegraaf*, Dutch-based *La Gazette de Hollande* could not understand why Schröder had been arrested and reported that by Thursday 9 December, colleagues in England had published articles under the headline 'How our Friends in the Netherlands are Treated'.[107] To compound this, Van Aalst was visited on 21 December by the French ambassador who indicated his belief that Schröder's arrest was a 'political error'.[108] This was also the day on which Schröder was finally released. The days between his arrest and release saw *De Telegraaf* publish pages of letters in support of the editor, further articles about smuggling, more poems and cartoons mocking the government's handling of neutrality, all of which must have been a further challenge to the neutrality laws the arrest had tried to protect.

Upon his release, Schröder published an article about his seventeen days in prison. Just as Holdert had done, Schröder reaffirmed his determination to remain critical of the government and outlined four things his arrest had shown. First, the government had handled the Dutch traditions of free speech in a careless manner. Secondly, they had compromised themselves to the outside world. Thirdly, he recognised that he had had martyrdom thrust upon him, and promised not to misuse it. Finally, he noted:

> The Minister of Justice – and I will never forgive him for this – made my children, who had just greeted their father with joy, on St. Nicholas Eve, cry bitterly as he was treated like a criminal and taken away several moments later.
>
> But against all this, is the great, immeasurable advantage, that the true spirit, which inspires the Dutch people, could express itself in a manner which leaves no room for doubt. As you see, the scales are entirely in our favour.[109]

The Schröder affair highlights tensions within Dutch society during the First World War. While there were attempts to enforce neutrality in the press, by preventing overt criticism of the governments of the belligerents, these attempts sometimes provoked a strong reaction. There were sometimes very public acts against the neutrality laws and the government, such as those taken regularly by Schröder or Holdert, but Schröder's arrest seemed to act as a rallying call for hundreds of other individuals to send in letters of support and those critical of the government, smuggling or German aggression. For Van Aalst, the arrest provided a new and unwelcome challenge, provoking more attention and criticism of the *NOT* from the public and foreign diplomats – and creating a new set of meetings for him to attend. It demonstrated that Schröder was concerned at how his family had been treated and how his relationships had suffered. I so wanted Van Aalst to display some sense of this, but at least it also highlighted that football could still form part of my history – even when I had given up hope. Football would also come to the fore in 1917 when the streets of Amsterdam became sites for violent clashes and sporting space would be transformed once again.

Amsterdam rebels: summer 1917

Years before I had come across Van Aalst's diaries, one of the first books I read about the Netherlands was Geert Mak's *Amsterdam: A Brief Life of the City*. I always retained a fondness for this work, especially when I walked down the streets mentioned in it. Every now and then something I had read in the book would pop into my mind alongside a canal. In the hazy recollection of my own story, I remember the vibrant cover and how reading it marked the beginning of a new part of my life to which Van Aalst's diaries had become the latest addition. Now I found that elements of Van Aalst's diaries flashed into my mind as I walked through Amsterdam trying to piece together the locations, events and people he talked about. Reading Van Aalst's diaries and stories of Amsterdam made me think of one passage in Mak's work in particular:

> The First World War passed Amsterdam and Holland by. The Netherlands remained neutral, and the only thing that Amsterdam noticed was a collapse in trade, a brief panic in the banks, a stream of Belgian refugees, a handful of war profiteers, and hunger among the workers and their families.[110]

I was not so worried by the brevity of Mak's treatment of the First World War in the Netherlands. In constructing this history I had become aware of how historians have to select and ignore certain stories, sometimes ones which others find important. But as I thought about this passage and read Van Aalst's words I realised that there was at least one more story that I wanted tell: the story of the so-called *Aardappeloproer* (Potato riots). It was a story which allowed me to think about fears of revolution, hunger and panic and gave me the opportunity to place some female characters into what has been an overwhelmingly male narrative. It also gave me another chance to walk around Amsterdam and add to my own story.

> **30 June 1917**
> I told [Minister-President Cort van der Linden] that precisely a week ago, I had also had a discussion with the Queen and gave the impression that the dissatisfaction amongst the people was still rising and that I would not be surprised if, in Amsterdam at present, it leads to an outburst. The Minister said he would bear my remarks in mind.[111]

Those in the Dutch government could not say they had not been warned about the feelings in Amsterdam. Van Aalst writes at length about his meeting with the Queen at the *Huis-ten-Bosch* on 22 June. After initial pleasantries, Wilhelmina enquired about the economic situation and the living conditions of the Dutch people. Van Aalst had a stark warning:

22 June 1917
I informed the Queen, that, if the basic living needs of the People this winter are not met, I expect the greatest difficulties, yes, I would even dare talk of a revolt. Up to now everything had been passively endured; apparently people are not taking the state of affairs to heart, but I was convinced that, at some point, some occasion or another would lead to a general outburst of dissatisfaction, [and] it is also very doubtful that, in the case of internal riots, we could place much faith in the army.[112]

The Queen responded that she did not think that revolt was the way for people to deal with such matters. Politely disagreeing, Van Aalst suggested that the government had done nothing to improve the situation, despite his warnings to them, and that, in such circumstances, many felt that they had little option apart from strikes; he informed Wilhelmina that something had only been done when a group of Amsterdam women had waited to confront Cort van der Linden at his office.

Tensions about a lack of food had arisen in 1916 and become a rallying point for radical socialists. Amongst these were David Wijnkoop and Henriette Roland Holst, who had left the *SDAP* in 1909 and 1911 respectively to pursue other paths to a socialist future. In 1916, Roland Holst aligned herself with Wijnkoop's *SDP*. The two were part of the local *Revolutionair Socialistische Comité* (Revolutionary Socialist Committee, *RSC*) who, in contrast to the *SDAP*, were determined to fight against the war and its consequences. The increasing scarcity of food and a rise in prices were considered something that could be used to provoke unrest amongst the proletariat and in Amsterdam the *Plaatselijk Arbeidssecretariaat* (Local Labour Secretariat, *PAS*) became a site for protest. Hendrika van Zelm also became involved in the move for change and especially for the rights of women. In 1916, she led a number of women to the Amsterdam city hall to complain about conditions; later she would go to The Hague to complain to Cort van der Linden.[113]

The year 1916 saw a number of demonstrations and fellow *RSC* associate Cornelis Kitsz was also heavily involved in organising protests. During the 1916 demonstrations, he had addressed a group of Amsterdam women at the Haarlemmerpoort. The protests of mid-1916 had clearly worried the Municipality, which quickly imposed a ban on demonstrations in the city. The *RSC*, presided over by Wijnkoop, decided to abide by the prohibition and in a speech held at the *AIJC*, Kitsz backed this stance.[114] By 1917, material conditions had not improved. Coal was scarce and many buildings went without heating; Amsterdam's municipal archive and its museums were entirely closed, schools shut at midday and shops were forced to shut early. In February, a central kitchen was opened to deal with the paucity of food; however, small riots occurred between February and May and potatoes had become a symbol for wider scarcity.[115] The rumblings of discontent erupted in June.

On the morning of 28 June, many women from poorer areas in Amsterdam went in search of potatoes for the day's lunch. By 9 o'clock, it became clear that there were no potatoes, either old or new, to be found. In the Jordaan, to the west of the centre, hundreds of women with bags focused their search on warehouses on the Brouwersgracht, for any sign of a consignment of potatoes; they had no luck. To the south, on the Prinsengracht, a barge containing 200 sacks of potatoes destined for soldiers was found. Shouts rang out from around the barge alerting people in the surrounding area of the discovery and within ten minutes, women from the Jordaan had arrived and stripped the barge of its contents. By midday, Amsterdam police had stationed officers along the Westerstraat, running through the heart of the Jordaan in an attempt to calm the situation.[116] The desperate need for food was noted in the *Algemeen Handelsblad,* which provided reportage of the disturbances throughout the week. They noted that on the morning of the 28 July around 2,500 to 3,000 bags of potatoes had been delivered to the market, but that 'the need in Amsterdam is around 6[,000] to 7,500 [...] Let us hope that tomorrow the delivery is much higher'.[117] The following day the newspaper noted that 'calm has returned again', adding that people seemed content with the news that more food would arrive the next day.[118]

But, by 3 July, the situation had not improved. An organised protest had been arranged against the lack of potatoes, which commenced with a few thousand women on the Dam square the day before. Flanked by a small number of police, the protest marched past the city hall, onto the Spui and then crossed the Singel onto the Leidschestraat. Suddenly, as the police expected the procession to turn left, it headed right onto the Herengracht. As the procession reached the Herengracht, a number of female gold workers shouted abuse at those in the procession below. As a reprisal, some in the line broke from the march to destroy a mirror at the front of the gold shop of *Hoeker & Zoon*.[119]

Those who remained in the procession continued, first past the offices of *Het Volk* on the Keizersgracht, then to the Rozengracht and to the site of the *Groentemarkt* (vegetable market) on the Marnixstraat. The procession stormed the *Groentemarkt* and hundreds of women broke into the *Visser* vegetable warehouse, leaving it with assorted vegetables. The rumour spread that the police on the Marnixstraat could not contain the disturbance and that many individuals who had left towards the Elandsgracht and Nassaukade returned towards the Marnixstraat. Outside the warehouses of the *Groentemarkt,* the police attempted to hold back the protests with mounted and unmounted officers, firing blanks into the air; from the protesters' side, a handcart was hurled towards the police. Upon hearing the shots, many of those on the Nassaukade hurried towards the disturbance where rumours of women being arrested had spread, causing much consternation. Wijnkoop and Cornelis Kitsz's wife Wimpje, who had been leading the group, attempted to quell the anger of the crowd by insisting that no women had been detained and that the mayor had promised a return of potatoes; the pair urged the women to persuade their husbands to follow the example of those who worked at the *Holland Lloyd* shipping company, and had gone temporarily on strike.[120] Later in the week Wijnkoop and Cornelis Kitsz would call for a general strike in the city – this strike would see between 15,000 to 20,000 workers head to the picket lines.[121] On 5 July *De Tribune*, the *SDP* newspaper, noted that the strikes, which were directed at the 'blood and hunger regime' of Posthuma (Agriculture, Industry and Trade Minister) and Wibaut (Amsterdam's senior *SDAP* politician), had stopped all engineering earthworks in the city, as well as a number of munitions factories.[122]

Back at the *Groentemarkt* on the 3 July, young men who had joined the procession began to move towards the police, who again fired revolvers in the air. On the Elandsgracht, a crowd rushed towards the *Meermarkt* market where there was news of food. In the rush, a woman fell in the water clutching a cauliflower; she was rescued still clutching the cauliflower and removed to safety on a cart – a poignant and slightly absurd representation of the desperation in the city. All around the southern Jordaan, warehouses were fiercely guarded. By the evening, arguments had emerged in the area around the market. Inspector Lemkes requested the closure of the entrances to the *Meermarkt,* on the Elandsgracht, Kinkerstraat and Rozengracht, as a small group of young men began a confrontation with the police. For the rest of the evening, gunfire could be heard in the air as the police charged rioters. Finally, at midnight, the area returned to an uneasy calm with only occasional gunfire.[123]

Other parts of the city saw sporadic outbursts of violence. On the eastern docks, another group of women emerged as potatoes were being loaded on-board ships to England. The sight of potatoes being exported amidst the crisis provoked hundreds of women from the Kattenburg and Czaar Peterstraat neighbourhoods to storm one of the ships. The goods were stripped within thirty minutes and a second ship was only prevented from being ransacked by harbour police.[124]

The eastern islands remained the scene of violence for the rest of the evening as crowds of people and police clashed with a hail of stones and gunfire. On Czaar Peterstraat, a young man was dragged away covered in blood and other wounded men were taken to the café on the corner of the Blankenstraat. Four others were injured, as was a policeman. The army, who had been ordered onto the streets of Amsterdam to contain further violence, became involved in the area around Czaar Peterstraat. While some soldiers refused to shoot at the crowd, others fired as the crowd rushed. Early next morning, at 2 o'clock, it emerged that a man had been killed on the Hoogte Kadijk and a number of young men were in hospital seriously wounded. Two police officers had also been taken to hospital.[125]

On 2 July, Van Aalst was in meetings with evidently rattled government ministers and Amsterdam's business community. The protests had not gone unnoticed. Van Aalst expressed concern that potato and cattle exports had not stopped. In a special minister's meeting, the intended sale of 600,000 cattle to Germany was noted and the Minister of Finance stated that: 'if these cattle are exported [...] it would lead to a revolution in our country'.[126] Revolution had been a concern for the government since the civil disturbances in Russia in March 1917 and *De Tribune*'s 4 July front page, which included a translation of the Russian Bolsheviks' call to soldiers on the Russo-German front, cannot have eased fears.[127] Amongst the government, there were suggestions that the capital would need to be formally placed under a 'state of siege'. In his diary entry, Van Aalst reiterated his anger at the government's lack of decision-making and Minister-President Cort van der Linden's plan:

> **3 July 1917**
> [Finance Minister Treub] was totally in agreement with me, that the Government would only aggravate the situation in Amsterdam if, as Mr Cort van der Linden seems minded to do, Amsterdam were placed under a state of siege.[128]

Later in the day, he met with the Minister-President:

> Finally, I dissuaded Mr Cort [van der Linden] most strongly about placing Amsterdam under a state of siege, and informed him that one should bear in mind [the fact] that Amsterdam occupies a special place in the country and it would be difficult to subdue by military means.[129]

Those individuals in the initial protests had, perhaps unknowingly, won a number of concessions as it was agreed that Amsterdam would receive an increased number of potatoes every day. Van Aalst noted that the government had acted too slowly and that the decision was similar to the demand that a group of women had made a few months before.[130] Perhaps they should have been listened to.

In the days following the outbursts, Amsterdam saw more disturbances – not a unified action, or a revolution, but a number of sporadic individual acts. As the Bijenkorf shop advertised its summer sale on 4 July, the *Algemeen Handelsblad* reported the continued strike of boat workers in the western docks. Isolated incidents of small groups plundering local food warehouses also surfaced. In the Kattenburg, a group of women with kitchen knives stole a meat wagon, while a separate incident in the Korte Kerkstraat, south of the centre, saw the plundering of a chicken warehouse in spite of the attempts of the workers there to prevent it. Elsewhere in Kattenburg, a number of children emptied a warehouse of sugar and chocolate and others caused disturbances with the police in which fifteen people were injured. Shoe shops too were attacked, indicating that the issue was not purely about food, but one of a lack of goods in general and a worsening of many individual conditions. Around the *Groentemarkt*, a cigar shop was raided and the police response resulted in the death of four individuals.[131]

The following day more plundering occurred, as well as a wider strike. A further group emerged in the north of the Jordaan causing a disturbance at a public house, yet this time it was not a local group but one from Kattenburg, of whom some in the Jordaan appeared contemptuous. This group moved from the Jordaan to the centre of the city and raided another shoe shop.[132]

The *RSC* saw the strikes, revolts and looting as a reason to call a general meeting of workers. Not being given any space in the Municipality of Amsterdam, they chose the site of a 'spacious football pitch', thirty minutes from the centre, on the Kruislaan in the Watergraafsmeer.[133] While the various reports in the media outlets gave information on the speeches, the thousands in attendance and the declaration of a twenty-four-hour protest strike, they did not mention what I really wanted – the name of the football club, or the football pitch used. There are some references to 'De Meer', which was a name used for the Ajax pitches, but I cannot be sure if it refers to Ajax's home or is simply an affectionate term for the wider area.[134] Nevertheless, given that clubs had to pay rent for land, and with this gained a degree of control over it, it seems unlikely that the gathering of a large group – estimated at many thousands – occurred on a ground without the express consent of the club concerned, or the

Watergraafsmeer Municipality, possibly for financial remuneration. On the ground of the *AIJC*, which had previously been used for events as diverse as cricket, equestrianism and revolutionary speeches, army tents were erected during the week of the disturbances.[135] In growing, industrialising and crowded cities, space was becoming a valuable commodity. As open spaces became less numerous, those that existed became increasingly important in the daily life of the city in a variety of sometimes seemingly contradictory ways.

Frustratingly, and sadly, Van Aalst made no entries to his diary between 5 and 30 July 1917. By this point, the revolts are no longer mentioned – there would be no great quote to close my history on this matter either. On 6 July the old liberal politician Beaufort noted that calm had returned to Amsterdam and that the strikes had failed; revolution had been averted.[136] At least for now. In total, *Het Volk* reported on 6 July, eight people had died in the disturbances over the week – other sources put the total at ten deaths and 113 wounded.[137]

Fig 5.2 Today's Museumplein to the rear of the *Rijksmuseum* is still used as a recreational space, as it was when it formed the grounds of the *AIJC*, Amsterdam, 2016

Each one of these deaths had a story, although not all were reported. These deaths were not always directly connected to the quest for revolutionary socialism or obtaining food. One death struck me more than others; it seemed particularly tragic and pointless, seeming to fit in with my own sense of the absurdity of everyday life, one which does not always emerge in historical narrative. On 5 July, a week before her wedding day, seventeen-year-old Hendrika Sturm was in her father's house when a stray bullet entered through the window on the Brouwersgracht and struck her in the stomach. She was taken to the hospital with a severe wound, but was pronounced dead shortly afterwards. The same bullet wounded her fiancé.[138] It appears Sturm was not connected to the revolts, but was an unintended, accidental victim of a stray shot. While her story may be difficult to place in narratives which focus on the action of perceived groups, classes or actions, there must be place in history to represent such absurdities, things which do not fit with a wider narrative and for the historian to create their own narrative to ensure that they are represented.

This vignette represents how different individuals were involved in attempts to provoke revolution, to deal with the threat of it or simply to carry on their daily lives. Van Aalst's diary suggests that there were tensions in the government about how best to deal with the situation, that they feared a wider rebellion and that, at times, the government was not able to cope with such tensions. The vignette helps provide a representation of how hunger became an increasing problem in Amsterdam, how it could be linked to wider social issues and how the First World War did not pass the Netherlands by. It also demonstrates how sporting spaces could have different roles within the life of the city; as a regulated, demarcated and ordered space, it could be used by many different organisations for a range of different events – from revolution to state policing. The story highlights the painful absurdity of everyday life and how there must be room for historians to create their own personal narratives to incorporate previously ignored elements. It also shows that sport can be found in many histories that appear to have nothing to do with it.

New openings

This history has shown that form is essential in the production of historical content. How a history is designed, structured and written is not extraneous to the historical process, but is its silenced other. Naturally, information about the past is important; without Van Aalst's diaries, this history would have been profoundly different. Perhaps, if I had chosen the diaries of Ernst Heldring, I would have got my stories of sport after all. But there were many other things which profoundly influenced the production of this history: the form I intended it to take; my own limitations of language, patience and interest; limitations of time, space or access; my emotional reaction to Van Aalst's words and the memories I have of these interactions.

Just as important in the choice of vignettes were present concerns. When my initial aims of providing a history of sport in everyday life appeared to be impossible, I had to choose new stories to tell, for reasons of balance in the book and because of contemporary considerations of the past (I write this in the middle of the four-year long centenary commemorations of the First World War). Each of these aspects was influenced by personal and present concerns. Stories of sport demonstrated that even those people central to the organisation of clubs and stadia were not necessarily passionate about the game itself; for them, organisation was the game. Stories of trade allowed me to represent one of Van Aalst's key concerns, but also to provide a story of those who looked to break the rules in absurd or innovative ways. The stories of Belgian refugees were influenced by events in late 2015, which saw many new individuals make similar traumatic and difficult journeys and led to me to wonder if De Rooy's comment relating to Amsterdam in 1914, that 'pity usually only has a limited shelf life', is still the case?[139] The arrest of Schröder was not only a story of press freedom, but also a story of a sportsman (and, like me, a wicket-keeping batsman). And stories of disturbances in the summer of 1917 allowed me to present other voices which had been ignored, to represent the absurdity of everyday life, but also to demonstrate that sporting space was able to transform its purpose depending on the needs of those around it.

In each case, I wanted to represent histories, which were new to me, which I found interesting, which I thought could say something about the present and which demonstrated the fluidity of the process of history and my own place within it. I also wanted to highlight that the process of writing history is not a simple one, which when we go to the archive presents itself to us and emerges on the page without transformation. History is intimately connected to the personal memory and emotions of the author. While researching these vignettes, I spent a great deal of time walking around the streets of Amsterdam reflecting on what I had read and on my own story. Many of these thoughts do not appear in this history.

One of the great problems of history in its present form is its reliance on the printed word, not only because it masks the fluidity of language and the creative input of the reader, but because, all too often, it presents the process of history without the difficulties and the effort of construction and the impact research has on the historian. Again, all too often, the printed word presents a story as though it is a final and fixed idea, when, in truth, during the process of writing the historian has ignored or excluded elements; changed path, opinion or objective; and has moved on again once the task is complete. The tyranny of the printed word masks the fact that history is always in flux, always fluid and never complete. It is time to embrace this.

Finally, I must return to Van Aalst's diaries. I still cannot quite understand what his purpose was in writing them, or what they told me about him or that period in Amsterdam. Did I miss something because I wanted typed diaries instead of handwritten ones? Did typing the diaries after their writing change something? Had the printed word yet again given a false impression of a fluid and complicated source? Or was it just something to do with me? Sadly, as with many of the questions in these histories, I do not have answers. But having had time to reconsider, my genuine and prolonged frustration and annoyance with Van Aalst – or rather with his choice of subject and manner of writing – has subsided.

These diaries, while problematic, gave me the opportunity to represent different stories and different individuals, and to think about myself and the world around me in new ways. What then is the purpose of using diaries in historical research? It is certainly not that they give us magical access to the past; they are prone to the same problems as other forms of writing and perspective. But surely, their greatest purpose is the same as that of history itself: to provoke new ways of thought, new questions and to encourage new representations about ourselves and the world around us. For allowing me to do this and for giving me new openings, I feel the need to say a belated, and somewhat pointless 'thank you' to Cornelis. I only hope that my own writing can do the same for someone else.

6

Conclusion

London, The Hague and Amsterdam, 2016

I returned to the Netherlands in January 2016 to carry out some final checks on what I had written in these histories, to take photos and, for one last time in connection with this work, to visit the *KB* and the *NA* which were such an important part of my research. The windy passage between the station and the building has changed; it no longer seems so windy, perhaps due to the new taller buildings, or my own state of mind. As I walked into the familiar locker rooms of the *KB* and towards the media room, where I spent weeks finding and printing old Dutch newspapers and where I learnt how to use a microfiche machine without getting my fingers trapped in the mechanism, a new sense of trepidation hit me. It was not the excitement or nervousness of conducting research, of trying to find sources and useful examples, but of finally having to publish; to let other people in on the private mental processes which led me to write this book; to allow other people to see my ideas, some more complete and solid than others; and to open myself up to questions and criticism. As I have said throughout, history is a proposal, and while we cannot say whether a proposal is true or false, we can certainly point out where it is lacking or misguided. I am left with a double feeling: relief and excitement at having finished, and a sense of trepidation and nervousness about what happens next.

In these histories, I wanted to give different representations of how football was important in early twentieth-century Dutch society and to provoke thoughts about the role of football today. Just what were the discourses that operated and how can representing them help us think about the world around us? While I find conclusions or endings problematic, I would like to provide one final personal account of these histories.

The period between 1910 and 1920 saw some important developments in Dutch football. In this time, the game continued its popularisation and its move from being a game for 'well-to-do' boys in the west of the Netherlands towards a game in which a greater part of the population took part. Naturally, there were numerous diversions from this narrative, as those who opposed the game still found reason to worry at its development and those who liked the older form of the game worried that its nature may have been changing too much. However, during this period, football became an increasingly important part of life in the Netherlands, spreading certain discourses of values more widely and deeply within Dutch society. That football was increasingly important and increasingly accepted is demonstrated by the development of large multi-purpose sporting stadia in Dutch cities. Without the support of politicians and especially wealthy citizens (although in many cases these two groups were not mutually exclusive), or without an increasing recognition of the educative possibilities of football, these developments could not have happened. The greatest change between 1910 and 1920 was the wider acceptance of organised football as a positive force in the Netherlands and the rapid construction of stadia in cities where more pressing needs of housing and expansion often took decades to materialise. This indicates that football, and sport in general, was able to mobilise capital, power and people more efficiently and quickly than other aspects of urban planning.

And this was because football was part of wider discourses within society. For those in the *NVB*, and many investors outside of it, football was not purely a game separate from society but was an integral part of the wider drive to educate the young and construct a 'better' society. As with other cultural products, and organised activities, football was able to reproduce discourses of discipline in society; from the design of stadia to the organisation of leagues and matches, football brought order, ranking and segregation into the city and into the daily life of thousands of individuals. Through new functional stadia, football ensured that individuals embodied the concepts of discipline in how they moved in the city and in the sporting space. Through the imposition of timetables, training, exams and norms, football spread the idea of observation and relentless scrutiny. By the end of the 1910s the emergence of many new sporting spaces firmly constructed into the urban landscape meant that new theatres of observation had been established; the football stadium became not a panopticon, where a faceless individual could watch and monitor, but a space where everyone was being watched and monitored at all times.

And they were being evaluated against the sportsman, be it playing, officiating, administrating or spectating. The sportsman was an idea reproduced in the media which allowed a permanent evaluation of the individual against the ideal. It ranked, differentiated and allowed the individual to be recognised within the team, all while making the body more efficient and more useful. The period between 1910 and 1920 in Dutch football can be seen as one where functionality became central to the game: the functionality of football in society, of space in the stadium and of the individual in the team. This functionality was intended to reproduce efficient, respectful and docile citizens who would work hard; play fairly; value teamwork, honesty and respect for authority; and who would take these aspects from school to work to the playing fields. No area of modern life was without these disciplinary aspects. Football was vital because it gave the impression of freedom from work or school, while at the same time reproducing their discourses further and deeper within the body of the individual.

As I have made clear, these histories have agendas in mind. While I love sport, and I will continue to play it, I am deeply sceptical of the way it acts as a way to reproduce the discourses outlined above. I believe that such discourses only help reproduce power structures which favour state-organised institutions and which value the discourses of efficiency, utility and docility over freedom, creativity and cooperation. As I hope I have shown, sport is not, and never was, separate from daily life – even of those who had no interest in it. It plays an integral part in shaping the spaces around us, the ideas we have and the very way we move our body. Because of its popularity and its ability to command passionate loyalty and provoke feelings of gratification, sport is one of the most powerful ways of reproducing disciplinary discourses that exist in society; sport, politics and society do not need to 'mix', for they were already part of each other from the start. I hope that with these histories I can help others think about how sport reproduces such discourses in society and that someone will be able to suggest a way to change them; I fear they are too embodied within me for my own answers to be useful.

And these histories are also about a new possibility for history. Postmodernist ideas have shown that History (deliberately capitalised) can no longer survive as a discipline which believes it can describe the past or act as a form of empirical knowledge. I hope that these histories have highlighted the aspects of history which occur in the mind of the historian. But this is not to say history is of no use. Far from it. I believe, as I hope I have shown, that history can be a truly democratic enterprise – one which encourages every voice to be heard, however distasteful, obscure or quiet. I am sceptical of politics' ability to provide answers to the important questions of our time and I am sceptical of the idea that powerful organisations truly permit the individual to be heard. And, as is clear, I am sceptical of the ability of organised, 'professional' History, which resides in and is practised by those in institutions, to do this either. It is my belief that professional History is too enmeshed within organisational structures, with their own discourses, to be able to answer, or even ask many important questions.

The power of History, in which the professional historian is given authority to create perceptions of the past which can shape identities, ideologies and the world around us, as noted by Southgate, is something that must be challenged. However, history, the practice of thinking and creating stories about the past, does not belong to just professional historians, but it is something which we all do on a daily basis. With these histories, I hope I have shown that history can encourage creativity, can be about opening new debates and promoting a multiplicity of voices. There are many different ways to think about the past and there are an infinite number of stories to tell. Every history that is constructed is dependent on personal perspectives, concepts and ideas; they rely on present-day attitudes and on the views of the people who consume it. This makes it impossible to provide definitive accounts of the past, but it can provide new and creative proposals of how we can view the present.

History in the twenty-first century must be about inclusion, about encouraging everybody to take part in telling stories, about finding new ways to empower those previously without a voice and about finding ways to think about the value of such stories without criticising them for not having credited a reference properly or falling foul of the constructed power mechanisms of professional History. We must recognise that when we discuss proposals about the past, we are, in reality, discussing moral perspectives on the present. We should not reject any proposal because it does not fit with established methods, but only because it proposes a view of the world we disagree with.

History today must primarily be about the mix of personal creativity, imagination and perspectives, about trying to find new ways to represent the problems we face in the world around us or even ourselves. Surely, this has to be the primary task of all forms of knowledge. To fulfil this there must be more opportunities for every individual to produce histories in new and innovative ways which do not rely on books, articles or access to the media. History must become an experimental kitchen and one with an open door. Sometimes experiments do not work, but that does not mean we should not try. Nor does it mean that we should shy away from experiments that might not succeed. I have tried not to in this book. In this way, history will not only be relevant but essential to our everyday life.

I find it difficult to think of a way to end this work – one which is about encouraging new beginnings – without seemingly ending the discussion and turning the reader away, but I think it is time I stop and let someone else speak for a while.

These have been my histories, my proposals.

What do you think?

Notes

Chapter 1

1 Others, including Boban, Savićević, Baresi, Maldini, Costacurta, Albertini, Lentini, Donadoni and Papin all deserved to be mentioned too.

2 To avoid this work becoming almost a parody of postmodern works for its use of inverted commas, I will restrict my usage of them to the first appearance of a term, or where I believe that their exclusion will make my own meaning, or those of others, ambiguous.

3 For the sake of simplicity I will use 'postmodern' throughout this work to describe my own ideas and those which have been broadly linked to ideas of postmodernity.

4 Charles Jencks, 'What Then Is Post-Modernism?', in *The Post-Modern Reader*, ed. Charles Jencks (Chichester: Wiley, 2011), pp. 14–37, 20–1. Bowen Raddeker notes her own personal relationship with the rise of the postmodern in the 1980s and its popularisation in the field of academic history in Australia at this time in Hélène Bowen Raddeker, *Sceptical History: Feminist and Postmodern Approaches in Practice* (London: Routledge, 2007), pp. 2–3.

5 Bowen Raddeker, *Sceptical History*, pp. 6–7. Hayden White notes that discussions about the nature of history can be traced back to arguments between Kant and Herder in the eighteenth century. Hayden White, 'The Discourse of History', in Hayden White, *The Fiction of Narrative: Essays on History, Literature, and Theory, 1957–2007* (Baltimore, MD: Johns Hopkins University Press, 2010), pp. 187–202, 187.

6 Simon Malpas, *The Postmodern* (Abingdon: Routledge, 2005), pp. 5–6.

7 Jencks, 'What Then Is Post-Modernism?', p. 14.

8 Jencks, 'What Then Is Post-Modernism?', p. 16.

9 Malpas, *The Postmodern*, pp. 6–7.

10 Malpas, *The Postmodern*, p. 7.

11 Steven Best and Douglas Kellner, *Postmodern Theory: Critical Interrogations* (New York: Guilford Press, 1991), p. 2.

12 Jencks, 'What Then Is Post-Modernism?', p. 15.

13 Jencks, 'What Then Is Post-Modernism?', p. 35.

14 Malpas, *The Postmodern*, p. 6.

15 Bowen Raddeker, *Sceptical History*, p. 2.

16 Bowen Raddeker, *Sceptical History*, p. 2.

17 Jean-François Lyotard, *The Postmodern as Explained to Children, Correspondence 1982–1985* (London: Turnaround Press, 1992), pp. 24–25, and p. 30.

18 Keith Jenkins, *Why History?: Ethics and Postmodernity* (London: Routledge, 1999), p. 1.

19 Jean-François Lyotard, *The Postmodern Condition: A Report on Knowledge* (Manchester: Manchester University Press, 1984), p. xxiv.

20 Jenkins, *Why History?*, p. 1.

21 Bowen Raddeker, *Sceptical History*, p. 2.

22 One example of the debate within history in the 1990s was the Evans–Jenkins debate, which took on an increasingly personal and vicious tone. That I have not engaged with this debate, or the wider debate between historians, is partly because I believe the antagonistic, hyperbolic sometimes personal nature of the historiographical debate is unhelpful to history in general and also to the effort to outline my own approach. See Richard Evans, *In Defence of History*, (London: Granta, 2000) and Jenkins, *Why History?*

23 Malpas, *The Postmodern*, p. 4.

24 Beverley Southgate, *History Meets Fiction* (Harlow: Pearson Education, 2009), p. 194.
25 Alun Munslow, *Narrative and History* (Basingstoke: Palgrave Macmillan, 2007), p. 9.
26 Frank Ankersmit, *Historical Representation* (Stanford: Stanford University Press, 2001), pp. 80–1.
27 Ankersmit, *Historical Representation*, p. 54.
28 Jenkins, *Why History?*, pp. 134–143.
29 Jenkins, *Why History?*, p. 139.
30 Ankersmit, *Historical Representation*, pp. 40–41.
31 Ankersmit, *Historical Representation*, pp. 54–5.
32 Ankersmit, *Historical Representation*, p. 89.
33 Ankersmit, *Historical Representation*, p. 57.
34 Ankersmit, *Historical Representation*, p. 89.
35 Ankersmit, *Historical Representation*, pp. 92–3.
36 Ankersmit notes that representation has rules, criteria, or standards for scale, coherence and consistency which are not there in the represented. Ankersmit, *Historical Representation*, p. 44.
37 Frank Ankersmit, 'Historiography and Postmodernism', *History and Theory*, Vol. 28, No. 2 (May, 1989), pp. 137–53, 152.
38 One of these constructions is the period I have chosen to study. Ankersmit, de Certeau and Jenkins all indicate that 'periods' or 'movements' are constructed by historians in different ways, and this is one problem when attempting to link historical representations to the past.
39 Munslow, *Narrative and History*, p. 5.
40 Ankersmit, *Historical Representation*, p. 16.
41 A discussion on theoretical perspective on archives and their role is available in Marlene Manoff, 'Theories of the Archive from Across the Disciplines', *Portal: Libraries and the Academy*, Vol. 4, No. 1 (January, 2004), pp. 9–25.
42 Michel Foucault, *The Archaeology of Knowledge* (London: Routledge, 2002), p. 145.
43 Manoff, 'Theories of the Archive', pp. 10–13.
44 Manoff, 'Theories of the Archive', p. 14.
45 Michel de Certeau, *The Writing of History* (New York: Columbia University Press, 1988), p. 66.
46 De Certeau, *The Writing of History*, p. 72.
47 Manoff notes this: 'Whatever the archive contains is already a reconstruction – a recording of history from a particular perspective; it thus cannot provide transparent access to the events themselves.' Manoff, 'Theories of the Archive', p. 14.
48 Manoff, 'Theories of the Archive', p. 15.
49 Ben Highmore, *Michel de Certeau: Analysing Culture* (London: Continuum, 2006), p. 88.
50 De Certeau, quoted in Highmore, *Michel de Certeau*, p. 88.
51 Highmore, *Michel de Certeau*, p. 86.
52 Bowen Raddeker, *Sceptical History*, p. 19.
53 Bowen Raddeker, *Sceptical History*, pp. 19–20.
54 Munslow, *Narrative and History*, p. 87.
55 Munslow, *Narrative and History*, p. 88.
56 Munslow, *Narrative and History*, p. 87.
57 R. Barthes, 'The Reality Effect', in R. Barthes, *The Rustle of Language* (Berkeley and Los Angeles, CA: University of California Press, 1989), pp. 141–8.
58 Munslow, *Narrative and History*, p. 88.
59 Roland Barthes, 'The Discourse of History', in R. Barthes, *The Rustle of Language* (Berkeley and Los Angeles, CA: University of California Press, 1989), pp. 127–40, 138.
60 Barthes, 'The Discourse of History', p. 138.
61 Frank Ankersmit, *The Reality Effect in the Writing of History; The Dynamics of Historiographical Topology* (Amsterdam: Koninklijke Nederlandse Akademie van Wetenschappen, 1989), pp. 35–7.
62 Barthes, 'The Discourse of History', p. 140.
63 R. Barthes, 'The Death of the Author', in R. Barthes, *The Rustle of Language* (Berkeley and Los Angeles, CA: University of California Press, 1989), pp. 49–55, 53.
64 Barthes, 'The Death of the Author', pp. 53–54.
65 Munslow, *Narrative and History*, p. 88.
66 Bowen Raddeker, *Sceptical History*, pp. 19–22.
67 Ankersmit, 'Historiography and Postmodernism', p. 144.
68 Barthes, 'The Discourse of History', pp. 138–9.
69 Munslow, *Narrative and History*, p. 138.

70 Jenkins, *Why History?*, pp. 116–17.
71 Hayden White, 'Interpretation in History', *New Literary History*, Vol. 4, No. 2 (1973), pp. 281–314, 294.
72 Hayden White, 'The Question of Narrative in Contemporary Historical Theory', *History and Theory*, Vol. 23, No. 1 (February 1984), pp. 1–33, 20.
73 White, 'The Question of Narrative', p. 20.
74 Jenkins, *Why History?*, p. 120.
75 Ankersmit, *Historical Representation*, p. 29.
76 Munslow, *Narrative and History*, pp. 6, 134.
77 Ankersmit, *Historical Representation*, pp. 71–4.
78 Ankersmit, *Historical Representation*, pp. 71–4.
79 De Certeau, *The Writing of History*, p. 65.
80 De Certeau, *The Writing of History*, pp. 57–8.
81 De Certeau, *The Writing of History*, p. 58.
82 De Certeau, *The Writing of History*, p. 57.
83 De Certeau, *The Writing of History*, p. 64.
84 De Certeau, *The Writing of History*, pp. 65–6.
85 De Certeau, *The Writing of History*, p. 68.
86 Michel Foucault, *Discipline and Punish: The Birth of the Prison* (London: Penguin, 1991), p. 27.
87 Foucault, *Discipline and Punish*, p. 31. See also, Anne Schwan and Stephen Shapiro, *How to Read Foucault's Discipline and Punish* (London: Pluto Press, 2011), p. 48.
88 Munslow, *Narrative and History*, pp. 64–5.
89 Munslow, *Narrative and History*, Ch. 4: 'History as Expression', pp. 64–79.
90 Ankersmit, *Historical Representation*, p. 100.
91 Ankersmit, *Historical Representation*, Ch. 2: 'In Praise of Subjectivity', pp. 75–103.
92 Jenkins, *Why History?*, p. 1.
93 Geoffrey Roberts quoted in Jenkins, *Why History?*, p. 110.
94 Munslow, *Narrative and History*, p. 61.
95 Ankersmit, *Historical Representation*, p. 76.
96 Ankersmit, *Historical Representation*, p. 76.
97 Linda Gordon quoted in Douglas Booth, *The Field: Truth and Fiction in Sport History* (Abingdon: Routledge, 2005), pp. 219–20.
98 Ankersmit, *Historical Representation*, p. 99.
99 Ankersmit, *Historical Representation*, pp. 96–8.
100 In *Why History?*, Keith Jenkins suggests that he now questions his formerly positive view of the purpose of history and suggests that perhaps we do not need to keep referring to the past in order to build new futures – this is taken up elsewhere in this work. Jenkins, *Why History?*, pp. 4–7.
101 Foucault, *The Archaeology of Knowledge*, p. 120.
102 Callum Brown, *Postmodernism for Historians* (Harlow: Pearson Education, 2005), pp. 59–65.
103 Brown, *Postmodernism for Historians*, p. 60.
104 Brown, *Postmodernism for Historians*, pp. 59–62.
105 Brown, *Postmodernism for Historians*, pp. 63–64..
106 Brown, *Postmodernism for Historians*, p. 64.
107 Brown, *Postmodernism for Historians*, p. 64; and Foucault, *Discipline and Punish*.
108 Foucault, *Discipline and Punish*, Ch. 3: 'Docile Bodies', pp. 135–69.
109 Michel Foucault, 'Two Lectures', in Michel Foucault, *Power/Knowledge: Selected Interviews and Other Writings 1972–1977* (New York: Pantheon Books, 1980), pp. 78–109, 98.
110 Chris Shilling, *The Body and Social Theory* (London; Thousand Oaks, CA; New Delhi: Sage, 2003), p. 66.
111 Booth, *The Field*, p. 195.
112 Tony Schirato, *Sports Discourse* (London: Bloomsbury Academic, 2013), p. 10.
113 Pierre Bourdieu, 'From Rules to Strategies', in Pierre Bourdieu, *In Other Words: Essays Towards a Reflexive Sociology* (Cambridge: Polity Press, 1990), pp. 59–75, 61–3.
114 C. L. Stevenson, 'Sport as a Contemporary Social Phenomenon: A Functional Explanation', *International Journal of Physical Education*, Vol. 11, No. 3 (1974), pp. 8–14, 8.
115 David Rowe, 'Introduction: Mapping the Media Sports Cultural Complex', in *Critical Readings: Sport, Culture and the Media*, ed. David Rowe (Buckingham: Open University Press, 2004), pp. 1–22, 5–9 and Eric Dunning, Sport Matters: Sociological Studies of Sport, Violence and Civilisation, (London: Routledge, 2001), p. 1.

116 David Winner, *Brilliant Orange: The Neurotic Genius of Dutch Football* (London: Bloomsbury, 2000); and Simon Kuper, *Ajax, the Dutch, the War: Football in Europe during the Second World War* (London: Orion, 2003).

117 Such as those on German football by Ulrich Hesse-Lichtenberger, *Tor!: The Story of German Football* (London: WSC Books, 2002); on FC Barcelona by Jimmy Burns, *Barça: A People's Passion* (London: Bloomsbury, 1999); and Italian football by John Foot, *Calcio: A History of Italian Football* (London: Harper Perennial, 2007).

118 Postmodernism in sport has focused on placing the ignored in history and providing an often deliberately provocative output, designed to break down traditional identity structures. Rail highlights that concepts of race, gender, class and nationality have been fertile areas of study, and so too have deconstructing the language-games within sporting discourses. Caudwell has deconstructed the relationship between concepts of female behaviour, gender and sexuality, indicating that it is fluid and dependent on context; the notion of 'women' as a defined group is, therefore, questionable and part of a privileged narrative. More on postmodern contributions can be found in Genevieve Rail's excellent summary in 'Postmodernism and Sport Studies', in *Theory, Sport & Society*, ed. J. Maguire and J. Young (Bingley: Emerald, 2002), pp. 179–207; J. Caudwell's work can be found in J. Caudwell, 'Women's Football in the United Kingdom: Theorizing Gender and Unpacking the Butch Lesbian Image', *Journal of Sport and Social Issues*, Vol 23, No. 4 (1999), 390–402.

119 Booth, *The Field*, p. 210.

120 Booth, *The Field*, p. 75.

121 Booth, *The Field*, p. 76.

122 Booth, *The Field*, p. 76.

123 Booth, *The Field*, p. 80.

124 Booth, *The Field*, p. 80.

125 Booth, *The Field*, p. 177.

126 Eindhoven is currently the only other Dutch city with more than one professional club – FC Eindhoven and PSV Eindhoven.

127 Jan Buursink, 'The Cultural Strategy of Rotterdam', *Cybergeo: European Journal of Geography*, Colloque Les Problèmes culturels des grandes villes, 8–11 December 1997, article 115, accessed online at http://cybergeo.revues.org/1203; and A. Harding 'Amsterdam and Rotterdam', in *European Cities towards 2000: profiles, policies and prospects*, ed. A. Harding et al. (Manchester: Manchester University Press, 1994), pp. 18–44.

128 Annet Tiessen-Raaphorst (ed.), *Rapportage sport 2014* (The Hague: Sociaal en Cultureel Planbureau, 2015), p. 11.

129 Tiessen-Raaphorst (ed.), *Rapportage sport 2014*, p. 128.

130 Tiessen-Raaphorst (ed.), *Rapportage sport 2014*, pp. 104–5.

131 Tiessen-Raaphorst (ed.), *Rapportage sport 2014*, pp. 89–90.

132 Tiessen-Raaphorst (ed.), *Rapportage sport 2014*, p. 163.

133 Mark Poster, *Cultural History and Postmodernity: Disciplinary Readings and Challenges* (New York: Columbia University Press, 1997), p. 9.

Chapter 2

1 Small sections of this work have appeared in Nicholas Piercey, 'Football Grounds, Memory and Cultural History in Amsterdam and Rotterdam from 1910 to 1920: The Football Stadium and Ground as a Historical Resource', in *Memorialkultur im Fußballsport: Medien, Rituale und Praktiken des Erinnerns, Gedenkens und Vergessens. Irseer Dialoge. Kultur und Wissenschaft Interdisziplinar, Band 17*, ed. M. Herzog (Stuttgart: Kohlhammer, 2013), pp. 287–309.

2 The architects behind the new station indicated their idea: 'The new station is not only larger, brighter and more orderly than the former, but also has an international feel; it beautifully complements both the efficiency of the hi-speed stop and Rotterdam city's bold ambitions for urban development and renewal.' Website of *De Zeen Magazine*, 'Rotterdam Centraal Station Reopens with a Pointed Metal-Clad Entrance', http://www.dezeen.com/2014/03/22/rotterdam-centraal-station-benthem-crouwel-mvsa-architects-west-8/.

3 Architect Winy Maas outlined his vision: 'Rotterdam has a big working class population, so the building needs to be pop. We didn't want that contemporary poshness, or for it to feel like Harrods food court.' Website of *The Guardian*, 'Rotterdam's Markthal: Superdutch goes

Supersized in Psychedelic Marketplace', https://www.theguardian.com/artanddesign/architecture-design-blog/2014/oct/02/-sp-rotterdam-markthal-superdutch-market-mvrdv.

4 Website of Feyenoord Rotterdam, 'Feyenoord kiest voor vernieuwbouwde Kuip FFC', https://www.feyenoord.nl/nieuws/nieuwsoverzicht/feyenoord-kiest-voor-vernieuwbouwde-kuip-ffc.

5 Cor Wagenaar, *Town Planning in the Netherlands since 1800: Responses to Enlightenment Ideas and Geopolitical Realities* (Rotterdam: 010 Publishers, 2011), pp. 20–2.

6 Schirato, *Sports Discourse*, p. 10.

7 Michel Foucault, 'Space, Knowledge and Power', in Michel Foucault, *Power: The Essential Works of Michel Foucault* (London: Allen Lane, 2001), Vol. III, pp. 349–64, 361.

8 This information was obtained by a personal visit to *Amsterdams Historisch Museum* (now known as the Amsterdam Museum), Kalvestraat, Amsterdam in December 2009.

9 Karl Baedeker, *Belgium and Holland including the Grand-Duchy of Luxembourg* (Leipzig: Karl Baedeker Publishing, 1910), pp. 367–70.

10 Wagenaar, *Town Planning in the Netherlands*, p. 143.

11 Lukas Wintershoven, *Demografisch Eeuwboek Amsterdam; Ontwikkelingen tussen 1900 en 2000* (Amsterdam: Dienst Ruimtelijke Ordening, 2000), pp. 14–15. An overview of developments in Dutch spatial planning before and around 1900 can be found in Jan Bank and Maarten van Buuren, *Dutch Culture in a European Perspective, III: 1900: The Age of Bourgeois Culture* (Assen: Royal Van Gorcum; Basingstoke: Palgrave Macmillan, 2004), Ch. 3, 'Urban Planning', pp. 105–36.

12 Quoted in Geert Mak, *Amsterdam: A Brief Life of the City* (London: The Harvill Press, 2001), p. 207.

13 Piet de Rooy, 'De Geest van omverwerping 1851–1876', in *Geschiedenis van Amsterdam: Hoofdstad in aanbouw 1813–1900*, ed. Remieg Aerts and Piet de Rooy (Amsterdam: SUN, 2006), vol. III, pp. 341–431, 375–9.

14 Wintershoven, *Demografisch Eeuwboek Amsterdam*, p. 15.

15 Ernst Heldring quoted in Piet de Rooy. 'Het middelpunt van het Vaderland 1901–1914', in *Geschiedenis van Amsterdam: Tweestrijd om de Hoofdstad 1900–2000*, ed. Piet de Rooy (Amsterdam: SUN, 2007), Vol. IV, pp. 17–70, 42.

16 Wintershoven, *Demografisch Eeuwboek Amsterdam*, p. 16.

17 Baedeker, *Belgium and Holland*, p. 369.

18 Wintershoven, *Demografisch Eeuwboek Amsterdam*, pp. 17–22 and Wagenaar, *Town Planning in the Netherlands*, pp. 206–207.

19 Wagenaar, *Town Planning in the Netherlands*, pp. 206–8. For more on the development of health provision in Amsterdam see Annet Mooij and Ruud Stokvis, 'De Gezonde stad', in *Amsterdam in de Tweede Gouden Eeuw*, ed. Martha Bakker et al. (Bussum: Thoth; Amsterdam: Genootschap Amstelodamum, 2000), pp. 263–91.

20 Wagenaar, *Town Planning in the Netherlands*, pp. 208–11.

21 Foucault, 'Space, Knowledge and Power', pp. 350–2.

22 Wintershoven, *Demografisch Eeuwboek Amsterdam*, pp. 27–9.

23 Boudien de Vries, 'Voluntary Societies in the Netherlands, 1750–1900', in *Civil Society, Associations and Urban Places: Class, Nation and Culture in Nineteenth-Century Europe*, ed. Graeme Morton, Boudien de Vries and R. J. Morris (Aldershot: Ashgate, 2006), pp. 103–16, 112.

24 De Vries, 'Voluntary Societies in the Netherlands', p. 114.

25 Website of the Concertgebouw, Amsterdam, 'Historie', https://www.concertgebouw.nl/uw-bezoek/gebouw-geschiedenis/historie.

26 De Vries, 'Voluntary Societies in the Netherlands', p. 113.

27 Maurits van Rooijen, *De Wortels van het Stedelijk Groen: een studie naar ontstaan en voortbestaan van de Nederlandse groene stad* ([n.p]: Erasmus Drukkerij, 1990), pp. 141–6.

28 Wintershoven, *Demografisch Eeuwboek Amsterdam*, p. 20.

29 Van Rooijen, *De Wortels van het Stedelijk Groen*, p. 174.

30 De Rooy. 'Het middelpunt van het Vaderland 1901–1914', pp. 67–70; and Website of Parlement en Politiek, 'Sociaal- Democratische Arbeiderspartij (SDAP)', https://www.parlement.com/id/vh8lnhrpfxu8/sociaal_democratische_arbeiderspartij.

31 Website of Parlement en Politiek, 'Sociaal-Democratische Arbeiderspartij (SDAP)', https://www.parlement.com/id/vh8lnhrpfxu8/sociaal_democratische_arbeiderspartij.

32 Joh. C. Breen, 'Kroniek van Amsterdam van 1 November 1908 tot 31 October 1909', *Jaarboek der vereeniging Amstelodamum*, No. 8 (1910), 1–30, 21–22.

33 De Vries, 'Voluntary Societies in the Netherlands', pp. 111–12. This is often linked to the concept of *verzuiling* (pillarisation), where social and cultural life became increasingly divided between Liberal-Neutral, Socialist, Protestant or Catholic world-views, with different organisations being set up by individuals connected to each group. The concept of *verzuiling* has been used particularly to relate to the period in the late nineteenth century and early twentieth century in Dutch life.

34 Website of Parlement en Politiek, 'Vrijzinnig-Democratische Bond (VDB)', https://www.parlement.com/id/vh8lnhrp8wti/vrijzinnig_democratische_bond_vdb.
35 Paul van de Laar, *Stad van formaat: geschiedenis van Rotterdam in de negentiende en twintigste eeuw*, (Zwolle: Waanders, 2000), pp. 204–207.
36 Anon., *Algemeen Adresboek der Gemeente Rotterdam 1910* (Rotterdam: M. Wyt & Zonen, 1910), pp. viii–ix (pages unmarked in the original).
37 Cor Wagenaar and Marinke Steenhuis, 'Laboratorium Spangen', in *Interbellum Rotterdam: Kunst en cultuur 1918–1940*, ed. Marlite Halbertsma and Patricia van Ulzen (Rotterdam: NAI Uitgevers, 2001), pp. 179–202, 181.
38 Van de Laar, *Stad van formaat*, p. 275.
39 Baedeker, *Belgium and Holland*, pp. 300–10.
40 Van de Laar, *Stad van formaat*, pp. 243–247.
41 Wagenaar, *Town Planning in the Netherlands*, p. 212. For population figures and dates of Rotterdam annexations see: Stadsarchief Rotterdam, Bevolkingscijfers van Rotterdam vanaf 1868, http://www.stadsarchief.rotterdam.nl/bevolkingscijfers-van-rotterdam-vanaf-1868.
42 Wagenaar, *Town Planning in the Netherlands*, pp. 212–213.
43 Josef Vos, *Recreatie in Rotterdam: tussen burger en bestuur* (Amsterdam: Boom, 1998), pp. 35–6.
44 Vos, *Recreatie in Rotterdam*, pp. 47–8.
45 Van Rooijen, *De Wortels van het Stedelijk Groen*, pp. 147–8.
46 Vos, *Recreatie in Rotterdam*, pp. 45–46.
47 Vos, *Recreatie in Rotterdam*, pp. 36–8.
48 C. Miermans, *Voetbal in Nederland: Een onderzoek naar de maatschappelijke en sportieve aspecten* (Assen: Koninglijke van Gorcum en Comp. N.V., 1955), p. 81.
49 Bank and Van Buuren, *Dutch Culture in a European Perspective*, III, p. 234.
50 Miermans, *Voetbal in Nederland*, p. 82.
51 Miermans, *Voetbal in Nederland*, pp. 83–4.
52 Mooij and Stokvis, 'De Gezonde stad', pp. 279–90.
53 Bank and Van Buuren, *Dutch Culture in a European Perspective*, III, p. 244.
54 Matty Verkamman, *Oranje Toen en Nu: 1905–1914, 2000/2001* (Houten: Premium Press, 2001), p. 9.
55 Miermans, *Voetbal in Nederland*, pp. 98–103.
56 For details on the regional bonds and their competitions see, *Voetbal-Jaarboekje 1909/1910*, compiled by Nederlandsche Voetbalbond (Amsterdam: Nederlandsche Voetbalbond, 1909), XII (1909/1910), pp. 241–64.
57 Bank and Van Buuren, *Dutch Culture in a European Perspective*, III, p. 244.
58 Mooij and Stokvis, 'De Gezonde stad', p. 289.
59 Miermans, *Voetbal in Nederland*, pp. 94–7.
60 *Voetbal-Jaarboekje 1913/1914*, compiled by Nederlandsche Voetbalbond (Amsterdam: Nederlandsche Voetbalbond, 1913), XVI (1913/1914), p. 272.
61 Although a team from Rotterdam, 'Concordia', finished top of the inaugural 1888/89 league, the seven teams in the competition did not play an equal number of games, with Concordia playing seven and Excelsior Harlem only one. This competition is often not considered to count as an official title.
62 Vos, *Recreatie in Rotterdam*, p. 36.
63 *Voetbal-Jaarboekje 1909/1910*, pp. 315–34.
64 *Voetbal-Jaarboekje 1909/1910*, pp. 259–61.
65 Mooij and Stokvis, 'De Gezonde stad', pp. 288–9.
66 *Voetbal-Jaarboekje 1909/1910*, pp. 315–34.
67 *Voetbal-Jaarboekje 1909/1910*, pp. 315–34.
68 Private Archive of the *Olympisch Station Amsterdam* (*OSA*), letter, Amsterdam, January 1909.
69 *OSA*, letter, Amsterdam, 21 November 1908 and Anon., 'Stadsnieuws', *Algemeen Handelsblad*, 26 November 1908, Avond, Eerste, p. 2.
70 *OSA*, letter, Amsterdam, 10 December, 1908 See also memos sent in November and December 1908 to J.H. Scheltema. *OSA*, Memos dated: 23 November 1908, 25 November 1908, 2 December 1908.
71 Verkamman, *Oranje Toen en Nu*, pp. 97–9.
72 Anon., 'Holland – England 0–1', *Algemeen Handelsblad*, 18 April 1911, Ochtend, Tweede, p. 6. Images of the match can be found here: http://www.delpher.nl/nl/tijdschriften/view?coll=dts&identifier=dts%3A1665049%3Ampeg21%3A0004&pres%5Bmaxperpage%5D=36.
73 BOB, 'Holland–England', *De Revue der Sporten*, Jaar 4, No. 49, 19 April 1911, pp. 772–9, 778.

74 BOB, 'Holland–England', *De Revue der Sporten*, Jaar 4, No. 49, 19 April 1911, pp. 772–9, 778.
75 BOB, 'Holland–England', *De Revue der Sporten*, Jaar 4, No. 49, 19 April 1911, pp. 772–79, 778–9.
76 E.D., 'De Holland–England Wedstrijd', *Algemeen Handelsblad*, 20 April 1911, Ochtend, Eerste, p. 2.
77 Wagenaar, *Town Planning in the Netherlands*, p. 224; and Van Rooijen, *De Wortels van het Stedelijk Groen*, p. 182.
78 Burgemeester and Wethouders of Amsterdam quoted in J. Hoven and M. J. Adriani Engels, *Vijftig jaar N.V. het Nederlands sportpark 'Olympisch Stadion' te Amsterdam, 17 mei 1962* (Amsterdam: N.V. het Nederlands sportpark 'Olympisch Stadion', 1962), p. 7.
79 *OSA*, Printed Report from E. R. Harkema, early 1912.
80 Hoven and Adriani Engels, *Vijftig jaar*, p. 7.
81 C.J.K van Aalst et al., 'Nederlandsch Sportpark te Amsterdam', *Het Centrum*, 1 March 1912, Tweede, p. 1.
82 C.J.K van Aalst et al., 'Nederlandsch Sportpark te Amsterdam', *Het Centrum*, 1 March 1912, Tweede, p. 1.
83 Anon., 'Het Anti-Revolutionair beginsel', *Het Volk*, 2 March 1912, Tweede, p. 3.
84 Anon., 'Het Anti-Revolutionair beginsel', *Het Volk*, 2 March 1912, Tweede, p. 3.
85 Miermans, *Voetbal in Nederland*, pp. 133–41.
86 Cees Zevenbergen, *Rotterdams Voetbalglorie 1886–1986: kroniek van een eeuw stedelijke voetbalhistorie* (Rijswijk: Sijthoff Handelsdrukkerijen; Rotterdam: Gemeentelijke Archiefdienst, 1986), p. 40.
87 Miermans, *Voetbal in Nederland*, pp. 133–41.
88 Verkamman, *Oranje Toen en Nu*, pp. 12–13.
89 Zevenbergen, *Rotterdams Voetbalglorie*, pp. 191–2.
90 Anon., 'Hollandsche Voetballers in Engeland', *Algemeen Handelsblad*, 19 April 1906, Avond, Derde, pp. 9–10.
91 Matty Verkamman, *90 jaar op het kasteel*, ed. Matty Verkamman et al. (Rotterdam: [n.p], 2007), p. 31.
92 Verkamman, *90 jaar op het kasteel*, p. 31.
93 Wagenaar and Steenhuis, 'Laboratorium Spangen', p. 182.
94 Rotterdam, *Stadsarchief Rotterdam* (*SAR*), Rotterdamse Voetbal- en Atletiek Vereeniging Sparta (Archive 257), Notulen van bestuursvergaderingen: September 1913–September 1915 (Part 24), minutes of meeting dated 3 September 1913.
95 Wagenaar and Steenhuis, 'Labatorium Spangen', p. 182.
96 Anon., 'Gemeenteraad', *NRC*, 12 December 1913, Ochtend, A, p. 1. Plans in the Rotterdam archive indicate that the designation of the recreational space was not decided, suggesting that it had been 'potentially earmarked for an ice rink'. See *SAR*, Archive 257, Stukken betreffende de vaststelling door de gemeente Rotterdam van de huurprijs van de grond, gepacht door Sparta, in de polder Spangen (Part 211), Plan entitled: *'Plan van Exploitatie der Gemeentelijke terreinen in den Spangenschen polder'*.
97 Anon., 'Gemeenteraad', *NRC*, 12 December 1913, Ochtend, A, p. 1.
98 In 1912, an ARP member tried to ban the playing of football in public spaces in Rotterdam on Sundays, while at the same time the head of Rotterdam police had noted that he felt instances of drunken behaviour had fallen on Sundays because of football. Zevenbergen, *Rotterdams Voetbalglorie*, pp. 44–5.
99 E. Wiersum, 'Dagelijksche kroniek 1913', in *Rotterdamsch Jaarboekje 1914*, ed. E. Wiersum (Rotterdam: W. L. & J. Brusse, 1914), pp. xiii–xxix, xxix; and Anon., 'Gemeenteraad', *NRC*, 12 December 1913, Ochtend, A, p. 1.
100 *SAR*, Archive 257, Part 211, letter dated 13 October 1914.
101 *SAR*, Archive 257, Part 24, minutes of meeting dated 20 April 1915.
102 Anon., 'Het Sportpark', *Het Volk*, 27 March 1912, Eerste, p. 3.
103 C.J.K van Aalst et al., 'Nederlandsch Sportpark te Amsterdam', *Het Centrum*, 1 March 1912, Tweede, p. 1
104 *OSA*, Papers entitled 'Lyst van Inteekenaren op het kapitaal van Maatschappy "Nederlandsch Sportpark"'.
105 C. Fasseur, 'CREMER, Jacob Theodoor', in *Biografisch Woordenboek van Nederland*, ed. J. Charité ('s Gravenhage: Martinus Nijhoff, 1979), Vol. I, pp. 122–5.
106 N. A. van Hoorn, 'EEGHEN, Samuel Pieter van', in *Biografisch Woordenboek van Nederland*, ed. J. Charité ('s Gravenhage,: Instituut voor Nederlandse Geschiedenis, 1989), Vol. III, pp. 157–9; and Jasmijn Bus, 'Familie van Eeghen', in *Nederlandse ondernemers 1850–1950: Amsterdam*, ed. Joop Visser, Matthijs Dicke and Annelies van der Zouwen (Zutphen: Walburg Pers, 2013), pp. 99–109, 106–9.

107 J. Kymmell, 'AALST, Cornelis Johannes Karel van', in *Biografisch Woordenboek van Nederland*, ed. J. Charité (Amsterdam: Elsevier, 1985), Vol. II, pp. 1–2; and Ton de Graaf, 'Karel van Aalst', in *Nederlandse ondernemers 1850–1950: Amsterdam*, ed. Joop Visser, Matthijs Dicke and Annelies van der Zouwen (Zutphen: Walburg Pers, 2013), pp. 31–5.
108 Joh. de Vries, 'Ernst Heldring', in *Nederlandse ondernemers 1850–1950: Amsterdam*, ed. Joop Visser, Matthijs Dicke and Annelies van der Zouwen (Zutphen: Walburg Pers, 2013), pp. 155–9.
109 Anon., 'A. Roelvink', *NRC*, 9 October 1927, Ochtend, D, p. 1.
110 Website of the Digitale Bibliotheek voor de Nederlandse Letteren, Jaarboek van de Maatschappij der Nederlandse Letterkunde 1929, 'Levensbericht van Mari Paul Voûte: 1856–1928, by E. J. Voûte, http://www.dbnl.org/tekst/_jaa003192901_01/_jaa003192901_01_0013.php.
111 Website of Gustav-Mahler.eu, 'Charles Ernest Henri Boissevain (1868–1940)', http://www.gustav-mahler.eu/index.php/moreformenu/personen/414-boissevain-charles-ernest-henri-1868–1940.
112 Website of RKD Nederlands Instituut voor Kunstgeschiedenis, Edwin vom Rath, https://rkd.nl/nl/explore/artists/421693.
113 Paula van der Houwen 'Willem Burger', in *Nederlandse ondernemers 1850–1950: Rotterdam*, ed. Joop Visser, Matthijs Dicke and Annelies van der Zouwen (Zutphen: Walburg Pers, 2014), pp. 62–7.
114 A. Hoynck van Papendrecht, *Gedenkboek A. van Hoboken & Co.: 1774–1924* (Rotterdam: [n.p], 1924), pp. 17–18, 147–53.
115 Van der Houwen, 'Willem Burger', p. 65.
116 Joost Jonker, 'KRÖLLER, Anthony George', in *Biografisch Woordenboek van Nederland*, ed. K. van Berkel ('s Gravenhage: Instituut voor Nederlandse Geschiedenis, 2008), Vol. VI, pp. 258–61; and Ariëtte Dekker, 'Anton Kröller', in *Nederlandse ondernemers 1850–1950: Rotterdam*, ed. Joop Visser, Matthijs Dicke and Annelies van der Zouwen (Zutphen: Walburg Pers, 2014), pp. 156–61.
117 Erik Boonstoppel, 'Familie Mees', in *Nederlandse ondernemers 1850–1950: Rotterdam*, ed. Joop Visser, Matthijs Dicke and Annelies van der Zouwen (Zutphen: Walburg Pers, 2014), pp. 189–201, 197–8.
118 Cora Boele, 'Familie Van Ommeren', in *Nederlandse ondernemers 1850–1950: Rotterdam*, ed. Joop Visser, Matthijs Dicke and Annelies van der Zouwen (Zutphen: Walburg Pers, 2014), pp. 234–43.
119 Anon., 'Dr D. P. Hoyer', *NRC*, 23 February 1926, Ochtend, C, p. 1.
120 F. J. M. van de Ven, 'BERG, Samuel van den', in *Biografisch Woordenboek van Nederland*, ed. J. Charité ('s Gravenhage: Instituut voor Nederlandse Geschiedenis, 1989), Vol. III, pp. 48–9; and Leni Ottevanger with Doreen Arnoldus, 'Sam van den Bergh', in *Nederlandse ondernemers 1850–1950: Rotterdam*, ed. Joop Visser, Matthijs Dicke and Annelies van der Zouwen (Zutphen: Walburg Pers, 2014), pp. 43–9.
121 W. F. Lichtenauer, 'HINTZEN, George Hermann', *Biografisch Woordenboek van Nederland*, ed. J. Charité (Amsterdam: Elsevier, 1985), Vol. II, pp. 230–2; and Marjan Zijlmans 'George Hintzen', in *Nederlandse ondernemers 1850–1950: Rotterdam*, ed. Joop Visser, Matthijs Dicke and Annelies van der Zouwen (Zutphen: Walburg Pers, 2014), pp. 129–33.
122 Foucault, *Discipline and Punish*, pp. 141–9.
123 Cornelis J. K. van Aalst and W. A. Holdert, 'Prijsvraag voor een stadion uitgeschreven door de Maatschappij "Het Nederlandsch Sportpark" te Amsterdam', *Architectura*, Vol. 20, No. 19 (11 May 1912), pp. 154–6.
124 Van Aalst and Holdert, 'Prijsvraag', p. 155.
125 John Bale, 'The Spatial Development of the Modern Stadium', *International Review for the Sociology of Sport*, Vol. 28, No. 2–3 (June 1993), pp. 121–33, 130.
126 Verkamman, *Oranje Toen en Nu*, p. 159.
127 H. P. Berlage et al., 'Prijsvragen. Stadion-prijsvraag', *Bouwkundig Weekblad*, Vol. 32, No. 31 (3 August 1912), pp. 377–378, 378.
128 Leo Lauer, 'De vorderingen bij den bouw van het Stadion te Amsterdam', *De Revue der Sporten*, Jaar 7, No. 25, 4 November 1913, pp. 386–389.
129 Anon., 'Het Nederlandsch Sportpark', *NRC*, 8 March 1914, Ochtend, C, p. 1.
130 Anon., 'Opening Sparta-Stadion', *NRC*, 16 October 1916, Ochtend, A, p. 1.
131 Anon., 'Nederland–Duitschland Diagram', *Algemeen Handelsblad*, 4 April 1914, Avond, Derde, p. 9.
132 Anon., 'Nederland–Duitschland 4–4', *De Courant*, 6 April 1914, Eerste, p. 2.
133 Anon., 'Nederland–Duitschland 4–4', *De Courant*, 6 April 1914, Eerste, p. 2.
134 See Anon., 'De Weg naar het Stadion', *Algemeen Handelsblad*, 6 April 1914, Avond, Eerste, p. 1; and Anon., 'Holland – Duitschland', *Het Volk*, 6 April 1914, Eerste, p. 2.

135 Anon., 'Nederland–Duitschland 4–4', *De Courant*, 6 April 1914, Eerste, p. 2.
136 Anon., 'Nederland–Duitschland 4–4', *De Courant*, 6 April 1914, Eerste, p. 2.
137 Images from the 1914 Netherlands versus Germany game can be found in *De Revue der Sporten* at http://www.delpher.nl/nl/tijdschriften/view?coll=dts&identifier=dts%3A1668046%3Ampeg21%3A0005&pres[maxperpage]=36.
138 Anon., 'Nederland–Duitschland 4–4, *De Courant*, 6 April 1914, Eerste, p. 2.
139 Nicholas Piercey, 'Investment, Advertisement, and Sponsorship: Business in Dutch Football 1910–1920', *Dutch Crossing*, Vol. 35, No. 1 (March 2011), pp. 89–104, 99–100.
140 Anon., 'Opening Sparta-Stadion', *NRC*, 16 October 1916, Ochtend, A, p. 1; and Ch.A. Cocheret, "Sparta!": *een Rotterdamse voetbalclub 1888–1963* (Rotterdam: Nijgh & Van Dietmar, 1963), p. 45.
141 Wagenaar and Steenhuis, 'Laboratorium Spangen', pp. 184–185. Images of the new Sparta stadium of 1916 can be found in *De Revue der Sporten* at http://www.delpher.nl/nl/tijdschriften/view?coll=dts&identifier=dts%3A1670006%3Ampeg21%3A0006&pres%5Bmaxperpage%5D=36.
142 Ch.A. Cocheret, *"Sparta!"*, p. 48.
143 Wagenaar and Steenhuis, 'Laboratorium Spangen', pp. 193–4.
144 Website of VOC, 'Geschiedenis', http://www.v-o-c.nl/algemeen/geschiedenis.
145 Zevenbergen, *Rotterdams Voetbalglorie*, pp. 51–2.
146 Website of Feyenord Rotterdam, 'Historie: 1914–1923', https://www.feyenoord.nl/de-club/geschiedenis. An image of the new Feyenoord ground in 1917 can be found as the top picture in *De Revue der Sporten* at http://www.delpher.nl/nl/tijdschriften/view?coll=dts&identifier=dts%3A1670047%3Ampeg21%3A0007&pres%5Bmaxperpage%5D=36.
147 Rotterdam, *SAR*, Sportclub Feyenoord (Archive 256), 'De Feyenoorder', officieel tijdschrift van de sportclub 'Feyenoord', 1917–1923 (Part 36), publication dated 25 August 1917, pp. 1–2, 1.
148 Rotterdam, *SAR*, Archive 256, Part 36, p. 1.
149 Rotterdam, *SAR*, Archive 256, Part 36, p. 1.
150 Rotterdam, *SAR*, Archive 256, Part 36, pp. 1–2.
151 Website of CVV, now defunct, http://www.cvvmercurius.nl/index.php?option=com_content&task=view&id=2&Itemid=201 (last accessed 19 March 2010).
152 *Voetbal-Jaarboekje 1913/1914*, p. 334; and Zevenbergen, *Rotterdams Voetbalglorie*, p. 53.
153 Website of Transvalia, now defunct, '*Beknopte Geschiedenis Transvalia*', http://www.transvaliazw.nl/overige/historie/historie.htm (last accessed 29 May 2011).
154 Anon., 'Inwijding van het Stadion'. *Het Volk*, 25 May 1914, Tweede, p. 8.
155 Anon., 'Een groote sportvereeniging in Amsterdam', *NRC*, 19 July 1914, Ochtend, B, p. 2.
156 Anon., 'Sportterrein', *NRC*, 19 July 1914, Ochtend, B, p. 1.
157 Anon., 'Nederland–Zweden 3–1', *NRC*, 10 June 1919, Ochtend, A, p. 2.
158 Anon., 'Sportterrein aan den Amstelveenscheweg', *NRC*, 29 December 1914, Ochtend, B, p. 2.
159 Hoven and Adriani Engels, *Vijftig jaar*, pp. 10–19.
160 An image of Ajax's stadium in 1912 can be found in *De Revue der Sporten* at http://www.delpher.nl/nl/tijdschriften/view?coll=dts&identifier=dts%3A1666040%3Ampeg21%3A0008&pres%5Bmaxperpage%5D=36.
161 Anon., 'Sportnieuws', *Het Volk*, 1 July 1918, Eerste, p. 4.
162 Anon., 'Sportnieuws', *Het Volk*, 1 July 1918, Eerste, p. 4.
163 More on the development of *Plan Zuid* and the work of the Amsterdam School can be found in Maristella Casciato, *The Amsterdam School* (Rotterdam: 010 Publishers, 2003), pp. 122–155.

Chapter 3

1 Southgate, *History Meets Fiction*, p. x.
2 Michel de Certeau, 'History: Science and Fiction', in Michel de Certeau, *Heterologies: Discourse on the Other* (Minneapolis: University of Minnesota Press, 1986), pp. 199–221, 219.
3 De Certeau, 'History: Science and Fiction', p. 201.
4 Please see Ch. 1 in this volume for an outline of the ideas in this section. The ideas outlined here are addressed in the following places: Munslow, *Narrative and History*, pp. 6 and 134; White, 'The Question of Narrative in Contemporary Historical Theory'; White, de Certeau, *The Writing of History*. In addition, L. O. Mink discusses the different nature of knowledge produced by narrative and literary forms of research in comparison to scientific and philosophical work. See Louis O. Mink, 'History and Fiction as Modes of Comprehension', *New Literary History*, Vol. 1, No. 3 (1970), pp. 541–58.

5 Hayden White, 'Introduction: Historical Fiction, Fictional History, and Historical Reality', *Rethinking History*, Vol. 9, No. 2/3 (2005), pp. 147–57, 148–50.
6 See Richard Slotkin, 'Fiction for the Purposes of History', *Rethinking History*, Vol. 9, No. 2/3 (2005), pp. 221–36; and Linda Orr, 'When History and Fiction Are Mixed Up: My Book Manuscript on Jean Zay and His Family', *Rethinking History*, Vol. 9, No. 2/3 (2005), pp. 255–73.
7 Orr, 'When History and Fiction Are Mixed Up', pp. 255–73.
8 Orr, 'When History and Fiction Are Mixed Up', pp. 271–2.
9 In his "afterword' Demos notes that historians who work in a specific area for so much of their life may come to understand more than sources can represent and that there can be a 'ring-true test' of whether a history sounds plausible or not. He suggests that historians use non-source-based elements to improve the understanding of the past given by their work. This is not my intention with this chapter and I have outlined my position about historical understanding and the role of the historian in constructing the past in Ch. 1. J. Demos, 'Afterword: Notes From, and About, the History/Fiction Borderland', *Rethinking History*, Vol. 9, No. 2/3 (2005), pp. 329–35.
10 E. Wiersum (ed.), *Rotterdamsch Jaarboekje 1915* (Rotterdam: W. L. & J. Brusse, 1915), opposite p. xxiii.
11 All *Algemeen Adresboeken* between 1808 and 1939 are fully available online thanks to the *SAR*. They can be found here: http://www.stadsarchief.rotterdam.nl/collectie/adresboeken.
12 For more details on Rotterdam clubs (as well as other sporting organisations) and fully interactive searches, please visit the excellent 'Databank Sport' from *Huygens Instituut voor Nederlandse Geschiedenis (ING)*, http://resources.huygens.knaw.nl/sportbondenclubsperiodieken/gids/search.
13 Southgate, *History Meets Fiction*, p. 197.
14 In the semi-fictionalised section of the work which follows, Dutch words, organisations or concepts will not be italicised, as has been done elsewhere. However, newspapers, journals and book titles will remain in italics.
15 Maartje M. Abbenhuis, *The Art of Staying Neutral: The Netherlands in the First World War, 1914–1918* (Amsterdam: Amsterdam University Press, 2006), pp. 66–67.
16 *SAR* Fotocollectie, -2: Standbeeld van Erasmus, op de achtergrond het Middensteiger en het spoorwegviaduct, 4100_IX-1100-03-1,-2.
17 Baedeker, *Belgium and Holland*, p. 303.
18 Anon., 'In de Stad', *NRC*, Monday 3 August 1914, Avond, B, p. 1.
19 *SAR* Fotocollectie, Het Hang met de winkels van A. van der Nagel & Zonen (mode-artikelen), rechts de winkel van de firma Doodewaard (spiegels en lijsten), 4100_1978–2821.
20 *SAR* Fotocollectie, Gezicht op de Glashaven vanuit het zuidoosten. Op de voorgrond de Rederijbrug, op de achtergrond de Zuiderkerk. 4029_PBK-2209.
21 E. Wiersum, 'Dagelijksche kroniek 1914', in *Rotterdamsch Jaarboekje 1915*, ed. E. Wiersum (Rotterdam: W. L. & J. Brusse, 1915), pp. xiii–xxxvii, xxiii.
22 Anon., 'In de Stad', *NRC*, Monday 3 August 1914, Avond, B, p. 1.
23 *SAR* Fotocollectie, Witte Huis, ROTTERDAM, 4029_PBK-2007–123; Baedeker, *Belgium and Holland*, p. 308.
24 E. Wiersum, 'Dagelijksche kroniek 1914', p. xxvi.
25 Der Kaiserliche Deutsche Gesandte, 'Mobilmachung angeordnet', *NRC*, 3 August 1914, Ochtend, B, p. 4; and Le Consul General de France a Rotterdam, 'L'Ordre général de mobilisation de l'armée Française a été décrété', *NRC*, 3 August 1914, Ochtend, B, p. 4.
26 Thalia Theatre, 'Schouwburgen, Concerten, Tentoonstellingen enz.', *NRC*, 3 August 1914, Avond, A, p. 4.
27 Baedeker, *Belgium and Holland*, p. 304.
28 Anon., 'Telegram', *NRC*, 3 August 1914, Ochtend, B, p. 3.
29 More can be found on this organisation via the *ING*, 'Verenigingen voor armenzorg en armoedepreventie in de negentiende eeuw', http://resources.huygens.knaw.nl/armenzorg/gids/vereniging/2776914523.
30 Concerns about food and prices appeared regularly in the *NRC* during this week. An article relating to food concerns is Anon., 'Levensmiddelen', *NRC*, 3 August 1914, Avond, B, p. 1. A Proclamation from the mayor relating to a law to regulate food prices can be found at Burgemeester Zimmerman, 'Proclamatie', *NRC*, 5 August 1914, Avond, C, p. 4.
31 *SAR* Fotocollectie, Rotterdam Delftschevaart, 4029_PBK-6528.
32 *SAR* Fotocollectie, Rotterdam Delftsche Vaart, 4029_PBK-2005–446.
33 *SAR* Fotocollectie, Stationsweg met Delftschepoort ROTTERDAM, 4029_PBK-2007–21.
34 The Retours digital magazine for railway history has an excellent guide to the Rotterdam Hofplein station, http://retours.eu/en/08-decorations-hofplein-station-rotterdam/#10.

35 Anon., 'Scheveningen', *NRC*, 2 August 1914, Ochtend, A, p. 4.
36 *SAR* Fotocollectie, Rotterdam / Koninginnebrug / ca. 1910, 4029_PBK-1991–107.
37 Van de Laar, *Stad van formaat*, p.139.
38 *SAR* Fotocollectie, ONTPLOFFING VAN HET S.S. "GUTENBERG". DE KETEL IN EEN DER STRATEN GEWORPEN, 4029_PBK-1983–1256.
39 Baedeker, *Belgium and Holland*, p. 309.
40 Anon., 'De bekende Sparta-doelverdediger G. van Driel', *De Revue der Sporten*, Jaar 5, No. 24, 25 October 1911, p. 371.
41 *SAR* Fotocollectie, Feestverlichting op het Prinsenhoofd ter gelegenheid van de Onafhankelijkheidsfeesten van 17 november 1913, 4029_PBK-5787.
42 Anon., 'De Oorlog', *NRC*, 04 August 1914, Avond, C, p. 2.
43 Burgemeester Zimmerman, 'Proclamatie', *NRC*, 4 August 1914, Avond, C, p. 2.
44 *SAR* Fotocollectie, Groet uit Rotterdam Fontein Burgem. Hoffmanplein, Groet uit Rotterdam, 4029_PBK-1083.
45 Van de Laar, *Stad van format*, pp. 105–9.
46 Herman Romer, *Rotterdam in de jaren tien: 1910–1920* (Zaltbommel: Europese Bibliotheek, 1985), p. 78.
47 *SAR* Fotocollectie, Rosestraat met Tramstation, Rotterdam, 4029_PBK-1993–628.
48 *Voetbal-Jaarboekje 1913/1914*, p. 332.
49 Van de Laar, *Stad van format*, pp. 111–16.
50 Abbenhuis, *The Art of Staying Neutral*, pp. 43–5.
51 Anon., 'In de Stad', *NRC*, 1 August 1914, Avond, C, p. 1.
52 Anon., 'Hollandsche IJzeren Spoorweg Maatschappij', *NRC*, 1 August 1914, Ochtend, B, p. 4.
53 *SAR* Fotocollectie, Rotterdam Stationsweg – Delftsche Poort, 4029_PBK-6638.
54 Anon., 'In de Stad', *NRC*, 1 August 1914, Avond, C, p. 1.
55 *SAR* Fotocollectie, Provenierssingel. Rotterdam, 4029_PBK-5851.
56 On 3 August, the *NRC* reported that the amount of telephonic traffic on 31 July and 1 August 1914 was greatly increased compared to normal figures. Anon., 'In de Stad: Telefoon- drukte', *NRC*, 3 August 1914, Avond, B, p. 1.
57 Anon., 'Schouwbergen en Concerten', *NRC*, 1 August 1914, Ochtend, B, p. 3.
58 Anon., 'Dienstvervanging door vouwen', *NRC*, 3 August 1914, Avond, B, p. 1.
59 *SAR* Fotocollectie, Eendrachtsweg Groeten uit Rotterdam, 4029_PBK-2114.
60 Van de Laar, *Stad van format*, pp. 212–214.
61 Baedeker, *Belgium and Holland*, p. 302.
62 Anon., 'Verboden van uitvoer', *NRC*, 2 August 1914, Ochtend, B, p. 1.
63 Abbenhuis, *The Art of Staying Neutral*, p. 73.
64 Anon., 'In de Stad', *NRC*, 1 August 1914, Avond, C, p. 1.
65 *SAR* Fotocollectie, Rotterdam De Heuvel, 4029_PBK-5591.
66 Anon., 'Aan de Duitsche grens', *NRC*, 1 August 1914, Avond, C, p. 1; and Abbenhuis, *The Art of Staying Neutral*, p. 87.
67 An image of a match on the Heuvelveld in 1910 can be found in *De Revue der Sporten*, http://www.delpher.nl/nl/tijdschriften/view?coll=dts&identifier=dts%3A1665005%3Ampeg21%3A0005&pres%5Bmaxperpage%5D=36.
68 Baedeker, *Belgium and Holland*, p. 308
69 Holland-Amerika Lijn, 'Cuba-Mexico-New Orleans Dienst', *NRC*, 3 August 1914, Avond, B, p. 4.
70 Website of In the Winning Mood, now defunct, '*Sparta & historie: In de Geest van Bok de Korver*', http://www.itwm.nl/artikel.php?id=3567 (last accessed 29 May 2011).
71 Anon., 'Sport', *NRC*, 1 August 1914, Ochtend, B, p. 1.
72 Anon., '*De Revue der Sporten*', *NRC*, 4 August 1914, Ochtend, p. 4.
73 An image of the Schuttersveld in use in 1910 for a match between VOC and Ajax Leiden can be found in *De Revue der Sporten*, http://www.delpher.nl/nl/tijdschriften/view?coll=dts&identifier=dts%3A1665003%3Ampeg21%3A0002.
74 Romer, *Rotterdam in de jaren tien*, p. 75.
75 *SAR* Fotocollectie, Vrouwen op de Veemarkt, die wachten op de melk, 4100_XIV-109–02.
76 Anon., 'In de Stad', *NRC*, 4 Augsut 1914, Avond, C, p. 1.
77 A photo of football on the Veemarkt in 1912 can be found at http://www.delpher.nl/nl/tijdschriften/view?coll=dts&identifier=dts%3A1667029%3Ampeg21%3A0009&pres%5Bmaxperpage%5D=36.
78 *Voetbal-Jaarboekje 1909/1910*, pp. 176–7.
79 Baedeker, *Belgium and Holland*, p. 308.

80 'Proclamatie van Burgemeester en Wethouders, 6 Augustus 1914', in *Rotterdamsch Jaarboekje 1915*, ed. E. Wiersum (Rotterdam: W. L. & J. Brusse, 1915), p. xxv.
81 Anon., 'In de Stad', *NRC*, 7 August 1914, Avond, C, p. 1.
82 *SAR* Fotocollectie, Rotterdam. Noorderkerk, 4029_PBK-2123.
83 G. C. Van der Leck, 'De Rotterdamsche Melkinrichting', *NRC*, 3 August 1914, Avond, A, p. 4.
84 Koninklijke Confederatie Melkinrichting, 'Prijsverlaging', *NRC*, 6 August 1914, Avond B, p. 4.
85 De Leden der Vereeniging van Nederlandsche Papiergroothandelaren, 'Papier', *NRC*, 6 August 1914, Avond B, p. 3.
86 *SAR* Fotocollectie, Rotterdam Noordsingel, 4029_PBK-4950.
87 Het Bestuur der Rotterdamsche Broodbakkers Vereeniging, 'Aan de Burgerij', *NRC*, 4 August 1914, Avond, B, p. 4.
88 Anon., 'Roode Kruis', *NRC*, 3 August 1914, Ochtend, B, p. 1.
89 Anon., 'Vrouwen- en Mannencomité's', *NRC*, 7 August 1914, Avond, C, p. 3.
90 Romer, *Rotterdam in de jaren tien*, p. 15.
91 Burgemeester Zimmerman, 'Kennisgeving', *NRC*, 4 August 1914, Avond, A, p. 2.
92 *SAR* Fotocollectie, Lust-Hofstraat, Rotterdam, 4029_PBK-1993–1361.
93 Anon., 'In de Stad', *NRC*, 7 August 1914, Avond, C, p. 1.

Chapter 4

1 Pierre Bourdieu, *On Television* (New York: The New Press, 1998), p. 21.
2 Bourdieu, *On Television*, pp. 21–4.
3 Foucault, *Discipline and Punish*, pp. 133–228.
4 This chapter is intended to be a new, historically based addition to Foucauldian-inspired work in sports studies based on early Dutch football. I consider this an experimental chapter, based upon Foucault's concept of 'discipline' rather than as an exhaustive account of wider scholarship on Foucault in sport. However, a useful introduction to the use of Foucault's concept of 'discipline' in wider sporting research can be found in David L. Andrews, 'Posting Up: French Post-Structuralism and the Critical Analysis of Contemporary Sporting Culture', in *Handbook of Sports Studies*, ed. Jay Coakley and Eric Dunning (London: Sage, 2012), pp. 106–37, 121–26.
5 Ongoing scandals involving the International Association of Athletics Federations (IAAF) and the *Fédération Internationale de Football Association* (International Federation of Association Football, FIFA) in late 2015 were only the latest to involve major sporting organisations and their alleged complicity in drug-taking, bribery or dishonest payments.
6 Houlihan indicates that the links between sport and politics do not just involve states or governments and major sporting institutions, but can be viewed as going throughout the full range of sporting activity from local clubs upwards. His overview summarises a range of approaches and provides a useful bibliography. Barrie Houlihan, 'Politics and Sport', in *Handbook of Sports Studies*, ed. Jay Coakley and Eric Dunning (London: Sage, 2012), pp. 213–27.
7 Ruud Stokvis, 'Een genre in beweging: De ongemakkelijke verhouding tussen sport en journalistiek', in *Journalistieke cultuur in Nederland*, ed. Johannes Bardoel (Amsterdam: Amsterdam University Press, 2009), pp. 191–207, 193–4.
8 Miermans, *Voetbal in Nederland*, pp. 106–9.
9 Stokvis, 'Een genre in beweging', p. 195.
10 J. M. H. J. Hemels, 'MEERUM TERWOGT, Albert Hendrik Magdalus', in *Biografisch Woordenboek van Nederland*, ed. J. Charité ('s Gravenhage,: Instituut voor Nederlandse Geschiedenis, 1989), Vol. III, pp. 401–2.
11 Digitally preserved *De Revue der Sporten* editions (as well as many cited newspaper articles) can be accessed online via the Delpher website http://www.delpher.nl/. I considered that newspapers would provide a representation of sporting news for a wider sphere of people than purely those interested in the weekly periodicals and this was also a factor in my decision not to research sporting journals for this history.
12 Jan van de Plasse, *Kroniek van de Nederlandse dagblad -en opiniepers*, (Amsterdam: Cramwinckel, 2005), pp. 192–193.
13 Stokvis, 'Een genre in beweging', p. 195.
14 Anon., 'Sportnieuws', *Het Volk*, 29 January 1912, Eerste, p. 3.
15 Anon., 'Sportnieuws', *Het Volk*, 29 January 1912, Eerste, p. 3.

16 Foucault, *Discipline and Punish*, pp. 135–8.
17 Foucault, *Discipline and Punish*, pp. 138–41.
18 Foucault, *Discipline and Punish*, pp. 141–8.
19 Foucault, *Discipline and Punish*, pp. 145–9, 181–4.
20 Foucault, *Discipline and Punish*, pp. 149–56.
21 Anon., 'H.V.V.–Sparta (4–0)', *NRC*, 3 January 1910, Ochtend, B, p. 3.
22 Anon., 'D.F.C.–Sparta (1–1)', *NRC*, 14 November 1910, Avond, A, p. 1.
23 *De Zilverenbal* – The Silver Ball – was a summer tournament run in Rotterdam three weeks before the competitive season began involving all the First Division teams as well as the two promoted teams. It began in 1901. Zevenbergen, *Rotterdams Voetbalglorie*, p. 30. Other similar tournaments occurred in different cities in the Netherlands.
24 Foucault, *Discipline and Punish*, pp. 156–62.
25 Foucault, *Discipline and Punish*, pp. 166–7.
26 Foucault, *Discipline and Punish*, p. 180.
27 Foucault, *Discipline and Punish*, pp. 141–9, 164.
28 Anon., 'Sport en Wedstrijd: Sportoverdrijving', *Algemeen Handelsblad*, 15 January 1910, Ochtend, Eerste, p. 2.
29 Anon., 'Onderwijs', *Algemeen Handelsblad*, 26 August 1910, Ochtend, Eerste, pp. 1–2, 1.
30 Anon., 'Onderwijs', *Algemeen Handelsblad*, 26 August 1910, Ochtend, Eerste, pp. 1–2, 1.
31 Anon., 'Onderwijs', *Algemeen Handelsblad*, 26 August 1910, Ochtend, Eerste, pp. 1–2.
32 M. F. Graafland, 'Schoolvoetbal', *Maasbode*, 21 February 1910, Avond, Tweede, p. 2.
33 Anon., 'Schoolvoetbal in den Haag', *Algemeen Handelsblad*, 11 May 1913, Ochtend, Tweede, p. 6.
34 M. F. Graafland, 'Schoolvoetbal', *Maasbode*, 21 February 1910, Avond, Tweede, p. 2.
35 Reports on school football continued throughout the period, including Anon., 'Schoolwedstrijden van den R.V.B.', *Maasbode*, 6 April 1914, Avond, Derde, p. 2; and Anon., 'Schoolwedstrijden A.V.B.', *Algemeen Handelsblad*, 26 October 1919, Ochtend, Tweede, p. 6.
36 Foucault, *Discipline and Punish*, pp. 184–92.
37 Anon., 'Sparta–Ajax 0–5', *Maasbode*, 2 February 1914, Avond, Derde, p. 2.
38 Anon., 'Sparta–Ajax 2–1', *Maasbode*, 4 March 1918, Avond, Tweede, pp. 1–2, 2.
39 Anon., 'Sparta–Ajax 0–5', *Maasbode*, 2 February 1914, Avond, Derde, p. 2.
40 Anon., 'Sparta–Ajax (0–3)', *NRC*, 2 February 1914, Avond, A, p. 2.
41 Anon., 'Kampong–R.A.P. 5–0', *Algemeen Handelsblad*, 4 April 1910, Avond, Tweede, p. 6.
42 Anon., 'Sportnieuws', *Het Volk*, 8 April 1918, Eerste, p. 4.
43 Foucault, *Discipline and Punish*, pp. 177–80.
44 Anon., 'De Wedstrijden van Gisteren', *NRC*, 4 February 1918, Avond, A, p. 1.
45 Anon., 'Sparta–Ajax 2–1', *Maasbode*, 4 March 1918, Avond, Tweede, p. 2.
46 Anon., 'De Wedstrijden van Gisteren', *Algemeen Handelsblad*, 4 March 1918, Avond, Tweede, p. 7.
47 Anon., 'Ajax slaat Haarlem', *De Courant*, 4 February 1918, p. 5.
48 Foucault, *Discipline and Punish*, p. 184.
49 Anon., 'De Wedstrijden van Gisteren', *NRC*, 4 March 1918, Avond, A, p. 2.
50 Anon., 'De Wedstrijden van Gisteren', *Algemeen Handelsblad*, 4 March 1918, Avond, Tweede, p. 7.
51 Anon., 'Ajax in Rotterdam geslagen', *De Courant*, 4 March 1918, p. 6.
52 Their 'amateurism' may also have been questioned because they had begun a lengthy training schedule which, as *Het Volk* noted, had seen an improvement in their technique. Anon., 'Sportnieuws', *Het Volk*, 1 July 1918, Eerste, p. 4.
53 Richard Holt, 'The Age of the Gentleman Amateur', in Richard Holt, *Sport and the British: A Modern History* (Oxford: Clarendon Press, 1989), pp. 98–117, 98–107.
54 Anon., 'Nederlandsche Beroepsspelers', *NRC*, 28 February 1910, Avond, A, p. 1.
55 Anon., 'Een nieuwe vereeniging!', *De Courant*, 5 January 1914, p. 3.
56 Anon., 'De Jaarlijke vergadering van den N.V.B.', *De Courant*, 6 July 1914, p. 2.
57 Verkamman, *Oranje Toen en Nu*, p. 103.
58 In the 1920s the issue of amateurism would become a particularly explosive one in Dutch football, and some feared a split similar to the one which had occurred in English football in 1907. The year 1922 saw the formation of the 'Netherlandsche Corinthians', who modelled themselves on the English team of the same name and saw themselves as the protectors of 'proper' Dutch amateurism. They believed that the popularisation of football had seen it move away from its earlier purpose and towards the concept of winning at all costs, with an accompanying threat of financial rewards. Their organisation, which was open to all clubs established before 1900, was aimed at promoting the quality of Dutch football, but to those outside it looked more like an organisation aimed at stopping the growing influence

of the *volksvoetbal* clubs and preserving an elite form of the game. See Miermans, *Voetbal in Nederland*, pp. 148–57.

59 Foucault, *Discipline and Punish*, pp. 180–1.
60 Anon., 'A.F.C. – V.U.C 8 -0', *De Courant*, 7 November 1910, Ochtend, p. 3.
61 Anon., 'Rotterdam', *De Courant*, 14 November 1910, Avond, p. 6.
62 Anon., 'Sterren van het voetbalveld', *De Revue der Sporten*, Jaar 12, No. 22, 29 January 1919, p. 309.
63 Anon., 'Overzicht', *De Courant*, 5 December 1910, Ochtend, p. 2.
64 Anon., 'A.F.C.–Willem II', *Algemeen Handelsblad*, 3 June 1918, Avond, Tweede, p. 5.
65 For example the *NRC* in 1910 provided a detailed explanation of the play-offs, the league promotion and relegation restructuring, irregularities, the *NVB* magazine, meetings, an agreement to select a coach for the national team and a view on the possible association with the *Dutch BvLO*. Anon., 'Nederlandsche Voetbalbond', *NRC*, 21 November 1910, Avond, D, p. 3.
66 Anon., 'Nieuwjaars-wedstrijd', *De Courant*, 3 January 1910, Ochtend, p. 2.
67 Anon., 'Forward–Blauw-Wit 1–5', *De Courant*, 7 November 1910, Ochtend, p. 3.
68 Anon., 'Nederland–Duitschland 4–4', *Algemeen Handelsblad*, 6 April 1914, Avond, Derde, pp. 10–11, 10.
69 Anon., 'R.K. Voetbaldag te Arnhem', *Maasbode*, 31 January 1910, Avond, Eerste, p. 2.
70 Anon., 'De Holland–Belgie wedstrijd op het H.F.C. terrein?', De *Maasbode*, 28 February 1910, Avond, Tweede, p. 2.
71 Anon., 'De Scheepsvaartbekerwedstrijden', *De Courant*, 2 September 1918, p. 5.
72 Anon., 'V.O.C.–Vitesse', *Maasbode*, 6 April 1914, Avond, Derde, p. 1.
73 Anon., 'Voetbal', *NRC*, 2 November 1914, Avond, B, p. 3.
74 Anon., 'De Jaarlijke vergadering van den N.V.B.', *De Courant*, 6 July 1914, p. 2.
75 Anon., 'Jaarvergadering van den R.V.B.', *Maasbode*, 1 July 1918, Avond, Eerste, p. 2.
76 Anon., 'Nederlandsche Voetbalbond', *NRC*, 21 November 1910, Avond, D, p. 3.
77 *Voetbal-Jaarboekje 1913/1914*, pp. 305–312.
78 Anon., 'Federatie van Erkende Voetbalbonden', *De Courant*, 4 May 1914, p. 2.
79 E. L. Riehl, 'Het Omkoopingsgeval', *De Courant*, 6 May 1918, p. 6.
80 Miermans notes two main influences on Dutch football from the First World War. First, many existing players stopped playing and this meant some clubs disbanded. Secondly, the spread of individuals around the country brought a new audience into contact with the game and for servicemen there was more time to practice the game. Miermans, *Voetbal in Nederland*, pp. 119–25.
81 Zevenbergen, *Rotterdams Voetbalglorie*, p. 52.
82 Anon., 'Het Conflict in den N.V.B.', *De Courant*, 3 June 1918, p. 6.
83 Anon., 'De R.-K. Voetbalvereeniging in Nijmegen', *Het Volk*, 2 December 1918, Eerste, p. 2.
84 Anon., 'RK Sportvereeninging Graaf Willem II', *Maasbode*, 4 February 1918, Avond, Tweede, p. 2.
85 Anon., 'Duitschland–Belgie (0–3)', *Maasbode*, 17 May 1910, Avond, Tweede, p. 2.
86 Anon., 'De Scheepsvaartbekerwedstrijden: Blauw-Wit – R.C.H. (1–0)', *De Courant*, 2 September 1918, p. 5.
87 Anon., 'De Wedstrijden van Gisteren', *NRC*, 4 February 1918, Avond, A, p. 1.
88 Bale, 'The Spatial Development of the Modern Stadium', pp. 125–7.
89 Anon., 'Nederland–Duitschland 4–4', *Algemeen Handelsblad*, 6 April 1914, Avond, Derde, pp. 10–11, 11.
90 Anon., 'Holland–Duitschland', *Het Volk*, 6 April 1914, Eerste, p. 2.
91 The banning of a team of Sparta women wanting to play football against a touring English side in 1893 is mentioned in Zevenbergen, *Rotterdams Voetbalglorie*, p. 25. More on women in early Dutch sport (although little on football) can be found in J. Steendijk-Kuypers, *Vrouwen-Beweging: Medische En Culturele Aspecten Van Vrouwen In De Sport, Gezien In Het Kader Van De Sporthistorie (1880–1928)* (Rotterdam: Erasmus, 1999).
92 Anon., 'Sportnieuws', *Het Volk*, 3 June 1918, Tweede, p. 6.
93 Anon., 'De Scheepsvaartbekerwedstrijden: Blauw-Wit wint den beker', *Het Volk*, 2 September 1918, Eerste, p. 2.
94 Anon., 'Voetbal te Ambt-Almelo', *NRC*, 21 November 1910, Avond, A, p. 1.
95 Anon., 'Om den Zilveren Bal', *NRC*, 2 September 1918, Avond, A, p. 1.
96 Anon., 'Sportnieuws', *Het Volk*, 5 January 1914, Tweede, p. 8.
97 Anon., 'De Wedstrijden van Gisteren', *Algemeen Handelsblad*, 4 February 1918, Avond, Derde, p. 9.
98 Anon., 'De Wedstrijden van Paaschdagen', *Algemeen Handelsblad*, 2 April 1918, Ochtend, Tweede, p. 5.
99 Anon., 'H.V.V. in Duisburg', *NRC*, 5 September 1910, Avond, D, p. 2.

100 Anon., 'Nederland–Duitschland 4–4', *Algemeen Handelsblad*, 6 April 1914, Avond, Derde, pp. 10–11, 11.
101 Anon., 'Nederland–Duitschland: Een leekepraatje', *NRC*, 6 April 1914, Avond, D, p. 1.
102 Anon., 'Nederland–Duitschland: Een leekepraatje', *NRC*, 6 April 1914, Avond, D, p. 1.
103 It may not be a surprise to find that *Het Volk* did not present the game in the same way, instead taking time to mention a Dutch military band of 'doubtful quality'. Anon., 'Holland–Duitschland', *Het Volk*, 4 April 1914, Eerste, p. 2.
104 Anon., 'Sparta–Ajax 0–5', *Maasbode*, 2 February 1914, Avond, Derde, p. 2.
105 Anon., 'De Wedstrijden van Gisteren', *Algemeen Handelsblad*, 6 May 1918, Avond, Derde, p. 10.
106 Anon., 'De Scheepvaartbekerwedstrijden', *Het Volk*, 2 September 1918, Eerste, p. 2; and Anon., 'Sportnieuws', *Het Volk*, 3 June 1918, Tweede, p. 8.
107 Anon., 'H.V.V.–Sparta', *Maasbode*, 3 January 1910, Avond, Tweede, p. 1.
108 Anon., 'De Wedstrijden van Zondag', *Maasbode*, 24 October 1910, Avond, Tweede, p. 1.
109 Anon., 'R.K. Voetbalbond', *Maasbode*, 9 September 1910, Avond, Derde, p. 2; and Anon., 'R.K.V.B. afd. Nijmegen', *Maasbode*, 5 August 1918, Avond, Tweede, p. 2.
110 Anon., R.K.V.V. Graaf Willem II', *Maasbode*, 7 December 1914, Extra-Editie, Eerste, p. 2; Anon., R.K.V.V. 'Leonidas', *Maasbode*, 7 December 1914, Extra-Editie, Eerste, p. 2; Anon., 'R.K. Sportvereeninging Graaf Willem II', *Maasbode*, 4 February 1918, Avond, Tweede, p. 2; Anon., 'Velocitas II–R.K.V.V. Bredania 2–3', *Maasbode*, 4 March 1918, Avond, Tweede, p. 2.

Chapter 5

1 An image of C. J. K. van Aalst can be found via the *Stadsarchief Amsterdam* at http://beeldbank.amsterdam.nl/beeldbank/indeling/detail/start/2?q_searchfield=van+aalst.
2 A copy of the diary of C. J. K. van Aalst was kindly given to me by the *ING* in The Hague. An online version can be accessed at: resources.huygens.knaw.nl/retroboeken/vanaalst/. Throughout this history I will reference this source as: Van Aalst, 'Dagboeken', followed by the corresponding date and page number.
3 Personal email to *ING*, 15 March 2010.
4 Irina Paperno, 'What Can Be Done with Diaries?', *The Russian Review*, 63 (October 2004), pp. 561–73, 565.
5 Paperno, 'What Can Be Done with Diaries?', p. 565.
6 Rosi Braidotti, *The Posthuman* (Cambridge: Polity Press, 2013), p. 167.
7 Braidotti, *The Posthuman*, pp. 163–9.
8 Ton de Graaf, 'Dr. Cornelis Johannes Karel van Aalst: een Amsterdams zakenman en bankier', *Amstelodamum*, vol. 85 (1998), pp. 7–14, 7–8.
9 J. Kymmell, 'AALST, Cornelis Johannes Karel van', *Biografisch Woordenboek van Nederland*, ed. J. Charité (Amsterdam: Elsevier, 1985), Vol. II, pp. 1–2.
10 De Graaf, 'Dr. Cornelis Johannes Karel van Aalst', pp. 8–10.
11 Van Aalst, 'Dagboeken', 5 October 1914, p. 24.
12 Van Aalst, 'Dagboeken', 7 October 1914, p. 24.
13 Van Aalst, 'Dagboeken', 30 September 1914, p. 22.
14 Van Aalst, 'Dagboeken', 10 February 1916, p. 230.
15 L. Lauer, 'De Olympische Spelen der Oudheid', *De Revue der Sporten*, Jaar 9, No. 52, 6 September 1916, pp. 660–3, 663.
16 Anon., *De Revue der Sporten*, Jaar 9, No. 52, 6 September 1916, pp. 664–9.
17 Anon., *De Revue der Sporten*, Jaar 9, No. 52, 6 September 1916, p. 670.
18 An image of C. J. K. van Aalst (fourth from left) and Queen Wilhelmina at the Sportpark in July 1916 can be found in *De Revue der Sporten* here: http://www.delpher.nl/nl/tijdschriften/view?coll=dts&identifier=dts%3A1671041%3Ampeg21.
19 Van Aalst, 'Dagboeken', 13 July 1916, p. 282.
20 Van Aalst, 'Dagboeken', 15 July 1916, pp. 282–3.
21 Van Aalst, 'Dagboeken', 15 July 1916, p. 284.
22 Van Aalst, 'Dagboeken', 29 November 1915, p. 200; and 19 November 1914, p. 40. An image of Van Aalst (third from left, standing) and the board of the *AIJC* can be found in *De Revue der Sporten* at http://www.delpher.nl/nl/tijdschriften/view?coll=dts&identifier=dts%3A1671012%3Ampeg21.

23 Van Aalst, 'Dagboeken', 26 February 1916, p. 232.
24 S. Kruizinga, 'NOT Neutrality', in *Caught in the Middle: Neutrals, Neutrality and the First World War*, ed. J. den Hertog and S. Kruizinga (Amsterdam: Askant, 2011), pp. 85–103, 88.
25 Kruizinga, 'NOT Neutrality', pp. 88–91.
26 Kruizinga, 'NOT Neutrality', p. 102.
27 Van Aalst, 'Dagboeken', 17 September 1914, p. 10.
28 Abbenhuis, *The Art of Staying Neutral*, p. 169.
29 Van Aalst, 'Dagboeken', 12 September 1914, p. 6.
30 Van Aalst, 'Dagboeken', 20 November 1914, p. 41.
31 Van Aalst, 'Dagboeken', 3 September 1914, p. 2.
32 Kruizinga, 'NOT Neutrality', p. 91.
33 Van Aalst, 'Dagboeken', 9 September 1914, p. 4.
34 Van Aalst, 'Dagboeken', 23 March 1915, p. 119.
35 Van Aalst, 'Dagboeken', 6 December 1915, p. 206; and 11 December 1915, p. 207.
36 Van Aalst, 'Dagboeken', 30 May 1916, pp. 263–4.
37 Van Aalst, 'Dagboeken', 22 December 1914, p. 51.
38 Van Aalst, 'Dagboeken', 27 January 1915, p. 72.
39 Van Aalst, 'Dagboeken', 14 November 1914, pp. 39–40.
40 Van Aalst, 'Dagboeken', 21 December 1914, pp. 50–1.
41 Van Aalst, 'Dagboeken', 8 October 1914, p. 26.
42 E. de Roodt, *Oorlogsgasten: vluchtelingen en krijgsgevangenen in Nederland tijdens de Eerste Wereldoorlog* (Zaltbommel: Europese Bibliotheek, 2000), p. 142. More on the fall of Antwerp and subsequent refugees can be found in Susanne Wolf, *Guarded Neutrality: Diplomacy and Internment in the Netherlands during the First World War* (Leiden: Brill, 2013), pp. 47–60.
43 De Roodt, *Oorlogsgasten*, pp. 140–8.
44 De Roodt, *Oorlogsgasten*, pp. 148–50 and Wolf, *Guarded Neutrality*, pp. 53–60. Wolf provides excerpts from a Roosendaal resident's diary between 3 October and 9 October 1914, which demonstrate the rapid increase in refugees and the deteriorating situation in the city, pp. 53–4.
45 Anon., 'Voor Antwerpen: Hoe gruwelijk de oorlog is', *Algemeen Handelsblad*, 7 October 1914, Avond, Eerste, pp. 1–2, 2.
46 Anon., 'Steun voor de Belgische vluchtelingen', *Algemeen Handelsblad*, 7 October 1914, Avond, Eerste, p. 5.
47 Anon., 'Kunst', *Algemeen Handelsblad*, 8 October 1914, Ochtend, Eerste, p. 2.
48 Anon., 'D.F.C.–Sparta 1–1', *Algemeen Handelsblad*, 12 October 1914, Ochtend, p. 3.
49 Anon., 'Belgische Vluchtelingen', *Algemeen Handelsblad*, 9 October 1914, Ochtend, Eerste, p. 2.
50 Anon., 'Belgische Vluchtelingen', *Algemeen Handelsblad*, 9 October 1914, Ochtend, Eerste, p. 2.
51 Anon., 'Belgische Vluchtelingen', *Algemeen Handelsblad*, 9 October 1914, Ochtend, Eerste, p. 2.
52 Piet de Rooy, 'Oorlog en revolutie', in *Geschiedenis van Amsterdam: Tweestrijd om de Hoofdstad 1900–2000*, ed. Piet de Rooy (Amsterdam: SUN, 2007), Vol. IV, pp. 73–125 (excepting pp. 108–18) 79.
53 Anon.,'Belgische Vluchtelingen', *Algemeen Handelsblad*, 12 October 1914, Octendblad, pp. 2–3, 2. A collection of 250 guilders was also made across the city, see De Roodt, *Oorlogsgasten*, pp. 153–5.
54 De Roodt, *Oorlogsgasten*, pp. 161–2.
55 Administratie van het *Algemeen Handelsblad*, 'Lectuur voor de Vluchtelingen', *Algemeen Handelsblad*, 10 October 1914, Ochtend, Eerste, p. 1.
56 For example, Geert Jan Koops, on the Huygensstraat, offered a range of woollen products for refugees at extra-low prices. Geert Jan Koops, 'Voor de Vluchtelingen', *Algemeen Handelsblad*, 12 October 1914, Ochtend, p. 4.
57 Anon., 'Belgische Vluchtelingen', *Algemeen Handelsblad*, 12 October 1914, Ochtend, pp. 2–3, 2.
58 De Roodt, *Oorlogsgasten*, pp. 154–5.
59 H. G. de Booy-Boissevain, 'Belgische Vluchtelingen', *Algemeen Handelsblad*, 11 October 1914, Ochtend, Eerste, p. 1. Throughout the war, many other societies and organisations were established to help those disadvantaged by conflict. The *Centraal Comité voor Huisvesting* was part of a private organisation set up in Amsterdam to help Belgian (and other) victims of war and it distributed money in the southern provinces. This was called the *Nederlandsch Comité tot Steun van Belgische en Andere Slachtoffers* (Netherlands Committee for the Support of Belgian and Other Victims). To coordinate help and oversee many of the private organisations, the government initiated the *Centrale Commissie* under the guidance of Baron van Tuyll van Serooskerken (president of the Netherlands Olympic Committee). The *Centrale Commissie* was one of the most active organisations in coordinating help for those exiled in the Netherlands. See De Roodt, *Oorlogsgasten*, p. 141.
60 *Algemeen Handelsblad*, 11 October 1914, Ochtend, Tweede, p. 5.

61 Frhr. von der Schuetz, 'Belgische Vluchtelingen: Verzoeken om naar Antwerpen terug te keeren', *Algemeen Handelsblad*, 12 October 1914, Ochtend, p. 2.
62 De Roodt, *Oorlogsgasten*, p. 162.
63 Abbenhuis, *The Art of Staying Neutral*, p. 99.
64 De Roodt, *Oorlogsgasten*, pp. 165–168.
65 Abbenhuis, *The Art of Staying Neutral*, p. 97; and De Roodt, *Oorlogsgasten*, p. 147.
66 Abbenhuis, *The Art of Staying Neutral*, p. 99.
67 De Roodt, *Oorlogsgasten*, p. 173; and De Rooy, 'Oorlog en revolutie', p. 79.
68 See Van Aalst, 'Dagboeken', 10 October–11 October 1914, p. 27; and Van Aalst, 'Dagboeken', 29 October 1914, p.33.
69 Van Aalst, 'Dagboeken', 22 January 1915, p. 69.
70 Van Aalst, 'Dagboeken', 9 October 1914, p. 26.
71 Van Aalst, 'Dagboeken', 17 January 1915, p. 67.
72 Van Aalst, 'Dagboeken', 25 March 1915, p. 120; and 26 March 1915, p. 120.
73 Van Aalst, 'Dagboeken', 3 January 1916, p. 213.
74 Van Aalst, 'Dagboeken', 4 December 1915, pp. 202–3.
75 His arrest was the focus of an article on the website Sportsgeschiedenis, 'De arrestatie van Kick Schröder', by Jurryt van de Vooren. This was an inspiration for my own research into the affair. The article can be found at http://www.sportgeschiedenis.nl/2009/03/18/de-arrestatie-van-kick-schroder.aspx.
76 An image of Schröder can be found via the *Stadsarchief Amsterdam* at http://beeldbank.amsterdam.nl/beeldbank/weergave/record/?id=16-0076.
77 Anon., 'J. C. Schroder als Sportman', *Algemeen Handelsblad*, 20 December 1938, Ochtend, Derde, p. 6.
78 Anon., 'De Internationale Voetbalwedstrijd', *Rotterdamsch Nieuwsblad*, 8 February 1894, Tweede, p. 1. The *Bondselftal* was the 'Association Team' of the *NVB*. This was an 'unofficial' national team comprised of Dutch players which often played against foreign club teams. It is considered the forerunner of the 'official' Netherlands international team, whose first match was in 1905. The *Bondselftal* played a total of fifteen representative matches, with the last one against Corinthians in April 1906. Verkamman, *Oranje Toen en Nu*, pp. 12–14.
79 Verkamman, *Oranje Toen en Nu*, p. 13.
80 An image of Schröder (inset photo) as captain of the All Holland cricket team in 1909 can be found in *De Revue der Sporten* at http://www.delpher.nl/nl/tijdschriften/view?coll=dts&identifier=dts%3A1664012%3Ampeg21%3A0002&pres%5Bmaxperpage%5D=36.
81 Anon., 'Cricket', *Algemeen Handelsblad*, 16 May 1894, Ochtend, p. 1; and Anon., 'Cricket', *Algemeen Handelsblad*, 5 August 1913, Ochtend, Eerste, p. 2.
82 Anon., 'J. C. Schroder als Sportman', *Algemeen Handelsblad*, 20 December 1938, Ochtend, Derde, p. 6.
83 Anon., 'J. C. Schroder als Sportman', *Algemeen Handelsblad*, 20 December 1938, Ochtend, Derde, p. 6
84 Abbenhuis, *The Art of Staying Neutral*, p. 169.
85 Joan Hemel, *Een journalistiek geheim ontsluierd: de Dubbelmonarchie en een geval van dubbele moraal in de Nederlandse pers tijdens de Eerste Wereldoorlog* (Apeldoorn: Spinhuis Uitgevers, 2010), pp. 28–31.
86 Abbenhuis, *The Art of Staying Neutral*, pp. 169–71.
87 Abbenhuis, *The Art of Staying Neutral*, p. 170.
88 J.C. Schröder quoted in Jurryt van de Vooren, 'De arrestatie van Kick Schröder', http://www.sportgeschiedenis.nl/2009/03/18/de-arrestatie-van-kick-schroder.aspx; see also J.C. Schröders reply to a letter from F.E. Posthumus Meijjes, 'Geen "Legende"', *De Telegraaf*, 16 June 1915, Avond, Tweede, p. 8.
89 Jurrt van de Vooren, 'De arrestatie van Kick Schröder', http://www.sportgeschiedenis.nl/2009/03/18/de-arrestatie-van-kick-schroder.aspx.
90 Anon., 'De pers-camarilla te Amsterdam', *De Telegraaf*, Ochtend, Eerste, 27 November 1915, p. 4.
91 Anon., 'De hoofdredakteur van "De Telegraaf" gevangen genomen', *Het Volk*, 6 December 1915, Eerste, p. 2.
92 Anon., 'De hoofdredakteur van "De Telegraaf" gevangen genomen', *Het Volk*, 6 December 1915, Eerste, p. 2.
93 Van Aalst, 'Dagboeken', 5 December 1915, p. 204.
94 Van Aalst, 'Dagboeken', 5 December 1915, p. 204.
95 H. M. C. Holdert. 'Aan onze lezers!', *De Telegraaf*, 5 December 1915, Tweede, p. 5.

96 For an example of the letters sent to *De Telegraaf* throughout early December 1915 see, Anon., 'De gevangenemming van onzen Hoofdredacteur', *De Telegraaf*, 9 December 1915, Avond, Tweede, p. 5–6.
97 M. de Visser, *De Telegraaf*, 9 December 1915, Avond, Tweede, p. 5.
98 J. F. Niermeijer, *De Telegraaf*, 9 December 1915, Avond, Tweede, p. 5.
99 J. R. Heuckeroth, *De Telegraaf*, 9 December 1915, Avond, Tweede, p. 5.
100 R. C. Boer et al., 'Een adres van Amsterdamsche hoogleeraren', *De Telegraaf*, 9 December 1915, Avond, Tweede, p. 5.
101 Jurryt van de Vooren, 'De arrestatie van Kick Schröder', http://www.sportgeschiedenis.nl/2009/03/18/de-arrestatie-van-kick-schroder.aspx.
102 J. van Epen, 'Holland Schaam je!!!', *De Telegraaf*, 8 December 1915, Avond, Tweede, p. 6.
103 Martin Liket, 'In wiens naam … ?', *De Telegraaf*, 10 December 1915, Avond, Tweede, p. 6.
104 Across the week, Raemaekers produced several cartoons. Some can be found at Louis Raemaekers, *De Telegraaf*, 10 December 1915, Avond, Tweede, p. 5; Louis Raemaekers, *De Telegraaf*, 13 December 1915, Avond, Tweede, p. 5; Louis Raemaekers, *De Telegraaf*, 14 December 1915, Avond, Tweede, p. 5; Louis Raemaekers, *De Telegraaf*, 20 December 1915, Avond, Tweede, p. 5; Louis Raemaekers, *De Telegraaf*, 22 December 1915, Avond, Tweede, p. 5; Louis Raemaekers, *De Telegraaf*, 23 December 1915, Avond, Tweede, p. 5.
105 J. H. Speenhoff, 'Schröder in de Bajes', *De Telegraaf*, 9 December 1915, Ochtend, Tweede, p. 5.
106 Anon., 'De Fransche pers en onzen hoofdredachterur', *De Telegraaf*, 9 December 1915, Ochtend, Tweede, pp. 6–7.
107 Anon., 'Het was te voorzien!', *De Telegraaf*, 9 December 1915, Ochtend, Tweede, p. 6.
108 Van Aalst, 'Dagboeken', 21 December 1915, p. 209.
109 J. C. Schröder, 'Een drove Sinterklaasgrap', *De Telegraaf*, 22 December 1915, Avond, Tweede, p. 6.
110 Mak, *Amsterdam: A Brief Life of the City*, p. 224.
111 Van Aalst, 'Dagboeken', 30 June 1917, p. 479.
112 Van Aalst, 'Dagboeken', 22 June 1917, p. 471.
113 De Rooy, 'Oorlog en revolutie', pp. 82–3.
114 Marten Buschman, 'Kitsz, Cornelis' on the website of *Biografisch Woordenboek van het Socialisme en de Arbeidersbeweging in Nederland,* https://socialhistory.org/bwsa/biografie/kitsz.
115 De Rooy, 'Oorlog en revolutie', pp. 82–5.
116 Anon., 'Aardappelrelletjes', *Algemeen Handelsblad*, 28 June 1917, Avond, Derde, p. 10.
117 Anon., 'Aardappelrelletjes', *Algemeen Handelsblad*, 28 June 1917, Avond, Derde, p. 10.
118 Anon., 'Stadsnieuws, De rust weergekeerd', *Algemeen Handelsblad*, 29 June 1917, Avond Derde, p. 11.
119 Anon., 'Stadsnieuws', *Algemeen Handelsblad*, 3 July 1917, Ochtend, Eerste, pp. 2–3, 2.
120 Anon., 'Stadsnieuws', *Algemeen Handelsblad*, 3 July 1917, Ochtend, Eerste, p. 2.
121 De Rooy, 'Oorlog en revolutie', p. 85. See also *De Telegraaf*, 'De algemeene staking', 5 July 1917, Ochtend Eerst, p. 3.
122 Anon., 'Vervolg Nieuwstijdingen', *De Tribune: Rev. Soc. Volksblad,* 5 July 1917, p. 2.
123 Anon., 'Stadsnieuws', *Algemeen Handelsblad*, 3 July 1917, Ochtend, Eerste, p. 2.
124 Anon., 'Stadsnieuws', *Algemeen Handelsblad*, 3 July 1917, Ochtend, Eerste, p. 2.
125 Anon., 'Stadsnieuws', *Algemeen Handelsblad*, 3 July 1917, Ochtend, Eerste, pp. 2–3.
126 Van Aalst, 'Dagboeken', 3 July 1917, p. 482.
127 Anon., 'Een Manifest der Bolsjewiki aan de soldaten', *De Tribune: Rev. Soc. Volksblad,* 4 July 1917, p. 1.
128 Van Aalst, 'Dagboeken', 3 July 1917, p. 482.
129 Van Aalst, 'Dagboeken', 3 July 1917, p. 484.
130 Van Aalst, 'Dagboeken', 3 July 1917, p. 483.
131 Anon., 'Stadsnieuws, De relletjes', *Algemeen Handelsblad*, 4 July 1917, Ochtend, Eerste, pp. 2–3.
132 Anon., 'Stadsnieuws, De relletjes', *Algemeen Handelsblad*, 5 July 1917, Ochtend, Eerste, pp. 2–3, 2.
133 Anon., 'De Meeting in de Kruislaan', *De Tribune: Rev. Soc. Volksblad,* 5 July 1917, p. 4.
134 Anon., 'De aardappelennood', *Het Volk*, 5 July 1917, Eerste, pp. 2–3, 2 and Anon., 'De Meeting in de Kruislaan', *De Tribune: Rev. Soc. Volksblad,* 5 July 1917, p. 4.
135 Anon., 'Stadsnieuws, De relletjes', *Algemeen Handelsblad*, 5 July 1917, Ochtend, Eerste, p. 2.
136 Willem Hendrik de Beaufort, *Dagboeken en aantekeningen van Willem Hendrik de Beaufort 1874–1918, Tweede Band: 1911–1918* ('s-Gravenhage: Instituut voor Nederlandse Geschiedenis, 1993), 6 July 1917, pp. 926–7.
137 De Rooy, 'Oorlog en revolutie', p. 85.
138 Anon., 'Stadsnieuws, De relletjes', *Algemeen Handelsblad*, 6 July 1917, Avond, Tweede, p. 6.
139 Anon., 'De toestand van heden', *Het Volk*, 6 July 1917, Eerste, p. 3 and De Rooy, 'Oorlog en revolutie', p. 79.

References

Books, journals, articles

In the interests of space, the full details of each entry contained within biographical collections is not listed here, although a reference for each volume is provided. Details of each individual entry can be found in the notes for the relevant individual.

Aalst, C. J. K. van and W. A. Holdert, 'Prijsvraag voor een stadion uitgeschreven door de Maatschappij "Het Nederlandsch Sportpark" te Amsterdam', *Architectura*, Vol. 20, No. 19 (11 May 1912), pp. 154–6

Abbenhuis, M. M., *The Art of Staying Neutral: The Netherlands in the First World War, 1914–1918* (Amsterdam: Amsterdam University Press, 2006)

Andrews, D. L., 'Posting Up: French Post-Structuralism and the Critical Analysis of Contemporary Sporting Culture', in *Handbook of Sports Studies*, ed. J. Coakley and E. Dunning (London: Sage, 2012), pp. 106–37

Ankersmit, F., 'Historiography and Postmodernism', *History and Theory*, Vol. 28, No. 2 (May 1989), pp. 137–53

Ankersmit, F., *The Reality Effect in the Writing of History; The Dynamics of Historiographical Topology* (Amsterdam: Koninklijke Nederlandse Akademie van Wetenschappen, 1989)

Ankersmit, F., *Historical Representation* (Stanford: Stanford University Press, 2001)

Anon., *Algemeen Adresboek der Gemeente Rotterdam 1910* (Rotterdam: M. Wyt & Zonen, 1910)

Baedeker, K., *Belgium and Holland including the Grand-Duchy of Luxembourg* (Leipzig: Karl Baedeker Publishing, 1910)

Bale, J., 'The Spatial Development of the Modern Stadium', International Review for the Sociology of Sport, Vol. 28, No. 2–3 (June 1993), pp. 121–33

Bank, J. and M. van Buuren, *Dutch Culture in a European Perspective, III: 1900: The Age of Bourgeois Culture* (Assen: Royal Van Gorcum; Basingstoke: Palgrave Macmillan, 2004)

Barthes, R., 'The Death of the Author', in R. Barthes, *The Rustle of Language* (Berkeley and Los Angeles, CA: University of California Press, 1989), pp. 49–55

Barthes, R., 'The Discourse of History', in R. Barthes, *The Rustle of Language* (Berkeley and Los Angeles, CA: University of California Press, 1989), pp. 127–40

Barthes, R., 'The Reality Effect', in R. Barthes, *The Rustle of Language* (Berkeley and Los Angeles, CA: University of California Press, 1989), pp. 141–8

Beaufort W. H. de, *Dagboeken en aantekeningen van Willem Hendrik de Beaufort 1874–1918, Tweede Band: 1911–1918* ('s-Gravenhage: Instituut voor Nederlandse Geschiedenis, 1993)

Berkel, K. van, *Biografisch Woordenboek van Nederland* ('s Gravenhage: Instituut voor Nederlandse Geschiedenis, 2008), Vol. VI

Berlage, H. P. et al., 'Prijsvragen. Stadion-prijsvraag', *Bouwkundig Weekblad*, Vol. 32, No. 31 (3 August 1912), pp. 377–378

Best, S. and D. Kellner, *Postmodern Theory: Critical Interrogations* (New York: Guilford Press, 1991)

Booth, D., *The Field: Truth and Fiction in Sport History* (Abingdon: Routledge, 2005)

Bourdieu, P., 'From Rules to Strategies', in P. Bourdieu, *In Other Words: Essays Towards a Reflexive Sociology* (Cambridge: Polity Press, 1990), pp. 59–75

Bourdieu, P., *On Television* (New York: The New Press, 1998)

Bowen Raddeker, H., *Sceptical History: Feminist and Postmodern Approaches in Practice* (London: Routledge, 2007)

Braidotti, R., *The Posthuman* (Cambridge: Polity, 2013)

Breen, J. C., 'Kroniek van Amsterdam van 1 November 1908 tot 31 October 1909', *Jaarboek der vereeniging Amstelodamum*, No. 8 (1910), pp. 1–30

Brown, C., *Postmodernism for Historians* (Harlow: Pearson Education, 2005)

Burns, J., *Barça: A People's Passion* (London: Bloomsbury, 1999)

Casciato, M., *The Amsterdam School* (Rotterdam: 010 Publishers, 2003)

Caudwell, J., 'Women's Football in the United Kingdom: Theorizing Gender and Unpacking the Butch Lesbian Image', *Journal of Sport and Social Issues*, Vol. 23, No. 4 (1999), 390–402.

Certeau, M. de, 'History: Science and Fiction', in M. de Certeau, *Heterologies: Discourse on the Other* (Minneapolis: University of Minnesota Press, 1986), pp. 199–221

Certeau, M. de, *The Writing of History* (New York: Columbia University Press, 1988)

Charité, J. (ed.), *Biografisch Woordenboek van Nederland* ('s Gravenhage: Martinus Nijhoff, 1979), Vol. I

Charité, J. (ed.), *Biografisch Woordenboek van Nederland* (Amsterdam: Elsevier, 1985), Vol. II

Charité, J. (ed.), *Biografisch Woordenboek van Nederland* ('s Gravenhage: Instituut voor Nederlandse Geschiedenis, 1989), Vol. III

Cocheret, C. A., *"Sparta!": een Rotterdamse voetbalclub 1888–1963* (Rotterdam: Nijgh & Van Dietmar, 1963)

Demos, J., 'Afterword: Notes From, and About, the History/Fiction Borderland', *Rethinking History*, Vol. 9, No. 2/3 (2005), pp. 329–35

Dunning, E., *Sport Matters: Sociological Studies of Sport, Violence and Civilisation*, (London: Routledge, 2001)

Evans, R., *In Defence of History*, (London: Granta, 2000)

Foot, J., *Calcio: A History of Italian Football* (London: Harper Perennial, 2007)

Foucault, M., 'Two Lectures', in M. Foucault, *Power/Knowledge: Selected Interviews and Other Writings 1972–1977'* (New York: Pantheon Books, 1980), pp. 78–109

Foucault, M., *Discipline and Punish: The Birth of the Prison* (London: Penguin, 1991)

Foucault, M., 'Space, Knowledge and Power', in M. Foucault, *Power: The Essential Works of Michel Foucault* (London: Allen Lane, 2001), Vol. III, pp. 349–364

Foucault, M., *The Archaeology of Knowledge and The Discourse on Language* (London: Routledge, 2002)

Graaf, T. de, 'Dr. Cornelis Johannes Karel van Aalst: een Amsterdams zakenman en bankier', *Amstelodamum*, Vol. 85 (1998), pp. 7–14

Harding, A., 'Amsterdam and Rotterdam', in *European Cities towards 2000: profiles, policies and prospects*, ed. A. Harding et al. (Manchester: Manchester University Press, 1994), pp. 18–44

Hemel, J., *Een journalistiek geheim ontsluierd: de Dubbelmonarchie en een geval van dubbele moraal in de Nederlandse pers tijdens de Eerste Wereldoorlog* (Apeldoorn: Spinhuis Uitgevers, 2010)

Hesse-Lichtenberger, U., *Tor!: The Story of German Football* (London: WSC Books, 2002)

Highmore, B., *Michel de Certeau: Analysing Culture* (London: Continuum, 2006)

Holt, R., 'The Age of the Gentleman Amateur', in R. Holt, *Sport and the British: A Modern History* (Oxford: Clarendon Press, 1989), pp. 98–117

Houlihan, B., 'Politics and Sport', in *Handbook of Sports Studies*, ed. J. Coakley and E. Dunning (London: Sage, 2012), pp. 213–27

Hoven, J. and M. J., Adriani Engels, *Vijftig jaar N.V. het Nederlands sportpark 'Olympisch Stadion' te Amsterdam, 17 mei 1962* (Amsterdam: N.V. het Nederlands sportpark 'Olympisch Stadion', 1962)

Hoynck van Papendrecht, A., *Gedenkboek A. van Hoboken & Co.: 1774–1924* (Rotterdam: [n.p], 1924)

Jencks, C., 'What Then Is Post-Modernism?', in *The Post-Modern Reader*, ed. C. Jencks (Chichester: Wiley, 2011), pp. 14–37

Jenkins, K., *Why History?: Ethics and Postmodernity* (London: Routledge, 1999)

Kruizinga, S., 'NOT Neutrality', in *Caught in the Middle: Neutrals, Neutrality and the First World War*, ed. J. den Hertog and S. Kruizinga (Amsterdam: Askant, 2011), pp. 85–103

Kuper, S., *Ajax, the Dutch, the War: Football in Europe during the Second World War* (London: Orion, 2003)

Laar, P. van de, *Stad van formaat: geschiedenis van Rotterdam in de negentiende en twintigste eeuw* (Zwolle: Waanders, 2000)

Lyotard, J.-F., *The Postmodern Condition: A Report on Knowledge* (Manchester: Manchester University Press, 1984)

Lyotard, J.-F., *The Postmodern as Explained to Children: Correspondence 1982–1985* (London: Turnaround, 1992)

Mak, G., *Amsterdam: A Brief Life of the City* (London: The Harvill Press, 2001)

Malpas, S., *The Postmodern* (Abingdon: Routledge, 2005)

Manoff, M., 'Theories of the Archive from Across the Disciplines', *Portal: Libraries and the Academy*, Vol. 4, No. 1 (January 2004), pp. 9–25

Miermans, C., *Voetbal in Nederland: Een onderzoek naar de maatschappelijke en sportieve aspecten* (Assen: Koninglijke van Gorcum en Comp. N.V., 1955)

Mink, L. O., 'History and Fiction as Modes of Comprehension', *New Literary History*, Vol. 1, No. 3 (1970), pp. 541–58

Mooij, A. and R. Stokvis, 'De Gezonde stad', in *Amsterdam in de Tweede Gouden Eeuw*, ed. M. Bakker et al. (Bussum: Thoth; Amsterdam: Genootschap Amstelodamum, 2000), pp. 263–91

Munslow, A., *Narrative and History* (Basingstoke: Palgrave Macmillan, 2007)

Nederlandsche Voetbalbond, *Voetbal-Jaarboekje 1909/1910* (Amsterdam: Nederlandsche Voetbalbond, 1909), XII (1909/1910)

Nederlandsche Voetbalbond, *Voetbal-Jaarboekje 1913/1914* (Amsterdam: Nederlandsche Voetbalbond, 1913), XVI (1913/1914)

Orr, L., 'When History and Fiction Are Mixed Up: My Book Manuscript on Jean Zay and His Family', *Rethinking History*, Vol. 9, No. 2/3 (2005), pp. 255–73

Paperno, I., 'What Can Be Done with Diaries?', *The Russian Review*, Vol. 63 (October 2004), pp. 561–73

Piercey, N., 'Investment, Advertisement, and Sponsorship: Business in Dutch Football 1910–1920', *Dutch Crossing*, Vol. 35, No. 1 (March 2011), pp. 89–104.

Piercey, N., 'Football Grounds, Memory and Cultural History in Amsterdam and Rotterdam from 1910 to 1920: The Football Stadium and Ground as a Historical Resource', in *Memorialkultur im Fußballsport: Medien, Rituale und Praktiken des Erinnerns, Gedenkens und Vergessens. Irseer Dialoge. Kultur und Wissenschaft Interdisziplinar, Band 17*, ed. M. Herzog (Stuttgart: Kohlhammer, 2013), pp. 287–309

Plasse, J. van de, *Kroniek van de Nederlandse dagblad -en opiniepers* (Amsterdam: Cramwinckel, 2005)

Poster, M., *Cultural History and Postmodernity: Disciplinary Readings and Challenges* (New York: Columbia University Press, 1997)

Rail, G., 'Postmodernism and Sport Studies', in *Theory, Sport & Society*, ed. J. Maguire and J. Young (Bingley: Emerald, 2002), pp. 179–207

Romer, H., *Rotterdam in de jaren tien: 1910–1920* (Zaltbommel: Europese Bibliotheek, 1985)

Rooijen, M. van, *De Wortels van het Stedelijk Groen: een studie naar ontstaan en voortbestaan van de Nederlandse groene stad* ([n.p]: Erasmus Drukkerij, 1990)

Rooy, P. de, 'De Geest van omverwerping 1851–1876', in *Geschiedenis van Amsterdam: Hoofdstad in aanbouw 1813–1900*, ed. R. Aerts and P. de Rooy (Amsterdam: SUN, 2006), Vol. III, pp. 341–431

Rooy., P. de, 'Het middelpunt van het Vaderland 1901–1914', in *Geschiedenis van Amsterdam: Tweestrijd om de Hoofdstad 1900–2000*, ed. P. de Rooy (Amsterdam: SUN, 2007), Vol. IV, pp. 17–70

Rooy, P. de, 'Oorlog en revolutie', in *Geschiedenis van Amsterdam: Tweestrijd om de Hoofdstad 1900–2000*, ed. P. de Rooy (Amsterdam: SUN, 2007), Vol. IV, pp. 73–125 (excepting pp.108–18)

Roodt, E. de, *Oorlogsgasten: vluchtelingen en krijgsgevangenen in Nederland tijdens de Eerste Wereldoorlog* (Zaltbommel: Europese Bibliotheek, 2000)

Rowe, D., 'Introduction: Mapping the Media Sports Cultural Complex', in *Critical Readings: Sport, Culture and the Media*, ed. D. Rowe (Buckingham: Open University Press, 2004), pp. 1–22

Schirato, T., *Sports Discourse* (London: Bloomsbury Academic, 2013)

Schwan, A. and S. Shapiro, *How to Read Foucault's Discipline and Punish* (London: Pluto Press, 2011)

Shilling, C., *The Body and Social Theory* (London; Thousand Oaks, CA; New Delhi: Sage, 2003)

Slotkin, R., 'Fiction for the Purposes of History', *Rethinking History*, Vol. 9, No. 2/3 (2005), pp. 221–36

Southgate, B., *History Meets Fiction* (Harlow: Pearson Education, 2009)

Steendijk-Kuypers, J., *Vrouwen-Beweging: Medische En Culturele Aspecten Van Vrouwen In De Sport, Gezien In Het Kader Van De Sporthistorie (1880–1928)* (Rotterdam: Erasmus, 1999)

Stevenson, C. L., 'Sport as a Contemporary Social Phenomenon: A Functional Explanation', *International Journal of Physical Education*, Vol. 11, No. 3 (1974), pp. 8–14

Stokvis, R., 'Een genre in beweging: De ongemakkelijke verhouding tussen sport en journalistiek', in *Journalistieke cultuur in Nederland*, ed. J. Bardoel (Amsterdam: Amsterdam University Press, 2009), pp. 191–207

Tiessen-Raaphorst, A. (ed.), *Rapportage sport 2014* (The Hague: Sociaal en Cultureel Planbureau, 2015)

Verkamman, M., *Oranje Toen en Nu: 1905–1914, 2000/2001* (Houten: Premium Press, 2001)

Verkamman, M.(ed.), *90 jaar op het kasteel*, (Rotterdam: [n.p.], 2007)

Visser, J., M. Dicke and A. van der Zouwen (eds.), *Nederlandse ondernemers 1850–1950: Amsterdam* (Zutphen: Walburg Pers, 2013)

Visser, J., M. Dicke and A. van der Zouwen (eds.), *Nederlandse ondernemers 1850–1950: Rotterdam* (Zutphen: Walburg Pers, 2014)

Vos, J., *Recreatie in Rotterdam: tussen burger en bestuur* (Amsterdam: Boom, 1998)

Vries, B. de, 'Voluntary Societies in the Netherlands, 1750–1900', in *Civil Society, Associations and Urban Places: Class, Nation and Culture in Nineteenth-Century Europe*, ed. G. Morton, B. de Vries and R. J. Morris (Aldershot: Ashgate, 2006), pp. 103–16

Wagenaar, C., *Town Planning in the Netherlands since 1800: Responses to Enlightenment Ideas and Geopolitical Realities* (Rotterdam: 010 Publishers, 2011)

Wagenaar, C., and M. Steenhuis, 'Laboratorium Spangen', in *Interbellum Rotterdam: Kunst en cultuur 1918–1940*, ed. M. Halbertsma and P. van Ulzen (Rotterdam: NAI Uitgevers, 2001), pp. 179–202

White, H., 'Interpretation in History', *New Literary History*, Vol. 4, No. 2 (1973), pp. 281–314

White, H., 'The Question of Narrative in Contemporary Historical Theory', *History and Theory*, Vol. 23, No. 1 (February 1984), pp. 1–33

White, H., 'Introduction: Historical Fiction, Fictional History, and Historical Reality', *Rethinking History*, Vol. 9, No. 2/3 (2005), pp. 147–157

White, H., 'The Discourse of History', in H. White, *The Fiction of Narrative: Essays on History, Literature, and Theory, 1957–2007* (Baltimore, MD: Johns Hopkins University Press, 2010), pp. 187–202

Wiersum, E. 'Dagelijksche kroniek 1913', in *Rotterdamsch Jaarboekje 1914*, ed. Dr E. Wiersum (Rotterdam: W. L. & J. Brusse, 1914), pp. xiii–xxix

Wiersum, E., 'Dagelijksche kroniek 1914', in *Rotterdamsch Jaarboekje 1915*, ed. E. Wiersum (Rotterdam: W. L. & J. Brusse, 1915), pp. xiii–xxxvii

Winner, D., *Brilliant Orange: The Neurotic Genius of Dutch Football* (London: Bloomsbury, 2000)

Wintershoven, L., *Demografisch Eeuwboek Amsterdam; Ontwikkelingen tussen 1900 en 2000* (Amsterdam: Dienst Ruimtelijke Ordening, 2000)

Wolf, S., *Guarded Neutrality: Diplomacy and Internment in the Netherlands during the First World War* (Leiden: Brill, 2013)

Zevenbergen, C., *Rotterdams Voetbalglorie 1886–1986: kroniek van een eeuw stedelijke voetbalhistorie* (Rijswijk: Sijthoff Handelsdrukkerijen; Rotterdam: Gemeentelijke Archiefdienst, 1986)

Public archival resources

Rotterdam, Stadsarchief Rotterdam (SAR)

SAR, Archive 257: Rotterdamse Voetbal- en Atletiek Vereeniging Sparta.

Part 24: Notulen van bestuursvergaderingen: 1913 September–1915 September
- Minutes of meeting dated 3 September 1913
- Minutes of meeting dated 20 April 1915

Part 208: Stukken betreffende geldleningen ten laste van Sparta
- Document entitled 'Rentlooze leening 1915'

Part 211: Stukken betreffende de vaststelling door de gemeente Rotterdam van de huurprijs van de grond, gepacht door Sparta, in de polder Spangen
- Letter dated 13 October 1914
- Plan entitled: '*Plan van Exploitatie der Gemeentelijke terreinen in den Spangenschen polder*'

SAR, Archive 256: Sportclub Feyenoord

Part 36: 'De Feyenoorder', officieel tijdschrift van de sportclub 'Feyenoord', 1917–1923
Publication dated 25 August 1917

Please note that the Sportclub Feyenoord archive has been recently returned to Feyenoord. Please contact the Feyenoord Musuem for details.

SAR Fotocollectie

Material belonging to the '*SAR* Fotocollectie' can be consulted in the reading rooms of the *Stadsarchief Rotterdam*. Alternatively it can be accessed online using the given classification number in the *Beeld en Geluid* 'Nummer' section of the archive website: http://www.stadsarchief.rotterdam.nl/collectie/beeld-en-geluid

The Hague, *Nationaal Archief* (*NA*)

NA, Archive Number: 2.19.123, Het archief van de Koninklijke Nederlandse Voetbalbond (KNVB), 1889–1996:
Section 1.3.1.: Algemene Jaarverslagen:
Part 246: 1913/14–1915/16
Section 2.2.1.: Ledenadministratie:
Part 459: 1914–1915, Achilles–M.V.V.O.
Part 460: 1914–1915, N.A.C.–Z.S.C.

Uncatalogued private archival resources

Amsterdam, Uncatalogued Private Archive of the *Olympisch Stadion Amsterdam* (*OSA*):
OSA, Letter dated 'Amsterdam, Januari 1909'
OSA, 'Amsterdam, 21 November 1908'
OSA, Letter dated 'Amsterdam, 10 December, 1908'
OSA, Memos dated: 23 November 1908, 25 November 1908, 2 December 1908
OSA, Printed Report from E.R. Harkema, early 1912
OSA, 'Lyst van Inteekenaren op het kapitaal van Maatschappy "Nederlandsch Sportpark"'

Newspaper articles and sporting magazines archive

Owing to spatial constraints I will not list each newspaper or sporting magazine article cited in this bibliography. However, articles cited in this work from the following newspapers and magazines can be found via the online digital newspaper archive at http://www.delpher.nl/.

Algemeen Handelsblad
De Revue der Sporten
De Telegraaf
De Tribune: Rev. Soc. Volksblad
Het Centrum
Het Volk
Nieuwe Rotterdamsche Courant
Rotterdamsch Nieuwsblad

Articles cited from the following works, were consulted in the newspaper reading rooms of the *Koninklijke Bibliotheek*, in The Hague, the Netherlands.

De Courant
Maasbode

Online resources

Biografisch Woordenboek van het Socialisme en de Arbeidersbeweging in Nederland: Marten Buschman, 'Kitsz, Cornelis', by Marten Buschman, https://socialhistory.org/bwsa/biografie/kitsz

Buursink, J., 'The Cultural Strategy of Rotterdam', *Cybergeo: European Journal of Geography,* Colloque 'Les Problèmes culturels des grandes villes', 8–11 December 1997, article 115, http://cybergeo.revues.org/1203

Concertgebouw, Amsterdam, 'Historie', https://www.concertgebouw.nl/uw-bezoek/gebouw-geschiedenis/historie

De Zeen Magazine: Alyn Griffiths, 'Rotterdam Centraal Station Reopens with a Pointed Metal-Clad Entrance', http://www.dezeen.com/2014/03/22/rotterdam-centraal-station-benthem-crouwel-mvsa-architects-west-8/

Digitale Bibliotheek voor de Nederlandse Letteren: E. J. Voûte, 'Levensbericht van Mari Paul Voûte: 1856–1928, in Jaarboek van de Maatschappij der Nederlandse Letterkunde 1929, http://www.dbnl.org/tekst/_jaa003192901_01/_jaa003192901_01_0013.php

Feyenord Rotterdam, 'Historie: 1914–1923', https://www.feyenoord.nl/de-club/geschiedenis

Feyenord Rotterdam, 'Feyenoord kiest voor vernieuwbouwde Kuip FFC', https://www.feyenoord.nl/nieuws/nieuwsoverzicht/feyenoord-kiest-voor-vernieuwbouwde-kuip-ffc

The Guardian: Oliver Wainright, 'Rotterdam's Markthal: Superdutch goes Supersized in Psychedelic Marketplace', https://www.theguardian.com/artanddesign/architecture-design-blog/2014/oct/02/-sp-rotterdam-markthal-superdutch-market-mvrdv

Gustav-Mahler.eu, 'Charles Ernest Henri Boissevain (1868–1940)', http://www.gustav-mahler.eu/index.php/moreformenu/personen/414-boissevain-charles-ernest-henri-1868-1940

Huygens Instituut voor Nederlandse Geschiedenis, 'C. J. K. van Aalst Dagboeken', resources.huygens.knaw.nl/retroboeken/vanaalst/

Huygens Instituut voor Nederlandse Geschiedenis, 'Databank Sport', http://resources.huygens.knaw.nl/sportbondenclubsperiodieken/gids/search

Huygens Instituut voor Nederlandse Geschiedenis, 'Verenigingen voor armenzorg en armoedepreventie in de negentiende eeuw', http://resources.huygens.knaw.nl/armenzorg/gids/vereniging/2776914523

Parlement en Politiek, 'Sociaal-Democratische Arbeiderspartij (SDAP)', https://www.parlement.com/id/vh8lnhrpfxu8/sociaal_democratische_arbeiderspartij

Parlement en Politiek, 'Vrijzinnig-Democratische Bond (VDB)', https://www.parlement.com/id/vh8lnhrp8wti/vrijzinnig_democratische_bond_vdb

Retours: Arjan den Boer, 'Dutch Concrete and Art Nouveau', http://retours.eu/en/08-decorations-hofplein-station-rotterdam/

RKD Nederlands Instituut voor Kunstgeschiedenis, Edwin vom Rath, https://rkd.nl/nl/explore/artists/421693

Sportgeschiedenis: Jurryt van de Vooren, 'De arrestatie van Kick Schröder', http://www.sportgeschiedenis.nl/2009/03/18/de-arrestatie-van-kick-schroder.aspx

Stadsarchief Rotterdam, Adresboeken Database, http://www.stadsarchief.rotterdam.nl/collectie/adresboeken

Stadsarchief Rotterdam, Bevolkingscijfers van Rotterdam vanaf 1868, http://www.stadsarchief.rotterdam.nl/bevolkingscijfers-van-rotterdam-vanaf-1868

Stadsarchief Rotterdam, Digitale Stamboom Database, http://www.stadsarchief.rotterdam.nl/collectie/digitale-stamboom

VOC, 'Geschiedenis', http://www.v-o-c.nl/algemeen/geschiedenis

Defunct websites

CVV, http://www.cvvmercurius.nl/index.php?option=com_content&task=view&id=2&Itemid=201 [last accessed 19 March 2010]

In the Winning Mood, '*Sparta & historie*: *In de Geest van Bok de Korver*', http://www.itwm.nl/artikel.php?id=3567 [last accessed 29 May 2011]

Transvalia, '*Beknopte Geschiedenis Transvalia*', http://www.transvaliazw.nl/overige/historie/historie.htm [last accessed 29 May 2011]

Appendix

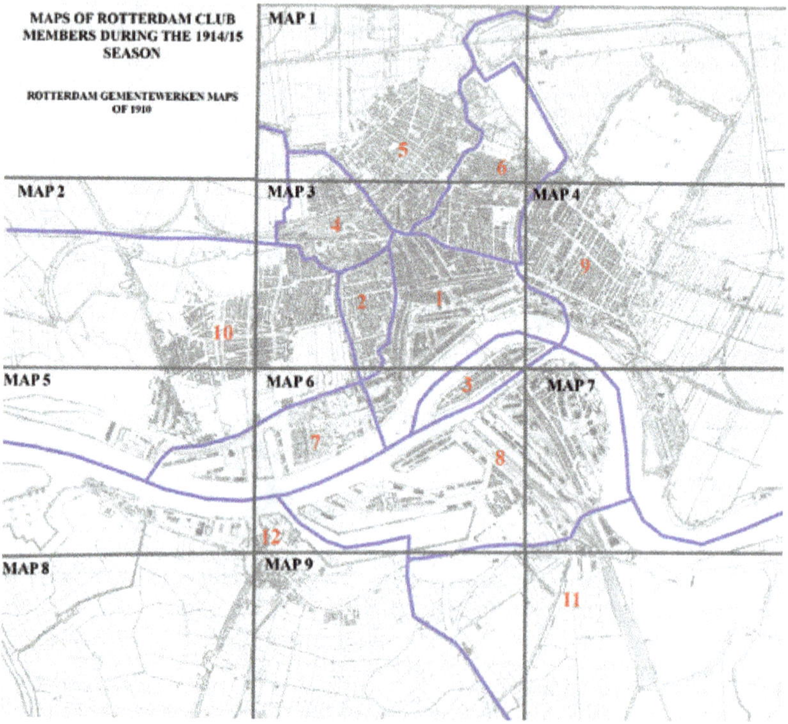

The maps in this Appendix provide a constructed representation of the registered addresses of members for the researched Rotterdam football clubs in the 1914/1915 season. The data has been placed onto a map from the Rotterdam *Gemeentewerken* of 1910, located in the *Stadsarchief Rotterdam*. To aid this representation I have divided Rotterdam into twelve different geographical zones. The divisions and their names do not necessarily correspond to formal divisions within the city. I outline the geographical parameters of the different areas below.

1: Stadsdriehoek
2: West Coolsingel
3: Noordereiland
4: Stationswijk
5: North
6: Crooswijk
7: Park
8: Feijenoord
9: East
10: West
11: Hillesluis
12: Charlois

Geographical parameters

1: Stadsdriehoek: The area is bordered from the Maas east of the Veerhaven, the Zalmhaven, Coolsingel canal north to (and including) Hofplein, following (and including) the Goudschesingel to (not including) the Oostplein and south of the Boerengat to the Maas.
2: West Coolsingel: The area west of the Coolsingel canal and east of the Westersingel canal, bordered to the north (and including) the Kruiskade.
3: Noordereiland: The island of Noordereiland situated between southern and northern Maas banks.
4: Stationswijk: The area north of (and not including) the Kruiskade, bordered to the west by the Westersingel through the Zoo, to the eastern rail exit of the Delftsche Poort Station, bordered to the north following (and including) the Waldenbergerweg and to the east (not including) of the Schiekade.
5: North: The area between (and including) the Schiekade and the Rotte with (not including) the Hofplein.
6: Crooswijk: The area to the east of the Rotte and to the north of the (not including) Goudschesingel, which is bordered on its eastern side by the Boezemsingel canal and returning to the Rotte.
7: Park: From the northern bank of the Maas at (and including) the Schiehaven, to the south (and including) the Westzeedijk, east of the Zalmhaven, west of the Veerhaven to the Maas.

8: Feijenoord: The area south of the Maas through the Maashaven, to the north of (and including) the Putsche to (and including) the Tweede Rosestraat and to the southern bank of the Maas at the Mallegat.
9: East: The area to the east of the Boezemsingel, through (and including) the Oostplein and joining the northern Maas through the Boerengat.
10: West: The area to the west of the Westersingel, south of the railway line, and bordered in the south (not including) by the Westzeedijk and the Schiehaven.
11: Hillesluis: The area south of the Maas bordered to the north by the Mallegat, following (not including) the Tweede Rosestraat and Putsche, joining (and including) the Breilschelaan to the intersection with the Dordtschestraatweg and bordered on its west by (including) the Dordtschestraatweg.
12: Charlois: South of the Maas river through the Maashaven and to the east (not including) the Dordtschestraatweg.

MAP 1
KEY
CVV
DVS
De Concordiaan
Feyenoord
Het Noorden
Leonidas
Lycurgus
Neptunus
RFC
Sparta
Transvalia
UDI
USC
VOC
EAST
CROOSWIJK
HILLEGERSBERG
NORTH
STATIONWIJK

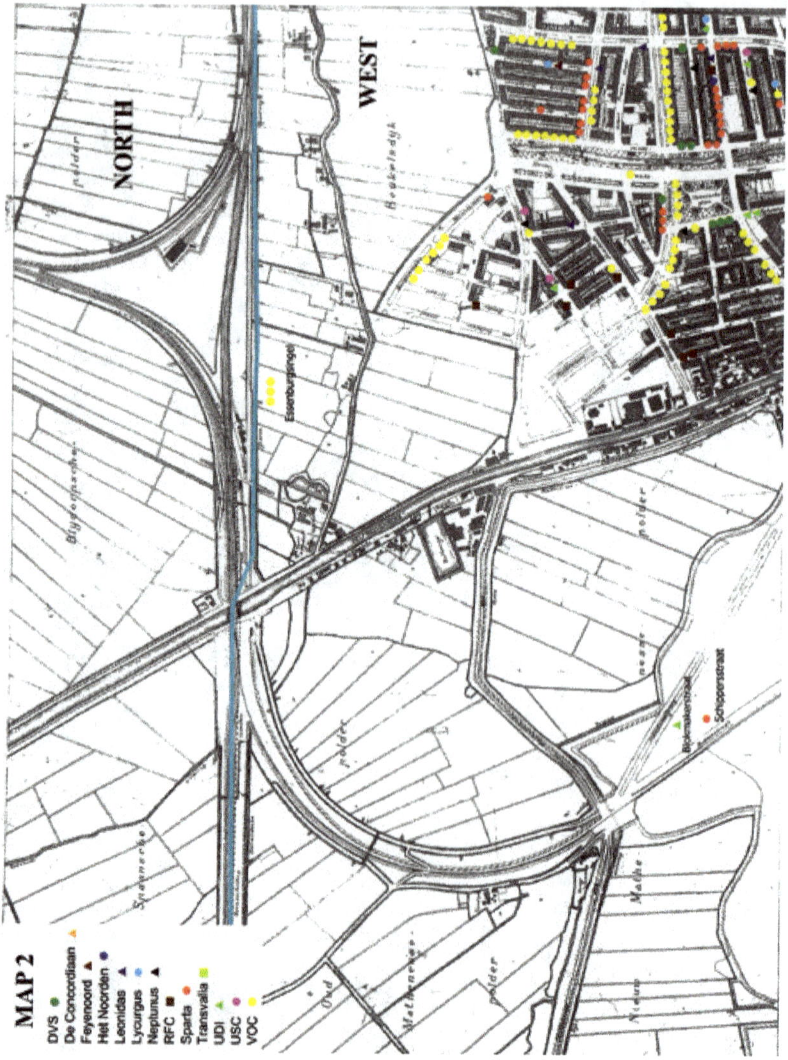
MAP 2
DVS
De Concordiaan
Feyenoord
Het Noorden
Leonidas
Lycurgus
Neptunus
RFC
Sparta
Transvalia
UDI
USC
VOC
NORTH
WEST

MAP 3
KEY
CW
DVS
De Concordiaan
Feyenoord
Het Noorden
Leonidas
Lycurgus
Neptunus
RFC
Sparta
Transvalia
UDI
USC
VOC
CROOSWIJK
STADSDRIEHOEK
NOORDEREILAND
NOORD
WEST COOLSINGEL
STATIONWIJK
WEST

MAP 4
KEY
CVV
DVS
De Concordiaan
Feyenoord
Het Noorden
Leonidas
Lycurgus
Neptunus
RFC
Sparta
Transvalia
UDI
USC
VOC
EAST

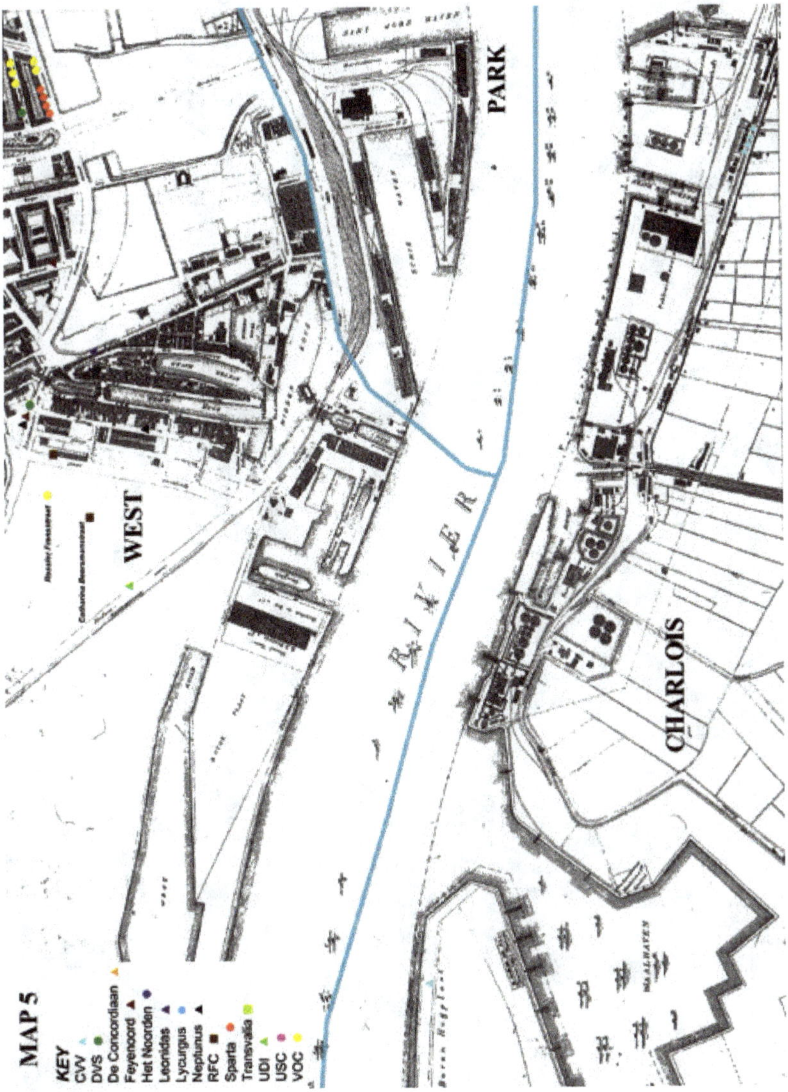
MAP 5
KEY
CVV
DVS
De Concordiaan
Feyenoord
Het Noorden
Leonidas
Lycurgus
Neptunus
RFC
Sparta
Transvalia
UDI
USC
VOC
WEST
PARK
RIVIER
CHARLOIS

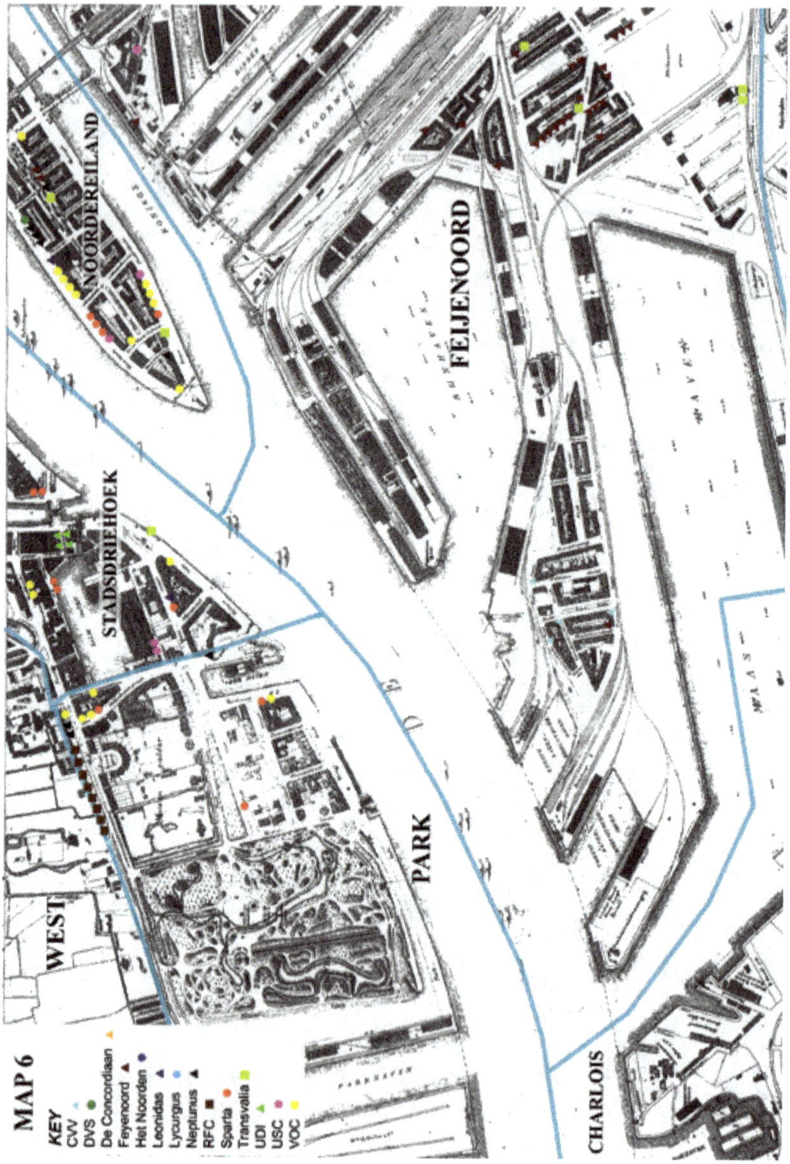
MAP 6
KEY
CVV
DVS
De Concordiaan
Feyenoord
Het Noorden
Leonidas
Lycurgus
Neptunus
RFC
Sparta
Transvalia
UDI
USC
VOC
NOORDEREILAND
STADSDRIEHOEK
FEIJENOORD
WEST
PARK
CHARLOIS

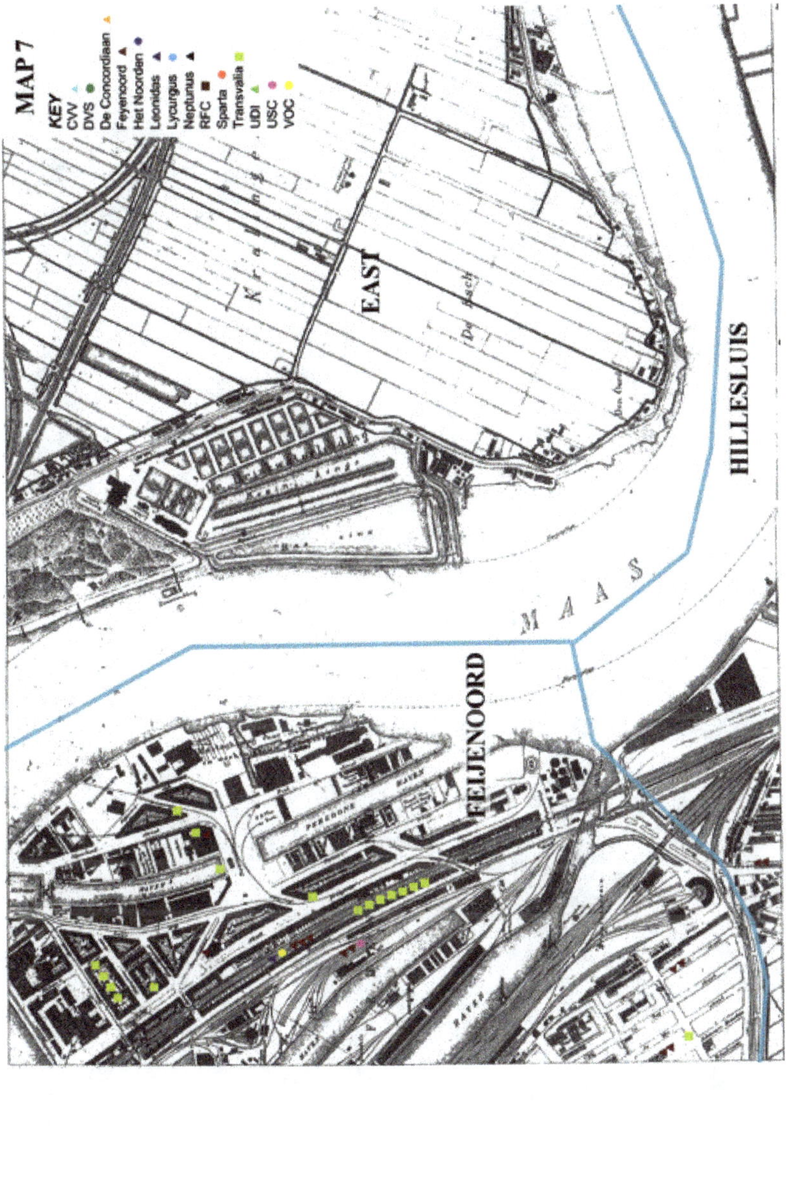
MAP 7
KEY
CW
DVS
De Concordiaan
Feyenoord
Het Noorden
Leonidas
Lycurgus
Neptunus
RFC
Sparta
Transvalia
UDI
USC
VOC
EAST
MAAS
FEIJENOORD
HILLESLUIS

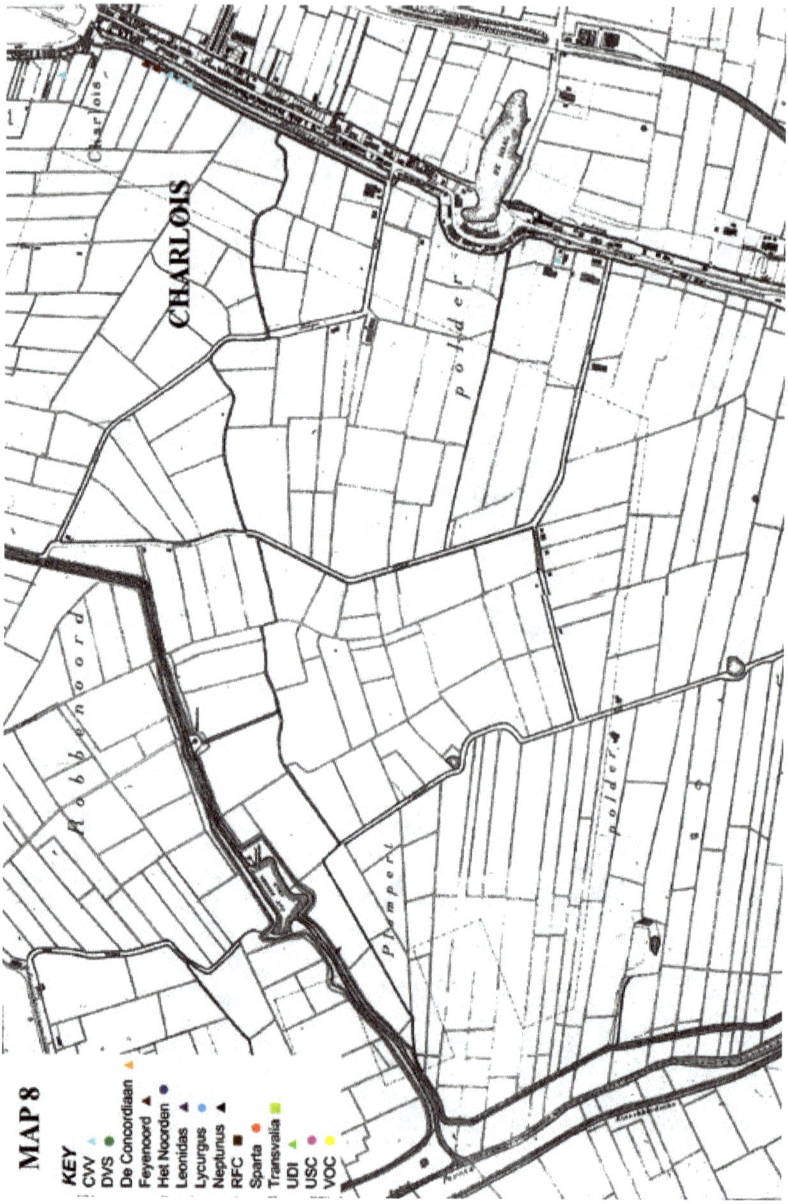
MAP 8
KEY
CW
DVS
De Concordiaan
Feyenoord
Het Noorden
Leonidas
Lycurgus
Neptunus
RFC
Sparta
Transvalia
UDI
USC
VOC
CHARLOIS

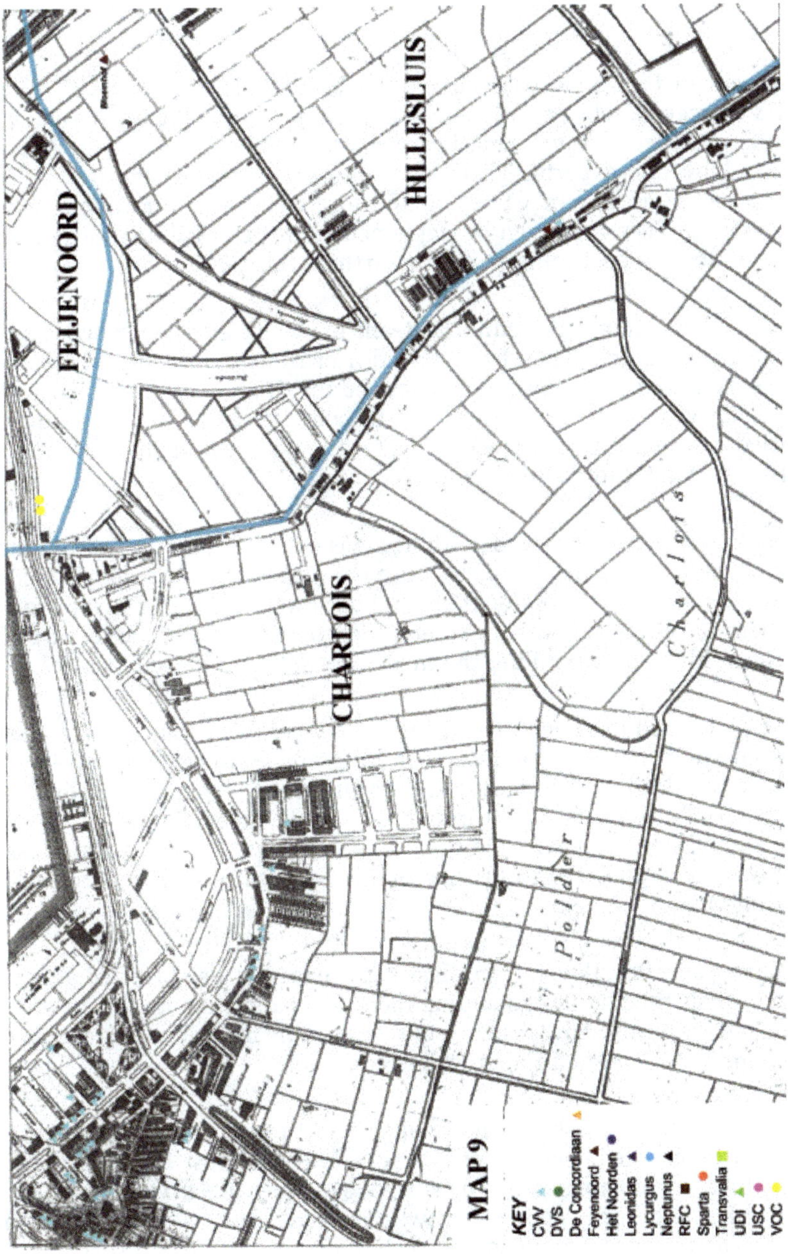
FEIJENOORD
HILLESLUIS
CHARLOIS
Polder
Charlois
MAP 9
KEY
CW
DVS
De Concordiaan
Feyenoord
Het Noorden
Leonidas
Lycurgus
Neptunus
RFC
Sparta
Transvalia
UDI
USC
VOC

Permissions

All chapters in this book were first published in FHAEDF, by UCL Press by Nicholas Piercey; hereby published with permission under the Creative Commons Attribution License or equivalent. Every chapter published in this book has been scrutinized by our experts. Their significance has been extensively debated. The topics covered herein carry significant information for a comprehensive understanding. They may even be implemented as practical applications or may be referred to as a beginning point for further studies.

We would like to thank the editorial team for lending their expertise to make the book truly unique. They have played a crucial role in the development of this book. Without their invaluable contributions this book wouldn't have been possible. They have made vital efforts to compile up to date information on the varied aspects of this subject to make this book a valuable addition to the collection of many professionals and students.

This book was conceptualized with the vision of imparting up-to-date and integrated information in this field. To ensure the same, a matchless editorial board was set up. Every individual on the board went through rigorous rounds of assessment to prove their worth. After which they invested a large part of their time researching and compiling the most relevant data for our readers.

The editorial board has been involved in producing this book since its inception. They have spent rigorous hours researching and exploring the diverse topics which have resulted in the successful publishing of this book. They have passed on their knowledge of decades through this book. To expedite this challenging task, the publisher supported the team at every step. A small team of assistant editors was also appointed to further simplify the editing procedure and attain best results for the readers.

Apart from the editorial board, the designing team has also invested a significant amount of their time in understanding the subject and creating the most relevant covers. They scrutinized every image to scout for the most suitable representation of the subject and create an appropriate cover for the book.

The publishing team has been an ardent support to the editorial, designing and production team. Their endless efforts to recruit the best for this project, has resulted in the accomplishment of this book. They are a veteran in the field of academics and their pool of knowledge is as vast as their experience in printing. Their expertise and guidance has proved useful at every step. Their uncompromising quality standards have made this book an exceptional effort. Their encouragement from time to time has been an inspiration for everyone.

The publisher and the editorial board hope that this book will prove to be a valuable piece of knowledge for students, practitioners and scholars across the globe.

Index

Printed in the USA
CPSIA information can be obtained
at www.ICGtesting.com
LVHW010815221023
761596LV00005B/504

9 798888 360378